PRAISE FC
DAY BY DAY THROUGH THE BIBLE

"Twenty years ago, as a pastor, I met Allen and first learned of the Ezra Project. Allen's passion then and now, and the goal of this series of reflections, is to get you into the Word of God day by day. I share that passion. Read the Bible, study it, meditate on it, memorize it, pray it through, listen to it preached— and let it lead you to the God of the Bible."

— **Dr. Donald W. Sweeting,** *chancellor,*
Colorado Christian University

"Instruction. Inspiration. Intercession. You'll experience all of these with *Day by Day Through the Bible: The Writings of the Major Prophets - Isaiah, Jeremiah & Ezekiel.* God communicated His wisdom through the major prophets, and now Allen J. Huth communicates it to you. Be instructed. Be inspired. And join Allen in a prayer of thanksgiving."

—**Dr. Woodrow Kroll,** *former president,*
Back to the Bible

"Allen Huth has spent years reading from God's Word and applying God's wisdom to his life. In *Day by Day Through the Bible,* Allen shares with us what God's Spirit has impressed upon his heart. As you read God's Word, and then read the wisdom Allen has received from God's Spirit through God's Word, your heart and soul will be fed in new ways – and you will find practical application of God's Word to your life."

—**John Snyder,** *lead pastor,*
Crossroads Community Church

"Reading the *Day by Day Through the Bible* series gets you excited to read the Word of God. I highly recommend this series for those who desire a fresh new way to see and hear from God in your daily devotion."

—David Love, *pastor,*
Calvary Castle Rock

"In *Day by Day Through the Bible,* Allen shares his personal journey through the Scriptures, and has challenged me to see *The Writings of the Major Prophets - Isaiah, Jeremiah & Ezekiel* in an entirely different light. He opened my heart and mind to the intimate call of God. I have a brand new exploratory manner of reading *The Writings of the Major Prophets - Isaiah, Jeremiah & Ezekiel.*"

—Denise Washington Blomberg,
AM91 Radio News Director

"You can really feel Allen's love for God's Word in these devotional lessons. His combination of real-life stories and practical applications make daily Bible reading fun and rewarding for anyone."

—Arlen Nordhagen, *entrepreneur, business owner,*
president of The Nord Foundation

"My favorite kind of book? The kind that explains insightful truths from scripture illustrated by relatable personal stories. Allen J. Huth has done that! He weaves threads from his well-worn Bible, his multiple journals, his extensive travels, and his experiences into a tapestry of lessons that will encourage you daily. I'll be quoting him many times!!"

—Robert J. Morgan, *best-selling gold-Illuminations,*
and gold-medallion winning author, speaker, Bible teacher

DAY *by* DAY
THROUGH THE
BIBLE

The Writings of the Major Prophets —
Isaiah, Jeremiah & Ezekiel

ALLEN J. HUTH

MEDIA.COM

DAY *by* DAY
THROUGH THE
BIBLE

Copyright © 2023 by Allen J. Huth

All rights reserved. No part of this book may be reproduced in any form or by any means—whether electronic, digital, mechanical, or otherwise—without permission in writing from the publisher, except by a reviewer, who may quote brief passages in a review.

Scripture quotations are from the ESV® Bible (The Holy Bible, English Standard Version®), copyright © 2001 by Crossway, a publishing ministry of Good News Publishers. Used by permission. All rights reserved.
Scripture quotations taken from the New American Standard Bible® (NASB), Copyright © 1960, 1962, 1963, 1968, 1971, 1972, 1973, 1975, 1977, 1995 by The Lockman Foundation. Used by permission. www.Lockman.org
Scripture taken from the New King James Version® (NKJV). Copyright © 1982 by Thomas Nelson. Used by permission. All rights reserved.

The views and opinions expressed in this book are those of the author and do not necessarily reflect the official policy or position of Illumify Media Global.

Published by
Illumify Media Global
www.IllumifyMedia.com
"Let's bring your book to life!"

Paperback ISBN: 978-1-959099-20-8

Typeset by Art Innovations (http://artinnovations.in/)
Cover design by Debbie Lewis

Printed in the United States of America

CONTENTS

FOREWORD

There was a time in my life when I struggled to read through the books of the Bible written by the prophets. Their writing often seemed intended for a different day and time, with little impact on my daily life. I struggled to understand the meaning of much of what was written, and certainly struggled to understand how it applied to my life.

More recently, as I read through Isaiah, Jeremiah, Lamentations, and Ezekiel, I reflected upon how much the challenges of the times in which these men lived resemble the culture in which we reside today. We can claim to be followers of God, and yet all too often, our lives do not reflect this. Our culture gives "lip service" to God, with many people turning to prayer when something tragic impacts us. The same people go on living as though God's love for them makes little difference.

Isaiah, Jeremiah, and Ezekiel were commissioned by God to stand in the gap during these trying times. God spoke through them to reach out to those He loved, pleading with the people to turn their hearts to God. We also are commissioned by God to stand in the gap for today's culture. While we may stand in the gap, we also know that the work to reconcile all mankind to God is His work. In Ezekiel 36:26-27, the Bible says, *"And I will give you a new heart, and a new spirit I will put within you. And I will remove the heart of stone from your flesh and give you a heart of flesh. And I will put my Spirit within you and cause you to walk in my statutes and be careful to obey my rules."*

More than twenty years ago, Allen J. Huth followed a call God placed on his heart and started the Ezra Project, a non-profit whose mission is stated very simply – "Connecting God's people to God's Word, by encouraging Christians to engage in the Bible daily." In pursuit of that mission, Allen has written the *"Day by Day Through the Bible"* series. In this book, Allen takes the writings of Isaiah, Jeremiah, and Ezekiel and shares insights that he gained in his life when he read from God's Word daily. Following this study guide will take you deeper into the meaning and impact these books can have in your life.

My prayer for you, as you follow through the daily study, is that God's Word will be your guide as you stand in the gap in today's culture. May God not only give you a new heart, may you also be blessed to see Him work through you to bring others to Christ.

—*Daniel J. Heighway*

Dan Heighway's career spanned more than three decades in various leadership roles in a Fortune 150 company. He now serves as the Executive Director of The Gideons International.

PREFACE

*T*he *Writings of the Major Prophets* is a guide of daily devotions in the four books attributed to Isaiah, Jeremiah, and Ezekiel, the so-called major prophets of the Old Testament. Done day by day, it will cover 115 days, because Isaiah and Jeremiah are consolidated into thirty-one days each:

- Isaiah, 66 chapters in 31 days
- Jeremiah, 52 chapters in 31 days
- Lamentations, 5 chapters in 5 days
- Ezekiel, 48 chapters in 48 days

Comments on Bible passages, life applications, and prayers are based on the audio daily devotion, ADDBIBLE, a free app that can be heard daily on your smartphone or tablet. The scripture verses are drawn from the English Standard Version (ESV) unless otherwise noted.

ADDBIBLE was recorded using written records from thirty-five years of my personal Bible reading journals. I started reading the Bible at fifteen years old and started journaling my quiet times in 1983. I have been blessed *"exceedingly abundantly"* (Eph. 3:20) by what God has revealed to me in His Word.

I count it an awesome privilege to share insights from my personal journals including personal stories of how God's Word has specifically impacted my life and short prayers we can pray together, all in 10-15 minutes per day.

This workbook is one of a series of *Day by Day Through the Bible* "Writings of" daily devotions featuring other Biblical authors like Moses, Solomon, the Minor Prophets, Mark, John, Paul, and more. Access them all by visiting ezraproject.net.

May God richly bless you as you enjoy a portion of God's Word each and every day. Abiding in the Word,

—Allen J. Huth, President
The Ezra Project

ABOUT ISAIAH, JEREMIAH, AND EZEKIEL[1]

In this workbook, we include the writings of three prophets, Isaiah, Jeremiah, and Ezekiel, considered the major Old Testament prophets. In another workbook, *The Writings of the Minor Prophets*, we cover the writings of the thirteen minor prophets: Daniel, Hosea, Joel, Amos, Obadiah, Jonah, Micah, Nahum, Habakkuk, Zephaniah, Haggai, Zechariah, and Malachi. The distinction of "major" or "minor," is primarily based on the size of their books, not the content of their messages.

Isaiah. Isaiah was one of the Jewish peoples most important prophets because his message was a unique blend of warnings against judgments, and the hope and comfort of salvation to come. His name means, "Yahweh is salvation." His father's name was Amoz. Isaiah may have been born in royalty. He was thoroughly schooled in the traditional forms and language of prophetic speech. Most likely, he was trained as a priest because his calling took place in the temple, in an area reserved for priests.

Isaiah was married and had two sons. His life experiences helped him understand poverty and the debauchery of the rich. He knew of the inequities and evils of society. Unlike Jeremiah, Isaiah says very little about himself. He may have been a very private man, but with close ties to other godly men like Micah and King Hezekiah. His life, and messages, may have been influenced by another prophet, Amos.

According to most scholars, he is attributed with writing all of the book that bears his name. Others suggest he only wrote chapters 1-39, and other anonymous prophets wrote chapters 40-66. The English Standard Version Study Bible supports Isaiah as the sole author (p.1234).

---

1   Much of About Isaiah, Jeremiah, and Ezekiel was gleaned from information found in Britannica.com and Got Questions.org. Other sources include *Calling America Back to The Bible*, by Dr. Woodrow Kroll, and the English Standard Version Study Bible.

According to Dr. Woodrow Kroll, former president of Back to the Bible, "Isaiah was to prophecy what Beethoven was to music and Shakespeare was to literature." Isaiah is well known for preaching naked and barefoot for three years

Jeremiah. Jeremiah had more to say about repentance than any other prophet. He is known as "the weeping prophet." He was born into a priestly family about 650 B.C. and grew up in a small village northeast of Jerusalem. He was a priest from a small town allotted to the tribe of Benjamin. Yet, he was close enough to Jerusalem to understand its people and their worship; but far enough away to be able to criticize what he saw happen there.

Jeremiah was forbidden by God to marry or have children. He was called by God at a young age, *"for I am only a youth"* (1:6); some say as young as seventeen, others about twenty-three years old. He is characterized as sensitive, introspective, and shy.

Jeremiah preached for over forty years without seeing any real success. He experienced rejection, depression, and discouragement. His hometown turned against him, his friends turned their back on him, so he may have been a very lonely man. He was taken to Egypt against his will after the fall of Jerusalem and was most likely stoned to death by his fellow countrymen in Egypt.

Also labeled "the prophet of doom," he was thrown into prison, his writings were cast into a fire, and he is attributed with only two converts in his forty years of ministry. Though the writings were burned, his faithful scribe Baruch re-wrote them, becoming the book that bears his name and the Book of Lamentations.

Ezekiel. Ezekiel's name means "strengthened by God," or "God strengthens." Ezekiel was like a Jewish street preacher. He used straight-forward language everyone could understand, whether they listened or not. According to Dr. Woodrow Kroll, Ezekiel was, "a man who did exactly and immediately whatever God asked him to do, even if it did not make sense at the time."

Ezekiel began his ministry in Palestine and lived in Jerusalem where he was trained to be a temple priest. He was among the Jews exiled to Babylon. There, he became a prophet, a watchman for the Lord. He used an array of visions, messages, poems, and dramas during his twenty-two years of street preaching to the Jews in

Babylon. One example is in chapter 5 where he chopped, burned, and scattered his own hair to illustrate God's message.

He was married but there is no record of children. When his wife died, God forbade him from weeping or mourning for her as another illustration of God's relationship with Israel. Jeremiah was an older contemporary of Ezekiel. Ezekiel clearly knew of Jeremiah and his messages. They probably never met as Jeremiah stayed in Jerusalem and Ezekiel was carted off to Babylon. Ezekiel probably never returned to Jerusalem. He died in captivity in Babylon.

As you will see in *The Writings of the Major Prophets*, God used unique men to deliver His unique messages to His people. Because these writings were preserved, those messages are in our hands today. Enjoy your 115-day journey with the major prophets of the Old Testament.

THIRTY-ONE DAYS IN ISAIAH

ISAIAH 1-3

Come Now, Let Us Reason Together

Today, we begin the prophetic Book of Isaiah. It is the second longest book of the Bible behind Psalms. Isaiah is sixty-six chapters. Verse 1 tells us the author, the message, and the timeframe, *"The vision of Isaiah the son of Amoz, which he saw concerning Judah and Jerusalem in the days of Uzziah, Jotham, Ahaz, and Hezekiah, kings of Judah."*

Isaiah is the author. His name means, "Yahweh is salvation," which gives us a glimpse into the message of the book. The central theme is God Himself and He does all things for His own sake. Isaiah announces God's charge against Israel. They have received much from God and should be grateful. But instead, they have despised God. By Isaiah's time, Israel no longer trusted in the promises of God. Instead, they aligned themselves with the promises of the world. Sound familiar?

The words in the first verse, *"in the days of Uzziah, Jotham, Ahaz, and Hezekiah,"* date Isaiah's writing around 740-680 B.C., during the decline of Israel and Judah. Isaiah, the greatest prophet of this era, chimes in with other prophets of this time about sin and judgment, but also writes some of the Bible's richest promises of a future Savior. Salvation is a key concept in this book. In one of its Hebrew forms, salvation is mentioned nearly once a chapter.

What to look for in the Book of Isaiah? A unique vision of God seated on His throne in power and glory, found in chapter 6. Prophecies concerning a virgin birth, found in chapters 7 and 9. A clear depiction of what Jesus accomplished on the cross of Calvary, found in chapter 53. We will go through the sixty-six chapters in thirty-one days. There will be multiple chapters daily, like today as we begin with chapters 1 through 3. Please read or listen to Isaiah 1-3.

COMMENTS

To help us through the Book of Isaiah, I will use three of my personal Bible reading journals. The first one will be from 1991, then ten years later, 2001, and another ten years later, 2011. Because of the length of today's chapters, I will just highlight a couple of verses out of each. I am going to go backwards from chapter 3 to chapter 1.

Isaiah 3:1 says, *"For behold, the Lord God of hosts is taking away from Jerusalem and from Judah support and supply."* Verse 8 tells us why, *"For Jerusalem has stumbled, and Judah has fallen, because their speech and their deeds are against the Lord, defying his glorious presence."* Isaiah 2:11 also tells us why, *"The haughty looks of man shall be brought low, and the lofty pride of men shall be humbled, and the Lord alone will be exalted in that day."*

Next, we see a very important future prophetic word in chapter 2, *"For out of Zion shall go forth the law, and the word of the Lord from Jerusalem. . . . and they shall beat their swords into plowshares, and their spears into pruning hooks; nation shall not lift up sword against nation, neither shall they learn war anymore"* (2:3-4). O, we long for that day.

Isaiah 1:2, *"Children have I reared and brought up, but they have rebelled against me."* And verse 4, *"Ah, sinful nation, a people laden with iniquity . . . They have forsaken the Lord, they have despised the Holy One of Israel."* Verses 15-17, *"When you spread out your hands, I will hide my eyes from you; even though you make many prayers, I will not listen . . . Wash yourselves; make yourselves clean; remove the evil of your deeds from before my eyes; cease to do evil, learn to do good."*

> **When you spread out your hands, I will hide my eyes from you; even though you make many prayers, I will not listen.**
>
> Isa. 1:15

Finally, verse 18 is a great, great verse, *"Come now, let us reason together, says the Lord: though your sins are like scarlet, they shall be as white as snow; though they are red like crimson, they shall become like wool."*

DIGGING DEEPER

Years ago, I heard a pastor preach on Isaiah. I have heard thousands of sermons in my fifty years of Christianity and remember few; but the time I heard that pastor quote Isaiah 1:18, I remember. *"Come now, let us reason together"* (v. 18), he proclaimed from the pulpit "Christianity is not blind faith; it can be reasoned!" At that time in my Christian life, I walked by faith, but not with much spiritual maturity. I did not understand Christianity could be reasoned. It stands the test of thoughtful interrogation; it is solid ground. That short phrase in 1:18 changed my life at a tender age. Praise God, for a faith that stands the test of reason.

Prayer

Father, as we close out the beginning of the Book of Isaiah, the first three chapters, You admonish us to come now and reason together. Christianity is not just about faith, it is reasonable, because You are a reasonable God.

As we go through the Book of Isaiah, let us use our minds, as well as our hearts, to understand what You have to say to Your people then, the people of Israel, and Your people today, us. *"Come now, let us reason together"* (1:18) through the Book of Isaiah. We ask for Your Holy Spirit's guidance. In Jesus' name, we pray. Amen.

MY THOUGHTS

ISAIAH 4-6

Here Am I, Send Me

Today, we are in Isaiah chapters 4-6. Isaiah reviews some history, then gets a glimpse of the throne room of God. Have you ever wondered what heaven is like? Please read or listen to Isaiah 4-6.

COMMENTS

Let's look at the journals from 1991, 2001, and 2011, concerning Isaiah 4-6. In 1991 (NASB), I wrote, "The vineyard of the Lord is the house of Israel and with all His care, it produced bad grapes, so it was laid waste, referring to chapter 5. Yet, in 5:25, *'For all this His anger is not spent, But His hand is still stretched out.'*" Then I quoted 6:8, *"Here am I. Send me!"*

Ten years later, in 2001, I was actually seeking direction about starting the Ezra Project. I read Isaiah 4-6, and wrote, "Looking for direction to only find that God looks to and fro to see who He can send. And Isaiah said, 'I am a sinner. A man of unclean lips; but cleanse me and send me.' If You are calling me, help me be willing to be sent to go." Concerning that journal entry, I was contemplating starting the Ezra Project in the fall of 2001. By God's leading, we did start the Ezra Project on April 1, 2002.

Let's look another ten years later, at my journal entry in 2011, "Even in judgment God is good and glorious, referring to 4:2." Then I looked at 5:13, "People go into exile for lack of knowledge." Next, I quoted 5:20, *"Woe to those who call evil good, and good evil."* We have a lot of that going on today. Judgement comes because they *"rejected the law of the Lord of Hosts, and despised the word of the Holy One of Israel"* (5:24). Then I referred to 6:5-7, "I pray before speaking every time, 'I am a man of unclean lips I need to be a clean vessel to be used of the Lord.'"

Woe To Those Who Call Evil Good, And Good Evil.

Isa. 5:20

Let's go back to a couple of a passages in chapter 5 and chapter 6. In chapter 5, there are some "woes." I want to review just a couple of those "woes":

> *Woe to those who rise early in the morning, that they may run after strong drink, who tarry late into the evening as wine inflames them! They have lyre and harp, tambourine and flute and wine at their feasts, but they do not regard the deeds of the Lord, or see the work of his hands.*

> *Therefore my people go into exile for lack of knowledge* (vv. 11-13).

Back then, they partied without regard to the deeds of the Lord. We see a lot of that today, a lot of partying without regard to the deeds of the Lord or the work of His hands. We should celebrate the goodness of God as much as we celebrate the skills, talents, and abilities of men.

Isaiah 5:20 is another "woe," *"Woe to those who call evil good and good evil."* We have much of that going on today. We cannot tell the difference between right and wrong. What appeared to be clearly wrong before, seems to be right today. And what seemed to be clearly right before, appears to be wrong today. So, *"Woe to those who call evil good and good evil"* (5:20).

Verse 21 is another woe, *"Woe to those who are wise in their own eyes, and shrewd in their own sight!"* What do you think about yourself? Are you wise in your own eyes or do you have a humble spirit before the Lord?

Verses 24 and 25 conclude the matter in chapter 5, *"for they have rejected the law of the Lord of hosts, and have despised the word of the Holy One of Israel. Therefore the anger of the Lord was kindled against his people, and he stretched out his hand against them and struck them."*

Part of our application from today is not to reject the law of the Lord. Do you despise the Word of God? May we never kindle the anger of the Lord against us so that God may not stretch out His hand against anyone of us.

DIGGING DEEPER

Let's conclude with some powerful concepts out of chapter 6. Isaiah gets a glimpse of the throne of God. That is amazing! He says, *"I saw the Lord sitting upon a throne, high and lifted up"* (v. 1). When Isaiah saw the throne room of God, he said, *"Woe is me! For I am lost; for I am a man of unclean lips, and I dwell in the midst of a people of unclean lips; for my eyes have seen the King, the Lord of hosts!"* (v. 5).

In the glorious presence of God, we are unclean. We are lost. Most likely, all of us will fall on our knees before Him and say, "Woe is me." But the mercy of God is demonstrated in this very scene. A seraphim from the very throne of God flies to Isaiah with a burning coal from the altar of God. He touches Isaiah's mouth and says, *"Behold, this has touched your lips; your guilt is taken away, and your sin atoned for"* (v. 7). Hallelujah! After that, what are you going to do? God speaks to Isaiah and says, *"Whom shall I send, and who will go for us?"* (v. 8). Isaiah says, *"Here I am! Send me"* (v. 8). If you saw the throne room of God and your lips were cleansed, your guilt was taken away, and your sin atoned for, you would probably do the same, shout, "Lord, here am I! Send me."

On a personal note, I get to speak on behalf of The Gideons International and on behalf of the Ezra Project frequently. Every time I get the opportunity to speak on behalf of the Lord, I pray these very verses in Isaiah 6. I pray God would take one of those burning coals from His throne of grace and touch my unclean lips and cleanse me so people do not hear from me, they hear from God Almighty. It is important to personalize the scriptures we read.

Prayer

Lord, thank You for a glimpse into heaven today. A glimpse into the very throne room of God. Thank You, Lord, we learned from there comes mercy, grace, and atonement for our sins. Thank You for forgiveness.

And surely this day, You are still looking to and fro to see who will go for You. May we respond, *"Here am I! Send me"* (6:8). Call us into Your service. Use us to further Your kingdom here on earth. We ask it, in Jesus' name. Amen.

MY THOUGHTS

ISAIAH 7 AND 8

A Virgin Will Conceive and Bear a Son

Today is day three on our thirty-one-day journey through the Book of Isaiah. We will cover chapters 7 and 8. Do you believe in the virgin birth? Please read or listen to Isaiah 7 and 8.

COMMENTS

In 1991, concerning chapter 7, I wrote about 7:14, "Prediction of Christ's virgin birth." In 2001, ten years later, I read Isaiah 7-9 and did not make a comment on Isaiah 7 or 8. Let's go to my next journal in 2011 where I quoted 7:9, *"If you are not firm in faith, you will not be firm at all."* Then I wrote, "Ahaz was invited to ask for a sign from God. He declined, *'The Lord himself will give you a sign'.* And Isaiah prophesies the virgin birth of Jesus, referring to verse 14."

Before we get to verse 14, let's go back to verse 9, *"If you are not firm in faith, you will not be firm at all."* How firm is your faith? Your immediate answer might be, "My faith is pretty firm." Normally our faith is pretty firm when things are comfortable. But how about when your Christianity is challenged? Or the culture around you becomes less Christian and even antagonist toward those of us of faith? Then how firm is your faith?

In recent days, my faith has been tested more than I want. I learned through the testing, my faith is firm. I am willing to stand against the cultural pressures of the day, to stand firm in my faith in biblical principles related to my Christianity. Again, *"If you are not firm in faith, you will not be firm at all"* (7:9).

> **If you are not firm in faith, you will not be firm at all.**
>
> **Isa. 7:9**

Now let's look at this great verse, 7:14, *"Therefore the Lord himself will give you a sign. Behold, the virgin shall conceive and bear a son, and shall call his name Immanuel."* In my English Standard Version Study Bible, there are a lot of footnotes related to this verse. Here is part of it:

> Although some claim that the word translated virgin refers generally to a "young woman," it actually refers specifically to a "maiden" – that is, to a young woman who is unmarried and sexually chaste, and thus has virginity as one of her characteristics. Thus when the Septuagint translators, 200 years before the birth of Christ, rendered *almah* here with Greek *parthenos* (a specific term for "virgin") they rightly perceived the meaning of the Hebrew term; and when Matthew applied this prophecy to the virgin birth of Christ, it was in accord with this well-established understanding of *parthenos* ("virgin") as used in the Septuagint and in other Greek writers (p. 1254).

Matthew, the gospel writer, verifies the meaning of this verse when he uses it directly in relationship to Jesus' birth, *"All this took place to fulfill what the Lord had spoken by the prophet: 'Behold, the virgin shall conceive and bear a son, and they shall call his name Immanuel'"* (Matt. 1:22-23). The word "Immanuel" is translated "God is with us." Continuing with the footnote, "Christian interpretation follows Matthew in applying this verse to the birth of Jesus. However, some aspects of Isaiah's prophecy also relate to the significance of the sign for Isaiah's own day" (p.1254).

Sometimes prophetic verses have a singular meaning and sometimes a double fulfillment. I said before, I am not a biblical scholar, I am not a pastor. I did not go to seminary, so I am not going to get into whether this is applicable to only the birth of Jesus or also to what Ahaz was facing at the time. That is why we go to church and that is why we get good study Bibles so we can read and hear from others about passages like this. I just know each time I read this verse and referred to it in my journal entries in ten-year increments, this verse applies to the virgin birth of Jesus. To that I say, praise the Lord!

DIGGING DEEPER

Before we close our time in Isaiah 7 and 8, I do want to refer to a verse in chapter 8. It is verse 19, *"And when they say to you, 'Inquire of the mediums and the necromancers who chirp and mutter,' should not a people inquire of their God?"*. The application from that verse is, who do you ask advice from? Today we ask Google everything. We ask Apple's Siri everything. We ask our friends. We get opinions from a lot of worldly sources. This verse reminds us, *"should not a people inquire of their God?"*

The application is, do not just go to those who, *"chirp and mutter,"* according to this verse, but also take your issues to the Lord. Look in His Word. Pray and seek the Lord. Inquire of God. Get biblical council, get godly wisdom, as you make decisions and choices in your life.

Prayer

Lord, we thank You for this passage today. Hundreds of years before it happened, You predicted the virgin birth of Jesus Christ, our Lord and Savior. We thank You for the reminder to not just go to worldly sources for advice, but also to inquire of You, our God.

You invited Ahaz to ask for a sign of the Lord and he refused. You invite us to inquire of You. May we not refuse, but may we come to You and listen for Your small, still voice that will help us make decisions, that will guide us in the steps we want and need to take in life. Thank You for Your promises we find in Your Word. In Jesus' name, we pray. Amen.

MY THOUGHTS

ISAIAH 9 AND 10

For to Us a Child Is Born

Today, we are in Isaiah chapters 9 and 10. We will discover one of the most quoted passages in all of the Bible; it is about Jesus. Do you know it? Please read or listen to Isaiah 9 and 10.

COMMENTS

Let's focus on a couple of wonderful verses in this passage today, starting with Isaiah 9:2, *"The people who walked in darkness have seen a great light; those who dwelt in a land of deep darkness, on them has light shone."* Maybe that is your very own testimony. Once you walked in darkness, then the light of the gospel came into your life, broke through the darkness, and now you see a great light. You turned your life over to the King of kings and Lord of lords, the Light of the world, Jesus Christ.

But if you are still walking in darkness, this verse is for you, *"The people who walked in darkness have seen a great light; those who dwelt in a land of deep darkness, on them has light shone"* (9:2). The light is shining on you now. Accept Jesus as your Lord and Savior.

Who is this Jesus? Isaiah 9:6-7 explain Him to us:

For to us a child is born, to us a son is given; and the government shall be upon his shoulder, and his name shall be called Wonderful Counselor, Mighty God, Everlasting Father, Prince of Peace. Of the increase of his government and of peace there will be no end, on the throne of David and over his kingdom, to establish it and to uphold it with justice and with righteousness from this time forth and forevermore. The zeal of the Lord of hosts will do this.

In the New Testament, Luke writes about the coming birth of Jesus in Luke 1:32-33, and refers back to these verses, *"He will be great and will be called the Son of the Most High. And the Lord God will give to him the throne of his father David, and he will reign over the house of Jacob forever, and of his kingdom there will be no end."* It is wonderful to see the powerful prophecies of the Old Testament fulfilled in the New Testament.

> **For all this his anger has not turned away, and his hand is stretched out still.**
>
> **Isa. 9:12**

There is another great promise in these verses today. Though Israel turned its back on God, and so often we do too verses like 9:12 and 9:21 say, *"For all this his anger has not turned away, and his hand is stretched out still."* God's mercy is always available to us if we will just turn back to Him.

In 10:21-22, Isaiah says, *"A remnant will return, the remnant of Jacob, to the mighty God. For though your people Israel be as the sand of the sea, only a remnant of them will return."* In other words, God always keeps a people to continue His promises.

Isaiah 10:25 says, *"For in a very little while my fury will come to an end, and my anger will be directed to their destruction,"* referring to those who oppose the nation of Israel, those who oppose the people of God.

Isaiah 10:27 says, *"And in that day his burden will depart from your shoulder, and his yoke from your neck."* In other words, God will relieve the pressure. He will restore His people Israel; He will restore you. What a message from the Prophet Isaiah that there will be a Savior who will come and establish His throne forever. And God will always keep a remnant to rebuild. And regardless of all the stuff we have done against the Lord, His anger has not turned away and His hand is stretched out still.

DIGGING DEEPER

Reach out to His stretched-out hand even this very moment. Quiet your heart before the Lord. Confess any rebellion, any disobedience, to Him right now. Allow His loving mercy to overflow you at this very moment. He loves you. He wants to restore you. He wants to forgive you. Reach out to His outstretched hand today.

Prayer

Father, we reach out to You. Thank You for always stretching out Your hand toward us. Thank You for Your love for us. I confess my rebellion, my disobedience, to You. Restore me to Your side today. In Jesus' name. Amen.

MY THOUGHTS

A Shoot from the Stump of Jesse

Today is day five in our thirty-one-day journey through the Book of Isaiah. We are going to look at three chapters, Isaiah 11-13. The wolf shall dwell with the lamb, thanks to the root of Jesse. Do you know who the root of Jesse is? Please read or listen to Isaiah 11-13.

COMMENTS

In my personal Bible reading journal, in 1991, as I read through these chapters, I wrote, "Concerning 11:6-10, the peace of God at the end. On 12:1, God forgives. Thank You, O God, for Your Word." On chapter 13, "God judges the nations of the world and each individual."

Let's go back and look at those verses concerning the peace of God in the future:

The wolf shall dwell with the lamb, and the leopard shall lie down with the young goat, and the calf and the lion and the fattened calf together; and a little child shall lead them. The cow and the bear shall graze; their young shall lie down together; and the lion shall eat straw like the ox. The nursing child shall play over the hole of the cobra, and the weaned child shall put his hand on the adder's den. They shall not hurt or destroy in all my holy mountain; for the earth shall be full of the knowledge of the Lord as the waters cover the sea.

In that day the root of Jesse, who shall stand as a signal for the peoples—of him shall the nations inquire, and his resting place shall be glorious (11:6-10).

The root of Jesse is described in the first two verses of Isaiah 11:

There shall come forth a shoot from the stump of Jesse, and a branch from his roots shall bear fruit. And the Spirit of the Lord shall rest upon him, the Spirit of wisdom and understanding, the Spirit of counsel and might, the Spirit of knowledge and the fear of the Lord.

My English Standard Version Study Bible footnote on 11:1 says about the shoot from the stump of Jesse:

After portraying the destruction of arrogant human evil as the felling of a vast forest (in the previous chapter), Isaiah presents the Messiah as a shoot or twig growing from a stump remaining after God's judgment. Jesse. The father of David. A greater David is prophesied. Unlike the human failure before him, especially King Ahaz, this son of Jesse bears the fruit of a new world (p. 1262).

> I will give thanks to you, O Lord, for though you were angry with me, your anger turned away, that you might comfort me.
>
> Isa. 12:1

Once again, Isaiah prophecies a Messiah, a Savior for the world. In the middle of all this bad news Isaiah has portrayed in the first few chapters of this book, chapter 12 is a reprieve. Maybe you are in a dry place, let's go back and read chapter 12. It is very short:

You will say in that day: "I will give thanks to you, O Lord, for though you were angry with me, your anger turned away, that you might comfort me.

"Behold, God is my salvation; I will trust, and will not be afraid; for the Lord God is my strength and my song, and he has become my salvation."

With joy you will draw water from the wells of salvation. And you will say in that day:

"Give thanks to the Lord, call upon his name, make known his deeds among the peoples, proclaim that his name is exalted.

"Sing praises to the Lord, for he has done gloriously; let this be made known in all the earth. Shout, and sing for joy, O inhabitant of Zion, for great in your midst is the Holy One of Israel."

Even in misery, even in judgement, even in destruction, there is time to praise the Lord. But then chapter 13 reminds us God is not happy with sin, disobedience, or disregard for Him or His Word:

Wail, for the day of the Lord is near; as destruction from the Almighty it will come (v. 6)!

Behold, the day of the Lord comes, cruel, with wrath and fierce anger, to make the land a desolation and to destroy its sinners from it (v. 9).

I will punish the world for its evil, and the wicked for their iniquity (v. 11).

In my journal in 2011, concerning Isaiah 13, I wrote about Babylon, "Babylon, the great city, *'will never be inhabited or lived in for all generations'* (v. 20). Israel exists today, but Babylon does not exist. God's plans and purposes will come to pass. Humankind cannot stop it."

DIGGING DEEPER

Jokingly, I have said, "Do you know any Babylonians? No, but you certainly know Jews. And you certainly know Israelites today, don't you?" The Word of God comes true. These prophesies have been realized, and we see it even this day in our lives.

Prayer

Lord, we thank You for the root of Jesse, a branch that will bear fruit forevermore. Our Savior Jesus is prophesied once again in these chapters in the Book of Isaiah. We also recognize why we need a Savior. Thanks to chapter 13, You remind us You are not pleased with sin, disobedience, or disregard, and You will judge the earth. But then we thank You in chapter 12, we can praise You. We can give You glory because You loved us enough to send a Savior. Thank You. In Jesus' name. Amen.

MY THOUGHTS

ISAIAH 14 AND 15

Satan?

Today, we are in Isaiah 14 and 15. In chapter 14, does Isaiah give us a glimpse of Satan? Please read or listen to Isaiah 14 and 15.

COMMENTS

Regarding Isaiah 14, some people say verses 12-15 not only relate to the king of Babylon but might be a reference to Satan himself. Let's look at those verses:

> "'I will ascend above the heights of the clouds; I will make myself like the Most High.' But you are brought down to Sheol, to the far reaches of the pit."
>
> Isa. 14:14-15

"*How you are fallen from heaven, O Day Star, son of Dawn! How you are cut down to the ground, you who laid the nations low! You said in your heart, 'I will ascend to heaven; above the stars of God I will set my throne on high; I will sit on the mount of assembly in the far reaches of the north; I will ascend above the heights of the clouds; I will make myself like the Most High.' But you are brought down to Sheol, to the far reaches of the pit*" (14:12-15).

The pride, the arrogance, the boastfulness of the king of Babylon and Satan are much alike. Both have been, or will be, destroyed by the Lord. There is judgement on Babylon, Assyria, and Moab in these chapters. These judgements on various nations will continue over the next few chapters of Isaiah.

DIGGING DEEPER

I break away from the text for a moment to talk about the Ezra Project, ADDBIBLE, and *Day by Day Through the Bible*. The whole purpose of our journey through the Book of Isaiah is so you stay connected to God's Word. Yes, some could read the Book of Isaiah a chapter at a time, and that would take sixty-six days. Over the years, I have read Isaiah a variety of ways, so I chose to go through the sixty-six chapters in thirty-one days. My prayer is that this approach keeps you involved; it keeps you engaged in the Word of God.

The purpose of ADDBIBLE and *Day by Day* is for busy people to stay connected to the Word of the Lord. I hope you not only enjoy these devotions but are being blessed by staying in the Word of God each and every day.

I realize when combining chapters, sometimes the readings are long, but it is more important to read or hear the Word of the Lord than to read or hear my comments about the Word of the Lord. I also encourage you to grab your Bible and go back through these books at a slower pace. My prayer again, is that you are blessed by staying connected to God's Word each and every day.

I encourage you to do two things. I encourage you to spread the Word. Turn your friends onto these daily devotions so they too can stay connected to God's Word on a daily basis. Secondly, maybe you would be led to help support this ministry with your prayers and with your financial support so we can continue to make the Bible available all over the world. Visit ezraproject.net and see how you can support the Ezra Project, ADDBIBLE, and *Day by Day Through the Bible*.

Prayer

Father, we thank You for Your Word. We thank You for the Prophet Isaiah. We thank You that You spoke these words into his heart and we get to read them thousands of years later. Bless each of us as we read or listen to Your Word. In Your name, we pray. Amen.

MY THOUGHTS

ISAIAH 16 AND 17

Pride, Arrogance, and Forgetfulness

Today is day seven of our journey through the Book of Isaiah in thirty-one days. Have you been guilty of pride, arrogance, or forgetting your relationship with God? Please read or listen to Isaiah 16 and 17.

COMMENTS

Chapter 16 is a continuation of chapter 15, an oracle concerning Moab. Who were the Moabites? We go all the way back to Genesis 19, the story of Lot and Sodom and Gomorrah, to find out the origin of the Moabites.

After Lot escaped the destruction of Sodom and Gomorrah, he lived in a town called Zoar. His two daughters escaped with him. Their story picks up in Genesis 19:30-37:

Now Lot went up out of Zoar and lived in the hills with his two daughters, for he was afraid to live in Zoar. So he lived in a cave with his two daughters. And the firstborn said to the younger, "Our father is old, and there is not a man on earth to come in to us after the manner of all the earth. Come, let us make our father drink wine, and we will lie with him, that we may preserve offspring from our father." So they made their father drink wine that night. And the firstborn went in and lay with her father. He did not know when she lay down or when she arose.

The next day, the firstborn said to the younger, "Behold, I lay last night with my father. Let us make him drink wine tonight also. Then you go in and lie with him, that we may preserve offspring from our father." So they made their father drink wine that night also. And the younger arose and lay with him, and he did not know when she lay down or when she arose. Thus both the daughters of Lot became pregnant by their father. The firstborn bore a son and called his name Moab. He is the father of the Moabites to this day.

Out of sexual immorality, the Moabites came into existence. After many, many years, they are being oppressed by Assyria, so they cry out to God. He answers in Isaiah 16:4-5:

When the oppressor is no more, and destruction has ceased, and he who tramples underfoot has vanished from the land, then a throne will be established in steadfast love, and on it will sit in faithfulness in the tent of David one who judges and seeks justice and is swift to do righteousness.

God's reply is indirect. As the Moabites plead for safety from Assyrian oppression, He refers to the Messianic throne of David, full of divine integrity, but He also will demand submission. *"We have heard of the pride of Moab—how proud he is!—of his arrogance, his pride, and his insolence; in his idle boasting he is not right"* (16:6). Pride and arrogance are Moab's sin.

Chapter 16 concludes with this message, *"And when Moab presents himself, when he wearies himself on the high place, when he comes to his sanctuary to pray, he will not prevail. This is the word that the Lord spoke concerning Moab in the past. But now the Lord has spoken, saying, 'In three years, like the years of a hired worker, the glory of Moab will be brought into contempt, in spite of all his great multitude, and those who remain will be very few and feeble'"* (16:12-14). God judges pride and arrogance.

Chapter 17 is an oracle concerning Damascus. The problem with Damascus is outlined in verse 17:10, *"For you have forgotten the God of your salvation and have not remembered the Rock of your refuge".* What will happen to Damascus? *"Damascus will cease to be a city and will become a heap of ruins"* (17:1).

Damascus was destroyed by Assyria in 732 B.C. But again, Isaiah projects ahead, *"In that day man will look to his Maker, and his eyes will look on the Holy One of Israel. He will not look to the altars, the work of his hands, and he will not look on what his own fingers have made"* (17:7-8).

> **For you have forgotten the God of your salvation and have not remembered the Rock of your refuge.**
>
> **Isa. 17:10**

DIGGING DEEPER

In these two chapters, God's judgment is on pride and arrogance and those who forget God. We all know God is the same yesterday, today, and forever. He is still very unhappy with pride, arrogance, and those who forget Him.

Out of these two tough chapters, our application is pretty simple. Check our pride barometer. Check our arrogance barometer. And remember the Lord and all He has done for us. Let's not get put in a position of judgment and potential destruction because of poor behavior before God.

Prayer

Lord, it appears these people cry out to You when they are desperate. We also cry out to You when we are desperate. In these instances, it appears You had enough and You destroyed them rather than answer their prayers. Let it not be so for us. Let us come to You with a repentant heart for our pride, our arrogance, and when we have forgotten You and have lived our own lives without You. May You hear our prayer and forgive us and restore our relationship with You. We do not deserve it any more than the Moabites or those in Assyria, but we ask it because You said we could. You are a God of mercy, and we thank You. In Jesus' name. Amen.

MY THOUGHTS

ISAIAH 18 AND 19

Hope

Today, we cover two more chapters of Isaiah, chapters 18 and 19. Are you on a downward spiral? Do you need hope? Please read or listen to Isaiah 18 and 19.

COMMENTS

In my journal in 1991, I wrote, "Not much going on here. These chapters are not easily understood; need to know a lot of history to relate to this." You may feel the same after these two chapters.

Ten years later, in 2001, I wrote a one-liner, "Judgment on nations. As a true prophet of God, it all had to come true."

Ten more years later, in 2011, I wrote, "Egypt will turn to the Lord? Was this ever fulfilled or is it still prophetic?"

Isaiah 18 is an oracle concerning Cush. My English Standard Version Study Bible footnote says, "Cush, also known as Nubia or Ethiopia (though not the same as modern Ethiopia), designates a region of northeast Africa along the Nile, which corresponds to present-day southern Egypt and northern Sudan, and is located northwest of present-day Ethiopia" (p. 1272). The interesting thing about chapter 18, is it refers to Gentile nations, *"All you inhabitants of the world, you who dwell on the earth, when a signal is raised on the mountains, look! When a trumpet is blown, hear!"* (18:3).

Then Isaiah projects into the future. *"At that time tribute will be brought to the Lord of hosts, from a people tall and smooth, from a people feared near and far, a nation mighty and conquering, whose land the rivers divide, to Mount Zion, the place of the name of the Lord of hosts"* (18:7). In the future, on that day, Gentiles will praise the Lord.

Chapter 19 is an oracle concerning Egypt. Egypt will suffer under the judgment of the Lord. Let's look at a couple of verses:

> *And I will stir up Egyptians against Egyptians, and they will fight, each against another and each against his neighbor, city against city, kingdom against kingdom; and the spirit of the Egyptians within them will be emptied out, and I will confound their counsel . . . and I will give over the Egyptians into the hand of a hard master, and a fierce king will rule over them, declares the Lord God of hosts* (19:2-4).

> *Where then are your wise men? Let them tell you that they might know what the Lord of hosts has purposed against Egypt* (19:12).

> *The Lord has mingled within her a spirit of confusion, and they will make Egypt stagger in all its deeds, as a drunken man staggers in his vomit. And there will be nothing for Egypt that head or tail, palm branch or reed, may do* (19:14-15).

But Isaiah projects past all this into the future:

> *In that day there will be an altar to the Lord in the midst of the land of Egypt, and a pillar to the Lord at its border. It will be a sign and a witness to the Lord of hosts in the land of Egypt. When they cry to the Lord because of oppressors, he will send them a savior and defender, and deliver them. And the Lord will make himself known to the Egyptians, and the Egyptians will know the Lord in*

that day and worship with sacrifice and offering, and they will make vows to the Lord and perform them. And the Lord will strike Egypt, striking and healing, and they will return to the Lord, and he will listen to their pleas for mercy and heal them (19:19-22).

The chapter concludes with, *"In that day Israel will be the third with Egypt and Assyria, a blessing in the midst of the earth, whom the Lord of hosts has blessed, saying, 'Blessed be Egypt my people, and Assyria the work of my hands, and Israel my inheritance'"* (19:24-25). On the day of this writing, that is certainly not the case, but what a glorious future it will be when Assyria, Egypt, and Israel all worship the Lord. When God calls *"Egypt my people, and Assyria the work of my hands, and Israel my inheritance"* (19:25), what a day that will be.

> **Blessed be Egypt my people, and Assyria the work of my hands, and Israel my inheritance.**
>
> **Isa. 19:25**

DIGGING DEEPER

Hallelujah! In the midst of judgement, Isaiah always brings hope. I hope these chapters have encouraged you today. If you are in the midst of a downward spiral with the Lord, there is hope. Come back to the Lord. His arms are open and He will receive You.

Prayer

Father, we thank You for the hope we receive from reading Your Word. Though these prophetic words have not all come to pass in our lifetime yet, they still may. When they do, the world will know that You are God, there is no other. Blessed be Your name. The name, in whom we pray. Amen.

MY THOUGHTS

ISAIAH 20-22

Does Isaiah Preach Naked?

Toaday, we cover Isaiah chapters 20-22. Listen very carefully to chapter 20. See what God asks Isaiah to do. Are you willing to do anything for God? Please read or listen to Isaiah 20-22.

COMMENTS

Let's look at Isaiah 20. In 2011, I wrote, "Isaiah is instructed by the Lord to walk naked and barefoot. He did so for three years. Was Isaiah really naked?" I quoted verse 4, *"with buttocks uncovered'. That sounds naked to me."*

What does the Word of God say? *"At that time the Lord spoke by Isaiah the son of Amoz, saying, 'Go, and loose the sackcloth from your waist and take off your sandals from your feet,' and he did so, walking naked and barefoot'"* (20:2). We do not question when you take your sandals off you are barefoot, so why do we question when you take your sackcloth off you are naked?

> "Go, and loose the sackcloth from your waist and take off your sandals from your feet, and he did so, walking naked and barefoot."
>
> Isa. 20:2

Why did the Lord ask Isaiah to do this? Scripture interprets scripture:

Then the Lord said, "As my servant Isaiah has walked naked and barefoot for three years as a sign and a portent against Egypt and Cush, so shall the king of Assyria lead away the Egyptian captives and the Cushite exiles, both the young and the old, naked and barefoot, with buttocks uncovered, the nakedness of Egypt. Then they shall be dismayed and ashamed because of Cush their hope and of Egypt their boast. And the inhabitants of this coastland will say in that day, 'Behold, this is what has happened to those in whom we hoped and to whom we fled for help to be delivered from the king of Assyria! And we, how shall we escape?'" (20:3-6)

God asked Isaiah to prophesy naked for three years to show the hopelessness of relying on Egypt or Cush or anybody else but the Lord.

DIGGING DEEPER

Who are you relying on? Are you relying on your employer? Are you relying on your friends? Are you relying on your spouse? Are you relying on your parents? The application from this message is rely on God and God alone. The world and all it has to offer is not dependable, but God is rock solid. Let's pray.

Prayer

Lord, sometimes we pray we will do anything You ask us to do, but after this chapter, we might exercise more caution when we pray like that. You asked Isaiah and other prophets to do some amazing things to communicate Your message to Your people. May it not take so much drama for us to hear what You have to say to us.

If we are depending on the things of the world, forgive us. Please do not strip everything away from us to teach us a lesson. Let us hear clearly from Your Word. May we depend on You and not the things of the world. Lord, guide and direct our steps. We ask it in Jesus' name. Amen.

MY THOUGHTS

The Whole Earth Is Judged

Today is day ten in our thirty-one-day journey through the Book of Isaiah and we will look at chapters 23 and 24. Not only individual nations, but the whole earth is subject to God's judgment. Do you want to be here when that happens? Please read or listen to Isaiah 23 and 24.

COMMENTS

In chapters leading up to Isaiah 24, nations were judged by the Lord. Here in chapter 24, the whole earth is judged. Let's take a look at some verses:

Behold, the Lord will empty the earth and make it desolate, and he will twist its surface and scatter its inhabitants (24:1).

The earth shall be utterly empty and utterly plundered; for the Lord has spoken this word (24:3).

The earth lies defiled under its inhabitants; for they have transgressed the laws, violated the statutes, broken the everlasting covenant. Therefore a curse devours the earth, and its inhabitants suffer for their guilt; therefore the inhabitants of the earth are scorched, and few men are left (24:5-6).

There is an outcry in the streets for lack of wine; all joy has grown dark; the gladness of the earth is banished (24:11).

The earth is utterly broken, the earth is split apart, the earth is violently shaken. The earth staggers like a drunken man; it sways like a hut; its transgression lies heavy upon it, and it falls, and will not rise again (24:19-20).

> The earth staggers
> like a drunken man;
> it sways like a hut.
> Isa. 20:20

Verse 21 concludes the matter, *"On that day the Lord will punish the host of heaven, in heaven, and the kings of the earth, on the earth."*

DIGGING DEEPER

All opposition to God, whether in heaven or on earth, will be judged. But, in the midst of the judgment, even of the whole earth, there is hope:

They lift up their voices, they sing for joy; over the majesty of the Lord they shout from the west. Therefore in the east give glory to the Lord; in the coastlands of the sea, give glory to the name of the Lord, the God of Israel. From the ends of the earth we hear songs of praise, of glory to the Righteous One (24:14-16).

After this chapter, what are you going to do? Are you going to fear the end of the world or are you going to look toward the glory of God? These things have yet to occur, but Isaiah is a prophet, and his words are true. These things will occur someday in the future.

It is interesting that virtually every generation thinks it is the last generation; yet still we tarry on the earth. I have never been a "sky-is-falling" Christian. I never really worry about the end of the age. I doubt if my worrying about it is going to speed it up or slow it down.

I used to want to be alive when Jesus came from the heavens back to the earth, but I forgot what condition the world will be in at that time. It will literally be hell on earth. We get a little glimpse of that in Isaiah 24.

Prayer

Lord, whether You come today, whether today is the day of salvation, or that day is thousands of years into the future, does not change my responsibility as I sojourn on the earth. The last thing You commanded us to do was be a witness for You in Jerusalem, Judea, Samaria, and the uttermost parts of the earth. Lord, help each one of us as we hear these things from Your Word, as we read the promises of scripture, be a bold witness for You.

Yes, one day the earth will be no more. That will happen according to Your perfect timetable. So, Lord, bless us as we sojourn on the earth as witnesses for You. Give us strength, power, and passion to share Jesus to those around us. In the name of the Lord, we pray. Amen.

MY THOUGHTS

ISAIAH 25 AND 26

Smooth

In our journey through the Book of Isaiah, today brings us to chapters 25 and 26. Is your life bumpy or smooth? Are you bouncing or gliding through life? Please read or listen to Isaiah 25 and 26.

COMMENTS

In 1991, I wrote about these chapters. I referred to 25:8, "Death and tears will be no more." Then quoted 26:7, *"The way of the righteous is smooth"* (NASB).

Ten years later, in 2001, I wrote, *"'You will keep him in perfect peace, Whose mind is stayed on You, Because he trusts in You'* (26:3 NKJV). I need Your perfect peace now, Lord."

In 2011, another 10 years later, I wrote, "God wins. He will reign from Jerusalem. Heaven on earth, referring to 25:6-9." Then, "Glory be His name." I quoted 26:3, *"You keep him in perfect peace whose mind is stayed*

> You keep him in perfect peace whose mind is stayed on you, because he trusts in you.
>
> Isa. 26:3

on you, because he trusts in you." And lastly, *"The path of the righteous is level; you make level the way of the righteous"* (26:7).

Isaiah 25 follows chapter 24. You might remember Isaiah 24 was the destruction of the whole earth. But there were no chapter breaks in the first renderings of the Bible, so chapter 25 continues after the destruction of the whole earth with *"O Lord, you are my God; I will exalt you; I will praise your name, for you have done wonderful things, plans formed of old, faithful and sure"* (25:1). Before the destruction of the earth, the question is: can you say that very phrase in that verse? Salvation, our relationship with God, is personal. Can you say, *"O Lord, you are my God; I will exalt you; I will praise your name"?* If not, make your relationship with God personal at the end of this devotion today.

Isaiah 25 also tells us God will reign from Jerusalem on earth. Let's look at 25:6-9:

On this mountain the Lord of hosts will make for all peoples a feast of rich food, a feast of well-aged wine, of rich food full of marrow, of aged wine well refined. And he will swallow up on this mountain the covering that is cast over all peoples, the veil that is spread over all nations. He will swallow up death forever; and the Lord God will wipe away tears from all faces, and the reproach of his people he will take away from all the earth, for the Lord has spoken. It will be said on that day, "Behold, this is our God; we have waited for him, that he might save us. This is the Lord; we have waited for him; let us be glad and rejoice in his salvation."

DIGGING DEEPER

Yes, in that day, death will be defeated forever; pain and tears will be defeated forever. We will rejoice in the God of our salvation. With the revelation of that truth in Isaiah 25, I hope we can all exclaim, *"You keep him in perfect peace whose mind is stayed on you, because he trusts in you. Trust in the Lord forever, for the Lord God is an everlasting rock"* (26:3-4). Make that your cry of your heart today. Trust in the Lord.

Those of us who do, look at 26:7, *"The path of the righteous is level; you make level the way of the righteous."* In my journal, I referred to it as, "Smooth." Is your life smooth? Are you on the path of righteousness? If your life is bumpy, if it is up and down, if it is all around, get on the path of righteousness before the Lord and let Him smooth out your path.

Isaiah 26 also proclaims, *"Your dead shall live; their bodies shall rise. You who dwell in the dust, awake and sing for joy!"* (26:19). What an assurance of our resurrection!

Prayer

Lord, I thank You for the assurance of a resurrection. Bodies will rise. The earth will give birth to the dead. Thank You, again, for the assurance of a resurrection. Life is not all there is. There will be life after death. The question is where will we spend it? In eternity with God in heaven or in eternity with Satan in hell?

For those of us who are sure of our salvation in You, we shout hallelujah! We look forward to eternity with You. But for those who are unsure, remind them, Lord, of what Your Word says in the New Testament, *"I am the way, the truth and the light, no man comes to the Father except through me"* (John 14:6).

Come to Jesus. Confess your sins. He is faithful and just to forgive your sins and cleanse you from all unrighteousness, so that you too can enjoy eternity in heaven with God. Lord, draw them to You today. We ask it, in Your name. Amen.

MY THOUGHTS

ISAIAH 27 AND 28

Mocking the Messenger

Today, we are in Isaiah 27 and 28. Israel mocks Isaiah. Have you ever mocked a man of God? Please read or listen to Isaiah 27 and 28.

COMMENTS

Referring to my personal Bible reading journals, I wrote in 1991, primarily concerning Isaiah 28 (NASB), *"For his God instructs and teaches him properly'* (28:26). *'His counsel is wonderful and . . . great'"* (28:29).

In 2001, I also focused more on Isaiah 28, referring to verses 24-25, "At some time we have to quit preparing the ground and actually plant the seed. We pray for people, but we don't share the gospel message with them. Plant." Isaiah 28:24-25 actually say:

Does he who plows for sowing plow continually? Does he continually open and harrow his ground? When he has leveled its surface, does he not scatter dill, sow cumin, and put in wheat in rows and barley in its proper place, and emmer as the border?

The point in my journal is clear. The ground is prepared. Plant the seed. It reminds me of similar phrase I have heard, "It's time to quit stirring and start painting."

In 2011, I wrote, *"'In that day'* (27:1). It must be the final days, the last days. The Lord is coming out from His place to punish the inhabitants of the earth for their iniquity." Then I referred to 28:16, "And God lays a new *'foundation in Zion, a stone, a tested stone, a precious cornerstone'*, Jesus Himself."

DIGGING DEEPER

In Isaiah 28, Israel is rejecting Isaiah's message. We see it in verses 9-10:

> For it is precept upon precept, precept upon precept, line upon line, line upon line, here a little, there a little.
>
> Isa. 28:10

To whom will he teach knowledge, and to whom will he explain the message? Those who are weaned from the milk, those taken from the breast? For it is precept upon precept, precept upon precept, line upon line, line upon line, here a little, there a little.

Israel is mocking the message of Isaiah, *"Therefore hear the word of the Lord, you scoffers, who rule this people in Jerusalem!"* (28:14). What does Isaiah want them to hear? What does God want them to hear? *"Therefore thus says the Lord God, 'Behold, I am the one who has laid as a foundation in Zion, a stone, a tested stone, a precious cornerstone, of a sure foundation: "Whoever believes will not be in haste"'"* (28:16).

My English Standard Version footnote on that verse says, "That sure foundation, embodied in Jesus Christ, is the good news that God saves as no one else can . . . Isaiah heaps terms upon terms to emphasize that God's salvation is worth believing in" (p.1289).

Israel struggled to believe. Do you struggle to believe? Israel struggled to commit their ways to the Lord. Do you struggle to commit your ways to the Lord? As we close, let's go back to a few verses, *"Give ear, and hear my voice; give attention, and hear my speech"* (28:23). *"For he is rightly instructed; his God teaches him"* (28:26). And the final verse of what we read today, *"This also comes from the Lord of hosts; he is wonderful in counsel and excellent in wisdom"* (28:29).

Do not be like Israel of old. Hear the Word of the Lord. Do not reject that tested stone, that precious cornerstone, that sure foundation, Jesus our Lord and Savior. If you have not done so, give your heart to Him today. And friends, if you did so, contact the ezraproject.net so we can pray for you. God bless you.

Prayer

Lord, we pray we will hear and listen to Your voice. We will not struggle to believe, and we will not struggle to commit our ways to You. We will give ear and attention to You. We will lean on You as our teacher and counselor. Speak to us Lord. In Jesus' name, we pray it. Amen.

MY THOUGHTS

This Is the Way, Walk in It

Today, we will cover Isaiah 29 and 30. Are you stubborn? Do you honor God with your lips but not your heart? If He showed you the way, would you walk in it? Please read or listen to Isaiah 29 and 30.

COMMENTS

Because of the length of today's chapters, I will only share from my journal in 2011, "Has it always been this way, that people substitute religion for relationship with God?" Then, "Do wonder upon wonder, Lord, referring to 29:14." I continued, "Humans question God all the time. Who do we think we are? Or more importantly, who do we think God is? God will reveal Himself clearly once again. We are a stubborn people who go about our own business, not God's plans. Isaiah was instructed to *write it before them on a tablet and inscribe it in a book . . . as a witness forever'* (30:8). We really don't want to hear from God. God wants us to come back to Him. He will help us get back on the right path and He will devour those who do not."

DIGGING DEEPER

Let's go back to 29:13, *"And the Lord said: 'Because this people draws near with their mouth and honor me with their lips, while their hearts are far from me'"*. Is your heart in your prayers? Is your heart in your praise? Is your heart in your faith in Jesus, or is your relationship just lip service?

How about 30:1, *"'Ah, stubborn children,' declares the Lord, 'who carry out a plan, but not mine, and who make an alliance, but not of my Spirit, that they may add sin to sin.'"* Are you working your plan, or God's plan for your life? Have you ever asked Him what His plan is for your life?

Think about what 30:8 really says, *"And now, go, write it before them on a tablet and inscribe it in a book, that it may be for the time to come as a witness forever."* What Isaiah heard from the Lord, and what he did back then, we hold in our hands or we listen to today. That is amazing!

Let's close with one more application:

Therefore the LORD waits to be gracious to you, and therefore he exalts himself to show mercy to you. For the LORD is a God of justice; blessed are all those who wait for him.

> **Therefore the LORD waits to be gracious to you, and therefore he exalts himself to show mercy to you.**
>
> **Isa. 30:18**

For a people shall dwell in Zion, in Jerusalem; you shall weep no more. He will surely be gracious to you at the sound of your cry. As soon as he hears it, he answers you. And though the Lord give you the bread of adversity and the water of affliction, yet your Teacher will not hide himself anymore, but your eyes shall see your Teacher. And your ears shall hear a word behind you, saying, "This is the way, walk in it," when you turn to the right or when you turn to the left (30:18-21).

Praise the Lord! He is gracious to us, merciful, and just. As soon as we cry out to Him, He answers! What a promise! Even in our adversity, or affliction, He hides no more! He will lead us out of such distress as a light to our path and a lamp to our feet saying, *"This is the way, walk in it."* If you need God's grace, His mercy, His justice, cry out to Him. If you are in distress, cry out to Him. He is the way, walk to Him today.

Prayer

God, thank You for preserving Your Word. Because You did so, we can read about the times of yesterday, the times we live in, and the days of tomorrow. We are reminded of Your stubborn children then and our own stubbornness now. But we are also reminded of Your grace, mercy, justice, and direction available from You to us, if we just cry out to You. We do so; we cry out to You this day! Hear our prayer, as You say You will, and show us the way, and Lord give us the desire and strength to walk according to Your way. Amen.

MY THOUGHTS

Don't Look to Egypt

Today, we are in Isaiah 31 and 32. From here to the end, we will be taking the rest of the Book of Isaiah two chapters a day. When you need help, who do you depend on: horses, chariots, your own strength, or the Lord? Please read or listen to Isaiah 31 and 32.

COMMENTS

In my personal Bible reading journals, of both 1991 and 2001, I read these chapters, but did not write anything about them. So let's move to 2011 when I read Isaiah 31-33 on the same day, and wrote, "Trust in man or God? Thirty-one makes the case to trust in God over man every time. Walk by faith in God, not by sight in man." Then I wrote, "Women take for granted the blessings of the Lord until they're removed, referring to 32:9-14." I continued, "When the Spirit returns, we experience fruit of the land, justice, righteousness, peace, quietness, trust, referring to 32:15-18."

Let's go back to chapter 31 for a very important principle in the Word of God. Though Isaiah is referring to Egypt, we can think about people or things we depend on today. As we read these verses again, replace Egypt with something you depend on yourself, *"Woe to those who go down to Egypt for help and rely on horses, who trust in chariots because they are many and in horsemen because they are very strong, but do not look to the Holy One of Israel or consult the Lord!"* (31:1). *"The Egyptians are man, and not God, and their horses are flesh, and not spirit. When the Lord stretches out his hand, the helper will stumble, and he who is helped will fall, and they will all perish together"* (31:3).

When you are in trouble, who do you depend on? Israel was depending on Egypt to save them. Yet God says, "No, Egypt is not going to save you. I am going to save you." Who is your Egypt? Is it your job? Is it your family? Is it the government? Who do you look to when you are in trouble to get you out of your situation? Do you look to man or do you look to God?

After Isaiah admonishes Israel for looking to Egypt, or looking to man, he gives them the solution:

> **Like birds hovering, so the Lord of hosts will protect Jerusalem; he will protect and deliver it; he will spare and rescue it.**
>
> Isa. 31:5

For thus the Lord said to me, "As a lion or a young lion growls over his prey, and when a band of shepherds is called out against him he is not terrified by their shouting or daunted at their noise, so the Lord of hosts will come down to fight on Mount Zion and on its hill. Like birds hovering, so the Lord of hosts will protect Jerusalem; he will protect and deliver it; he will spare and rescue it."

Turn to him from whom people have deeply revolted, O children of Israel. For in that day everyone shall cast away his idols of silver and his idols of gold, which your hands have sinfully made for you (31:4-7).

DIGGING DEEPER

Isaiah gives Israel the solution here in chapter 31. He gives us the same solution today. We are not to depend on men, or man, or this world to get us out of situations or circumstances. We are to turn our eyes toward the Lord and depend on the Lord of hosts who will deliver us.

Let's pay particular attention to verse 6, *"Turn to him from whom people have deeply revolted."* We have so much ungodliness today, so much anti-God today, but we as Christians need to turn to the Lord for our solutions.

What are you facing this very day? What is the challenge before you and your life today? Are you looking to the world for a solution or are you looking to the Word? Or are you looking to God for your solution? It is clear in Isaiah 31; we need to turn our eyes back to the Lord.

Isaiah 32:15-18 tell us what happens when we call upon the Lord, when the Holy Spirit is who we depend on to resolve our conflicts:

> *until the Spirit is poured upon us from on high, and the wilderness becomes a fruitful field, and the fruitful field is deemed a forest. Then justice will dwell in the wilderness, and righteousness abide in the fruitful field. And the effect of righteousness will be peace, and the result of righteousness, quietness and trust forever. My people will abide in a peaceful habitation, in secure dwellings, and in quiet resting places.*

O, the difference between the cares of this world and the peace of God when we depend on Him.

Prayer

Lord, we turn our attention to You. Or for some of us, we turn our attention back to You. Maybe we are under the circumstances. Maybe we are in the midst of a difficult trial. Lord, keep my eyes fixed on You. Do not let the world and the idolatry of this world try to tell me it can solve my problems. You and You alone can solve my problems today.

We ask, Lord, that You intervene, show Yourself, deliver us from anything we are facing today as we call upon You, as this chapter reminds us to do. When You respond, when You answer, may we be careful to give You all the praise and all the glory. For it is in Jesus' name, we ask it. Amen.

MY THOUGHTS

ISAIAH 33 AND 34

Walk with Him or Be Judged by Him

Isaiah chapters 33 and 34 offer a clear choice: walk with God or be judged by Him. How is your walk? Do you stay close to God, or wander away? Please read or listen to Isaiah 33 and 34.

COMMENTS

Isaiah 33 and 34 give us a pretty clear choice. One is to walk with the Lord and depend on the Lord. The other is to be judged by God Himself. First, let's look at the good news in chapter 33, *"O LORD, be gracious to us; we wait for you. Be our arm every morning, our salvation in the time of trouble"* (33:2). *"The LORD is exalted, for he dwells on high; he will fill Zion with justice and righteousness, and he will be the stability of your times, abundance of salvation, wisdom, and knowledge; the fear of the LORD is Zion's treasure"* (33:5-6). That is how it can be as we depend on the Lord.

Let's keep going, *"'Now I will arise,' says the LORD, 'now I will lift myself up; now I will be exalted'"* (33:10). Let's go on to verse 20. I often say the safest place on earth is Jerusalem. You might think I am crazy; however, all the world may disappear, but Jerusalem will be there at the end. *"Behold Zion, the city of our appointed feasts! Your eyes will see Jerusalem, an untroubled habitation, an immovable tent, whose stakes will never be plucked up, nor will any of its cords be broken."* Yes, Jerusalem may be the safest place on earth. It will be there in the end.

> **For the LORD is our judge; the LORD is our lawgiver; the LORD is our king; he will save us.**
>
> **Isa. 33:22**

Finally, *"For the LORD is our judge; the LORD is our lawgiver; the LORD is our king; he will save us"* (33:22). Isaiah 33 begs us to come back to the Lord, begs us to have a relationship with God Almighty. And He wants a relationship with us. He wants us and He wants to be our God.

But the contrast is Isaiah 34:

For the LORD is enraged against all the nations, and furious against all their host; he has devoted them to destruction, has given them over for slaughter. Their slain shall be cast out, and the stench of their corpses shall rise; the mountains shall flow with their blood. All the host of heaven shall rot away, and the skies roll up like a scroll (34:2-4).

DIGGING DEEPER

O, that we would not face the judgment of God. *"For the LORD has a day of vengeance, a year of recompense for the cause of Zion"* (34:8). *"He shall stretch the line of confusion over it, and the plumb line of emptiness"* (34:11). We need to stop here and ask, is that what your life is like, confusion and emptiness? If so, go back to Isaiah 33, call upon the name of the Lord. Get close to God once again. Let Him erase the confusion and fill your emptiness with His love.

There is more great advice in 34:16, *"Seek and read from the book of the LORD."* That is what we are doing. That is what *Day by Day Through the Bible* is all about, staying in the Word of the Lord. *"Seek and read from the book of the LORD."*

Prayer

Father, You give us a choice today. You give us the contrast of how You want us to be close to You and how You want to be close to us in Isaiah 33. But if not, and by our choice, then You will judge. You become furious, You become enraged, at those who do not want a relationship with You.

Lord, we pray, we commit to follow You, to stay close to You, to seek You. Hear our prayers, Lord. Guide our steps. Direct our paths. Help us be a light shining in the darkness of this world. Help us pull others toward You and away from Your judgment. Give us strength, Lord, and power to do this. In Jesus' name. Amen.

MY THOUGHTS

ISAIAH 35 AND 36

Who Do You Trust?

Isaiah 35 and 36 challenge us to trust in God. Who do you trust in? Self, family, friends, government, or God Almighty? Please read or listen to Isaiah 35 and 36.

COMMENTS

After reading chapters 35 and 36 (NASB) in 1991, I quoted one verse, *"Encourage the exhausted, and strengthen the feeble"* (35:3).

In 2001, I read Isaiah 33-36 on the same day, and wrote one entry about these chapters referring to chapter 36, "Who do we trust? Egypt, ourselves, our enemies, or God and His promises?"

In 2011, I wrote concerning these chapters, "After His judgement they shall see the glory of the Lord, the majesty of our God, referring to 35:2. Heaven on earth, referring to 35:5-10. A highway of holiness that only the redeemed can cross. Again, all will not make it to heaven, referring to 35:8-9." Then, "The world says, 'Don't trust in God', after seeing *'We trust in the Lord our God'* in 36:7. They lie and say it is from God, referring to 36:10. It promises peace and prosperity yet cannot deliver, referring to 36:16-17."

Chapter 35 gives us a little glimpse of heaven on earth. Does this sound like Jesus?

Then the eyes of the blind shall be opened, and the ears of the deaf unstopped; then shall the lame man leap like a deer, and the tongue of the mute sing for joy. For waters break forth in the wilderness, and streams in the desert; the burning sand shall become a pool, and the thirsty ground springs of water; in the haunt of jackals, where they lie down, the grass shall become reeds and rushes. And a highway shall be there, and it shall be called the Way of Holiness; the unclean shall not pass over it. It shall belong to those who walk on the way (35:5-8).

We thank the Lord throughout Isaiah there are glimpses of heaven. There are glimpses of the end times. There are glimpses of the future.

Before we look at chapter 36, I want to refer to a footnote in my English Standard Version Study Bible concerning the transitional aspects of the chapters we are in, and we will be in, for the next couple of days. Concerning chapters 36 through 39:8:

Historical Transition: "In Whom Do You Now Trust?" These chapters form a narrative bridge between the mostly poetic chapters 1-35 and 40-66. Chapters 36-37 look back to chapters 28-35, proving through Hezekiah that faith in God is met by his blessing. Chapters 38-39 provide context for chapters 40-55, as Hezekiah's folly dooms his nation to Babylonian exile. Against the backdrop of divine faithfulness (chapters 36-37) and human inconstancy (chapters 38-39), God stands forth as the only hope of his people (p. 1302).

As we look at chapter 36, we see the transition as Assyria knocks at the door of the walls of Jerusalem and they talk to King Hezekiah. The question the representative from Assyria asks the people of Jerusalem is, "Who do you trust? Are you going to trust your king, King Hezekiah, against the power of Assyria?" The Rabshakeh, the representative from Assyria, intentionally speaks to the hearers of all the people, not just to the representatives, so they can fear and tremble with what they hear.

DIGGING DEEPER

The application, the question, for us is the same today. Who do we trust in and who do we listen to? Verse 2 of Isaiah 36 says there is a great army approaching Jerusalem. Verses 4 and 5 say, *"On what do you rest this trust of yours? Do you think that mere words are strategy and power for war? In whom do you now trust."* A question all of us should consider in our heart of hearts. The Rabshakeh asks them, "Are you going to trust in your friends? Your neighbors? Are you really going to trust in Egypt, that broken reed of a staff?"

> **On what do you rest this trust of yours? Do you think that mere words are strategy and power for war? In whom do you now trust.**
>
> Isa. 36:5

Then he offers them a deal, "If you compromise with me, I will give you horses and we can have peace together."

Then he offers them the ultimate deception, the same Satan does to us today. *"Moreover, is it without the Lord that I have come up against this land to destroy it? The Lord said to me, 'Go up against this land and destroy it'"* (36:10). A falsity, a complete lie. That is what the enemy did then; that is what the enemy does today. He lies in our ears.

Lastly, he accuses the godly. He accuses King Hezekiah himself. He says to the people, *"Do not let Hezekiah deceive you, for he will not be able to deliver you. Do not let Hezekiah make you trust in the Lord by saying, 'The Lord will surely deliver us. This city will not be given into the hand of the king of Assyria.' Do not listen to Hezekiah"* (36:14-16). The same attacks come from the enemy today. He attacks godly people and says, "Don't listen to them. They don't know what they are talking about. Don't trust in God."

In Isaiah 37 and 38, we will see what Hezekiah does; what God does in response to these accusations from Assyria. But until then, what are you going to do? What is your response when Satan lies in your ears? The deception all around us is that Christianity is out-of-date. It is old-fashioned, irrelevant. It does not apply to our lives today. Does it sound any different than it was back in Isaiah's day? We have the same choice. Who are we going to trust? Are we going to trust in the words of men or are we going to trust in the Word of the Lord?

Prayer

Lord, may we push back from the lies of the enemy in our day just like Isaiah and Hezekiah did in their day. In Your name, we pray. Amen.

MY THOUGHTS

ISAIAH 37 AND 38

Hezekiah

Isaiah 37 and 38 contain the story of King Hezekiah. If you face the impossible, read or listen to these two chapters. Do you believe prayer can change things? Please read or listen to Isaiah 37 and 38.

COMMENTS

My journals from 1991, 2001, and 2011, reflect some thoughts on these two chapters. In 1991, I wrote about chapter 37, "Against all odds, God delivers His people. 185,000 die as Israel is saved. That's a big number."

> So now, O Lord our God, save us from his hand, that all the kingdoms of the earth may know that you alone are the Lord.
>
> Isa. 37:20

In 2001, I wrote, "God delivers Israel from Assyria against all odds. He destroys 185,000 soldiers and the king. Trust in the Lord. He then extends Hezekiah's life fifteen years."

In 2011, I wrote, "Hezekiah turned to the Lord for His help in time of need. God heard his prayer, saved Jerusalem, and punished Assyria. We need leaders who will turn to the Lord." And I quoted, *"So now, O Lord our God, save us from his hand, that all the kingdoms of the earth may know that you alone are the Lord"* (37:20). Then I wrote, "God said Hezekiah was to die. Then God said he would live an extra fifteen years. What happened in between? Hezekiah turned his face to the wall and prayed to the Lord. Can prayer change the mind of God?"

DIGGING DEEPER

These are amazing chapters of God's deliverance even when things look impossible. No matter what you are facing, look at these two chapters. Read or listen to them again and again when you face things that are against all odds because God delivers.

In this passage, we also learn God does not necessarily respond to the immediate crisis. *"Have you not heard that I determined it long ago? I planned from days of old what now I bring to pass"* (37:26). Nothing surprises God. Your circumstance does not surprise God. He already has an answer for you just like He had an answer for King Hezekiah. It was nothing for an angel of the Lord to strike down 185,000 Assyrians. It was nothing for God to add fifteen years to the life of King Hezekiah. It is nothing for God to solve your problem.

Prayer

Lord, we thank You for the power of Your Word, the hope we get from staying in the scriptures. Somebody may be facing an impossible task. May this passage give them hope. Nothing is impossible with God. Nothing.

Whether you face a corporate crisis like the town being under siege like Hezekiah with 185,000 Assyrians standing at the wall. Or whether you face a personal crisis like your own health, like Hezekiah did. Either one is solvable when you put your faith and trust in the Lord. Hezekiah went to the Lord. I hope you do too.

Lord, from these chapters, we believe prayer changes things. So, we pray, and we ask You to change the things that need to be changed in our lives. You will get the glory in our lives, just like You did in these chapters. In Jesus' name, we pray. Amen.

MY THOUGHTS

The Bigness of God

Today brings us to Isaiah 39 and 40. Chapter 40 is filled with descriptions of God Almighty. Do you wonder who God is? Do you wonder what He is really like? Please read or listen to Isaiah 39 and 40.

COMMENTS

In 1991, I focused on Isaiah 40 (NASB), as you probably just did too. I wrote, "Flesh is as grass. People are grass. *The grass withers, the flower fades, But the word of our God stands forever'* (40:8). STAY FOCUSED. God's Word stands forever. I am in the business of spreading His Word." Then I referred to the last few verses of chapter 40. "God does not get tired. He gives strength, increases power to those who wait upon Him."

Ten years later, in 2001, again focusing on chapter 40, I wrote, "40. One of the greatest chapters of scripture. It's about Jesus, us, end times, His Word, His kingdom, our strength in Him."

> The grass withers, the flower fades, but the word of our God will stand forever.
>
> Isa. 40:8

Another ten years later, in 2011, I wrote, "Hezekiah fades into selfishness. He got fifteen more years and peace in his days, but he exposed Jerusalem to Babylon."

I wrote again, "'*The grass withers, the flower fades, but the word of our God will stand forever*' (40:8). God's Word is eternal."

I finished with, "How big is God? He measured the waters in the hollow of His hand. '*Nations are like a drop from a bucket . . . coastlands like fine dust*' (40:15). He '*sits above the circle of the earth . . . its inhabitants are like grasshoppers*' (40:22), '*he blows on them, and they whither*' (40:24). '*His understanding is unsearchable*' (40:28). He is bigger than we can think or imagine."

There is a reference to John the Baptist in Isaiah 40:3, "*A voice cries: 'In the wilderness prepare the way of the Lord; make straight in the desert a highway for our God.'*" John the Baptist fulfills that prophecy.

Then there is the power verse, "*The grass withers, the flower fades, but the word of our God will stand forever*" (40:8). That is why we want to spend time in His Word because His Word does not change. His Word is still applicable today. His Word stands forever.

If you want to know what God is really like, read or listen to Isaiah 40:9-26, verses I quoted in my journal entry about the power and the bigness of God. Though He put Himself in a human body and called His name Jesus, God is way bigger than that.

DIGGING DEEPER

Let's close with a couple of descriptions of God. He measures the waters in the hollow of His hand. He weighs the mountains and the hills. "*Behold, the nations are like a drop from a bucket*" (40:15). The coastlands are like fine dust to God. Again, "*All the nations of the earth are nothing before him*" (40:17). He "*sits above the circle of the earth and its inhabitants are like grasshoppers*" (40:22). We think we are significant? We are like grasshoppers in His eyes.

Verse 25 says, "*To whom then will you compare me, that I should be like him? says the Holy One.*" There is none like God, no not one.

As we close Isaiah 40, let's gain some strength by applying the last few verses in our lives. Life at this turbo-charged pace can get us weary, but here is the strength of the Lord:

Have you not known? Have you not heard? The Lord is the everlasting God, the Creator of the ends of the earth. He does not faint or grow weary; his understanding is unsearchable. He gives power to the faint, and to him who has no might he increases strength. Even youths shall faint and be weary, and young men shall fall exhausted; but they who wait for the Lord shall renew their strength; they shall mount up with wings like eagles; they shall run and not be weary; they shall walk and not faint (40:28-31).

Prayer

Father, we thank You for a description of who You are. We all want to know about God. We all want to know who You are and about what You are like. The Word of God tells us that in this very chapter, Isaiah 40.

Your Word also tells us right here, You give power to the faint. You strengthen those who are weak. You renew the strength of those who are weary or feel exhausted. You say, *"but they who wait for the Lord shall renew their strength; they shall mount up with wings like eagles; they shall run and not be weary; they shall walk and not faint"* (40:31). May we be counted as those who wait on You, Lord. Strengthen us through Your Word this day. In Jesus' name, we ask it. Amen.

MY THOUGHTS

ISAIAH 41 AND 42

Jews Today, but No Babylonians

Today, we will cover chapters 41 and 42 of the Book of Isaiah. God said He would always protect His people Israel. Thousands of years later, there are still Jews, an amazing illustration of keeping His promise. Do you know any Babylonians? Please read or listen to Isaiah 41 and 42.

COMMENTS

In 2001, I wrote, "God promises to protect and help Israel. Israel is still in the world, what a testimony! Babylonians are no more, but Israel, tiny Israel, surrounded by Arabs who hate them and want to destroy them, still exists today. And so many world events end up including Israel. God has kept His promise."

In 2011, I wrote, "The Lord is the first and the last." Then, "God chose Israel. God protects Israel as His own. Idols can't deliver. Worship God." Then I wrote about 42:1-4, "Jesus?"

DIGGING DEEPER

Let's look at 42:1-4. Is this Jesus:

Behold my servant, whom I uphold, my chosen, in whom my soul delights; I have put my Spirit upon him; he will bring forth justice to the nations. He will not cry aloud or lift up his voice, or make it heard in the street; a bruised reed he will not break, and a faintly burning wick he will not quench; he will faithfully bring forth justice. He will not grow faint or be discouraged till he has established justice in the earth; and the coastlands wait for his law.

Next, let's look at a few encouraging verses from these two chapters:

I, the Lord, the first, and with the last; I am he (41:4).

Fear not, for I am with you; be not dismayed, for I am your God; I will strengthen you, I will help you, I will uphold you with my righteous right hand.

Isa. 41:10

Fear not, for I am with you; be not dismayed, for I am your God; I will strengthen you, I will help you, I will uphold you with my righteous right hand (41:10).

You shall seek those who contend with you, but you shall not find them; those who war against you shall be as nothing at all (41:12).

I am the Lord; that is my name; my glory I give to no other, nor my praise to carved idols. Behold, the former things have come to pass, and new things I now declare; before they spring forth I tell you of them (42:8-9).

I will turn the darkness before them into light, the rough places into level ground (42:16).

Prayer

Lord, we thank You that You are the same yesterday, today, and forever. We thank You for these encouraging words in our relationship with You. Applicable then, applicable to us this day. May Your righteous right hand uphold each and every one of us and may we give You the praise and the glory. In Your name, we pray it. Amen.

MY THOUGHTS

ISAIAH 43 AND 44

No Other

In Isaiah 43 and 44, Isaiah reminds again, God is God, there is no other. Yet we tend to stray toward worshipping idols that cannot save. Are you worshipping God alone, or do you still have idols drawing your attention away from the one true God? Please read or listen to Isaiah 43 and 44.

COMMENTS

In 1991, I read these two chapters (NASB) together. In my personal Bible reading journal, I simply quoted several verses:

I, only I, am the Lord, And there is no savior besides Me (43:11).

Do not call to mind the former things, Or consider things of the past. Behold, I will do something new (43:18-19).

I am the first and I am the last, And there is no God besides Me (44:6).

Is there any God besides Me, Or is there any other Rock? I know of none (44:8).

Concerning verses 12-20, I wrote, "Folly of idolatry. Didn't make sense to Israel like things that don't make sense today."

Ten years later, in 2001, I read these two chapters on the same day, and wrote, "God is God. There are no others. Idolatry. Man making images to worship is foolishness. We need to worship the creator, not His creation."

Another ten years later, in 2011, I wrote concerning these two chapters, "'*You are mine*' (43:1). Israel is the Lord's. He loves His nation and will preserve it through the ages and has."

I added, "My theme for the year has been let go of the past and prepare for our future. As I sit in our new home and read, I quote these verses, '*Remember not the former things, nor consider the things of old. Behold, I am doing a new thing; now it springs forth, do you not perceive it?*'" (43:18-19). I continued, "Though Israel burdened God with their sin and wearied Him with their iniquities, as we do, He '*blots out your transgressions for my own sake, and I will not remember your sins*' (43:25). God is God alone. Hallelujah." Lastly, I wrote, "The folly of idolatry concerning 44:9-20." And, "Cyrus. Predicted by name years before he was born. He will rebuild Israel."

> **Remember not the former things, nor consider the things of old. Behold, I am doing a new thing; now it springs forth, do you not perceive it?**
>
> **Isa. 43:18-19**

DIGGING DEEPER

Isaiah makes the case for one true God, "*Before me no god was formed, nor shall there be any after me. I, I am the LORD, and besides me there is no savior*" (43:10-11). "*I am the first and I am the last; besides me there is no god*" (44:6). "*Is there a God besides me? There is no Rock; I know not any*" (44:8). "*I am the LORD, who made all things, who alone stretched out the heavens, who spread out the earth by myself*" (44:24).

Because He is the one true God, He alone can save us from our sins, *"I, I am the Lord, and besides me there is no savior"* (43:11). *"I, I am he who blots out your transgressions for my own sake, and I will not remember your sins"* (43:25). *"I have blotted out your transgressions like a cloud and your sins like mist; return to me, for I have redeemed you"* (44:22).

Do you believe He is the one true God? Do you believe there are no others? Do you believe He alone can forgive sin and offer everlasting life? Let's pray.

Prayer

Lord, we thank You that in these chapters we realize, once again, You are the Savior, there is no other. These chapters, also remind us not to look back, but to look forward to the new things You are doing. And, Lord, You remind us of the folly of idolatry. You remind us of Your grace and Your forgiveness when You say, *"I have blotted out your transgressions like a cloud and your sins like mist; return to me, for I have redeemed you"* (44:22).

Lord, again, we thank You that You are our Savior, there is no other. We thank You that You remind us to look ahead, not backwards, to see the new things You are doing and we thank You that You forgive us. Thus, we thank You for Your Word, Your promises, Your encouragement in the Book of Isaiah. To God be the glory. In Jesus' name. Amen.

MY THOUGHTS

ISAIAH 45 AND 46

I Am God, There Is No Other

Today, we will cover chapters 45 and 46 of Isaiah where God proclaims numerous times, He is God, there is no other. Do you believe Him? Please read or listen to Isaiah 45 and 46.

COMMENTS

In my personal Bible reading journal in 1991 (NASB), I made referred to the phrase, *"I am God, and there is no other."* I noted it occurred in 45:5, 6, 18, 21, 22, and in 46:9. Then I referred back to a couple of other chapters. "Chapters 43-46 make it pretty clear there is but one God. And He identifies Himself pretty clearly."

Ten years later, in 2001, I had a similar theme as I read those chapters. I wrote, "I am the Lord, there is no other. There is no other God besides me. He says it over and over in these chapters and His Word. Yet, we do not listen and create idols and fake gods. Then we argue that what we have created must be true because we don't think it's right that there is only one God, one way to heaven."

Another ten years go by, in 2011, and I wrote similar things in my journal. I wrote, "God works through people who don't even know Him." I am thinking about Cyrus, who I will come back to in a moment. And then I wrote, "God is God. There is no other. He alone speaks truth. All the earth can be saved through Him." Then I wrote, "46:5-7 makes me think of Thailand. Statues of Buddha fashioned in gold by men and people worshipping a god who cannot move nor answer."

DIGGING DEEPER

Let's look at those verses I just referred to about the Buddhist statues in Thailand, 46:5-7:

> To whom will you liken me and make me equal, and compare me, that we may be alike? Those who lavish gold from the purse, and weigh out silver in the scales, hire a goldsmith, and he makes it into a god; then they fall down and worship! They lift it to their shoulders, they carry it, they set it in its place, and it stands there; it cannot move from its place. If one cries to it, it does not answer or save him from his trouble.

> To whom will you liken me and make me equal, and compare me, that we may be alike?
>
> Isa. 46:5

As I visited Thailand, and many other countries around the world, I saw this very thing take place. Man-made gods, man-made idols, people fall down and worship, but they cannot move, and they cannot answer.

In Isaiah 45:1, a person named Cyrus is mentioned. And as we closed out yesterday's reading on chapter 44, the last verse says, *"Cyrus, 'He is my shepherd, and he shall fulfill all my purpose'; saying of Jerusalem, 'She shall be built,' and of the temple, 'Your foundation shall be laid.'"* This Cyrus who Isaiah is referring to is the very Cyrus that is in the Book of Ezra. Isaiah is writing this prophesy around 740 to 680 B.C. Cyrus comes on the scene somewhere around 586 B.C., well over a hundred years later. So, Isaiah is prophesying of a Persian king who will allow Israel to rebuild Jerusalem a hundred years down the road.

The questions about prophesy are always, "Did it happen? Did it come true?" Was Cyrus a king over Persia? And as always in prophesy, the answer is yes. In my English Standard Version Study Bible footnote, it refers to Josephus, a Jewish historian. He "records a story in which Cyrus, reading Isaiah's prophecy, was so impressed with the divine power to tell the future that he eagerly sought to fulfill what was written about him" (p. 1322). Yes, there was a King of Persia named Cyrus, and yes, he allowed the people to come back from Babylon and rebuild the walls of Jerusalem and the temple in Jerusalem. Isaiah's prophesies are true.

Prayer

Lord, we thank You we can depend on Your Word. We thank You that Your Word is true. If it is true about King Cyrus, it is true about everything Isaiah has written. Therefore, it is true there is one God. There is no other. So, we worship You alone. And we thank You that when You say, "I will accomplish all my purpose, for I have purposed it and I will do it," we can depend on You and Your Word. We say thank You. In the name of Jesus. Amen.

MY THOUGHTS

ISAIAH 47 AND 48

Babylon

Today, we are in Isaiah 47 and 48. Babylon represents the culture of the world, then and now. Not much has changed has it? Please read or listen to Isaiah 47 and 48.

COMMENTS

In chapter 47, Isaiah condemns Babylon, which represents the culture of the world. We will look at a few descriptions of Babylon, but it also relates to our world today. *"Now therefore hear this, you lover of pleasures, who sit securely, who say in your heart, 'I am, and there is no one besides me'"* (47:8). We face a world of pleasures today, a world that thinks it is secure in itself, a world that says, *"I am, and there is no one besides me,"* a world that does not look to God anymore. Yet, verse 10 says, *"You felt secure in your wickedness; you said, 'No one sees me'; your wisdom and your knowledge led you astray, and you said in your heart, 'I am, and there is no one besides me.'"*

> You felt secure in your wickedness; you said, "No one sees me"; your wisdom and your knowledge led you astray, and you said in your heart, "I am, and there is no one besides me."
>
> Isa. 47:10

DIGGING DEEPER

Our world is a wicked world today. We see senseless acts of terror all around us on a regular basis. In our world today, it is worldly wisdom and worldly knowledge leading us far from God. Yet, we have so much pride; like the Babylonians say, *"I am, and there is no one besides me"* (47:8).

Verse 12 says, *"Stand fast in your enchantments and your many sorceries."* In our culture today, people will turn to anything but God. Verse 13 goes on to say, *"You are wearied with your many counsels; let them stand forth and save you."* Who does the world go to when they have problems? To Google, to Siri, to the internet, to therapists, to counselors? But who turns to the Lord anymore? It was the same in Babylon; it is the same today.

Isaiah finishes chapter 47 with verse 15, *"Such to you are those with whom you have labored, who have done business with you from your youth; they wander about, each in his own direction; there is no one to save you."* Will the world ever come to conclude we are wandering about in our own direction and that will not save us?

The question today for us: is the world getting better or is it getting worse? As we close, let us pray for our Babylon, the culture of our day.

Prayer

Almighty God, forgive us for the ways of the world and not following the ways of the Word. May we see the false hope the world offers. May we be the ones that turn people to You, the real place of hope.

Lord, we know You judged Babylon. It is no more. You also will judge our world, our culture, today. Use us, Lord, to turn people away from the ways of the world and toward the ways of the Word. Use us, Lord. In Jesus' name. Amen.

MY THOUGHTS

Is My Hand Shortened?

Today, we cover two more chapters of the Book of Isaiah, chapters 49 and 50. Do you believe God created you? Do you believe He has the power to deliver you? Please read or listen to Isaiah 49 and 50.

COMMENTS

Let's go back and look at a couple of verses in both of these chapters, beginning with 49:1, *"The Lord called me from the womb, from the body of my mother he named my name."* Do you believe that? Do you believe God created you? That He knew your name while you were in your mother's womb? I believe it. I also believe He purposes every one of us according to His will. He created us for a reason, a purpose, to fulfill His kingdom here on earth. So, let's be about His business.

I also like 49:6. It reminds me God's salvation has been from the beginning and it always included all people, *"I will make you as a light for the nations, that my salvation may reach to the end of the earth."* He is speaking to the Jews. He is speaking to the nation of Israel. He would make that nation a light for all nations. His salvation could reach the end of the earth. So God has always been inclusive. He always intended His salvation would reach to the ends of the earth, to all people.

Lastly, in chapter 50, verse 2 says, *"Is my hand shortened, that it cannot redeem? Or have I no power to deliver?"* No, His hand is not shortened. Salvation is in the power of His right hand. He offers it to all who will receive it from Him.

> Is my hand shortened, that it cannot redeem? Or have I no power to deliver?
>
> Isa. 50:2

DIGGING DEEPER

Why do we do these devotions? Why did we do ADDBIBLE, Audio Daily Devotion? We do both so people can connect with God's Word. When we connect with God's Word, we connect with God. That is our goal at the Ezra Project, to connect God's people to God's Word.

I spend time each and every day in God's Word. But surveys tell us busy-ness is what keeps people from God's Word. That is why we created ADDBIBLE, so if necessary, you can multitask. You can listen to God's Word a chapter a day and stay connected with God's Word.

The other two reasons people say they do not read or listen to the Bible is because they do not understand what it says, and it does not apply to their lives. In *Day by Day Through the Bible* and ADDBIBLE, we address those two issues, showing the Bible is understandable and relevant to our lives today.

Friends, that is what God has called us to do. We hope you are enjoying *Day by Day*. We hope it is touching your life, and you are growing spiritually. If so, we pray you will spread it to your friends, to your family, to those in your church, because you know people who are not spending time in God's Word on a daily basis. Turn them on to ADDBIBLE, or *Day by Day Through the Bible*.

Prayer

Father, help us connect God's people to God's Word. Help them be receptive to You and Your Word. Grant us favor as we share Your Word with others. Bless them as they engage in Your Word. Amen.

MY THOUGHTS

ISAIAH 51 AND 52

The Coming Salvation

Today, we are in Isaiah 51 and 52. Isaiah tells Israel salvation is on the way; it just may take longer than they think. Do you believe your salvation is on the way? Please read or listen to Isaiah 51 and 52.

COMMENTS

In 1991, I read Isaiah 52-55 on one day. I did not have any journal entries on chapters 51 and 52. Ten years later in 2001, I wrote about these chapters (NASB), "Isaiah must have been filled with the Holy Spirit to write such things." I made a statement, *"Thus says the Lord'* (50:1). To speak for God, you better be right." Another ten years later, in 2011, I wrote, "Heaven and earth will pass away but my salvation will be forever. Blessed are they who bring good news. All the ends of the earth shall see the salvation of our God, not just Jews."

DIGGING DEEPER

In Isaiah 51:4, God reminds us of what He wants from Israel and what He wants from us today, *"Give attention to me, my people, and give ear to me, my nation."* God wants our attention. He reminds us this world is temporary. Look at 51:6:

Lift up your eyes to the heavens, and look at the earth beneath; for the heavens vanish like smoke, the earth will wear out like a garment, and they who dwell in it will die in like manner: but my salvation will be forever and my righteousness will never be dismayed.

Why should we depend on something temporary when we can have a relationship with an eternal God? He puts it another way in 51:12, *"I, I am he who comforts you; who are you that you are afraid of man who dies, of the son of man who is made like grass."* He says you fear what men can do to you, but men are temporal like grass; they just blow away. Why not have a relationship with the one who stretched out the heavens and laid the foundations of the earth?

In Isaiah 52, He reminds Israel and Jerusalem of the coming salvation of the Lord. *"Awake, awake, put on your strength, O Zion; put on your beautiful garments, O Jerusalem, the holy city"* (52:1). In verse 3, He reminds them, *"For thus says the Lord: 'You were sold for nothing, and you shall be redeemed without money.'"*

> How beautiful upon the mountains are the feet of him who brings good news, who publishes peace, who brings good news of happiness, who publishes salvation.
>
> Isa. 52:7

There will come a day when they will hear His voice and understand it is He that will save them. Verse 7, *"How beautiful upon the mountains are the feet of him who brings good news, who publishes peace, who brings good news of happiness, who publishes salvation."* Verse 8 continues, *"The voice of your watchmen—they lift up their voice; together they sing for joy; for eye to eye they see the return of the Lord to Zion."* Yes, the Lord will return to Jerusalem. Yes, Jesus will reign from Jerusalem on earth.

But before He does, Isaiah reminds us He is going to suffer:

Behold, my servant shall act wisely; he shall be high and lifted up, and shall be exalted. As many were astonished at you—his appearance was so marred, beyond human semblance, and his form beyond that of the children of mankind—so

shall he sprinkle many nations. Kings shall shut their mouths because of him,
for that which has not been told them they see, and that which they have not
heard they understand (52:13-15).

Yes, before He went to the cross and on the cross, Jesus was marred, *"beyond*
human semblance, and his form beyond that of the children of mankind" (52:14). He
was barely recognizable. Tomorrow, Isaiah 53, is going to give us a great glimpse of
the suffering Messiah. But until then, we pray to the Lord.

Prayer

We thank You that You remind us salvation has been from the
beginning. It comes through Israel. It comes through the Jewish people, but
it comes to all mankind. We thank You that through prophets like Isaiah,
You tell us these things are so. Someday, You will reign from Jerusalem. But
until then, reign in our hearts. Make Yourself very real to us. Holy Spirit,
indwell us, we pray. In the name of Jesus. Amen.

MY THOUGHTS

ISAIAH 53 AND 54

The Suffering Messiah

Today, we are in Isaiah 53 and 54. Chapter 53 is one of the most prophetic and most quoted chapters of the Old Testament. Do you believe Isaiah is describing Jesus? If not, who? Please read or listen to Isaiah 53 and 54.

COMMENTS

In my personal Bible reading journal of 2001, I wrote a one-liner concerning Isaiah 53, "Jesus, Jesus, Jesus. What prophetic words." Ten years later in 2011, I wrote, "Jesus. Virtually every verse describes Jesus Christ. Yet, Isaiah wrote it hundreds of years before Jesus is born. Who else could it be?" Then I quoted some of the descriptions:

Despised and rejected by men (53:3)

With His stripes we are healed (53:5)

The Lord has laid on him the iniquity of us all (53:6)

Yet opened not his mouth (53:7)

Made his grave with the wicked and with a rich man in his death,
Although he had done no violence, and there was no deceit in his mouth (53:9)

Yet he bore the sin of many (53:12)

"Jesus, Jesus, Jesus! Hallelujah! Isaiah 53. A chapter about the suffering Messiah."

DIGGING DEEPER

Let's go back and look at these verses as we think about Jesus, our Lord and Savior. We begin with Isaiah 53:2, *"For he grew up before him like a young plant, and like a root out of dry ground; he had no form or majesty that we should look at him, and no beauty that we should desire him."* True, there are no descriptions of Jesus that He was six-foot-tall and weighed one-hundred eighty pounds, or He had blonde hair and blue eyes, or He had a beard or long hair. There are no descriptions of Jesus.

Verse 3, *"He was despised and rejected by men, a man of sorrows and acquainted with grief; and as one from whom men hide their faces he was despised, and we esteemed him not."* We know on the day He was sent to the cross, He was rejected by men. We know the night before in the Garden of Gethsemane, He prayed so much He sweated blood. He was sorrowful and He was acquainted with grief.

> He was despised and rejected by men, a man of sorrows and acquainted with grief; and as one from whom men hide their faces he was despised, and we esteemed him not.
>
> Isa. 53:3

Verse 4, *"Surely he has borne our griefs and carried our sorrows; yet we esteemed him stricken, smitten by God, and afflicted."* Yes, Jesus carried our sorrows to the cross.

Verse 5, *"But he was wounded for our transgressions; he was crushed for our iniquities; upon him was the chastisement that brought us peace, and with his stripes we are healed."* Anyone who has been a Christian very long has heard this verse describing Jesus.

Verse 6 tells us why He went to the cross, *"All we like sheep have gone astray; we have turned—every one—to his own way; and the Lord has laid on him the iniquity of us all."* Isaiah reminds us, *"for all have sinned and fall short of the glory of God"* (Rom. 3:23). Jesus went to the cross for the sins of all mankind. All of us, individually.

We go on to 53:7, *"He was oppressed, and he was afflicted, yet he opened not his mouth; like a lamb that is led to the slaughter, and like a sheep that before its shearers is silent, so he opened not his mouth."* We remember the trials of Jesus when many were accusing Him and He had nothing to say. He chose not to say anything, *"he opened not his mouth"* (53:7).

Verse 9, *"And they made his grave with the wicked and with a rich man in his death, although he had done no violence, and there was no deceit in his mouth."* We know He was crucified between two criminals, then He was buried in a tomb of a rich man, Joseph of Arimathea.

Verse 10 is a striking verse, *"Yet it was the will of the Lord to crush him."* We remember Jesus from the cross saying, *"My God, my God, why have you forsaken me?"* (Matt. 27:46). God allowed Jesus, His only begotten Son, to die on that cross because of verse 12, *"yet he bore the sin of many, and makes intercession for the transgressors."*

Isaiah wrote these words hundreds of years before Jesus ever sojourned on the earth. Isaiah, the prophet, wrote words that rang true. He described Jesus, the suffering Messiah.

Prayer

Lord, as we read Your Word, help us have great confidence in the things we read. The only way prophets like Isaiah can write truths like this is if You lay it in their hearts. You are the One who knows the end from the beginning. You designed the plan of salvation from the Garden of Eden.

We thank You that You sent Jesus, the suffering Messiah, for the forgiveness of our sins. Yes, for the forgiveness of the sins of the world. But, yes, for the forgiveness of my sins. Thank You for sending Jesus, the author and finisher of my faith. Because He died for me and rose again, we pray in Your name. Amen.

MY THOUGHTS

ISAIAH 55 AND 56

So Shall My Word Be

Today, we are in Isaiah 55 and 56. There is a very special passage in these two chapters. See if you can find it. How important is the Word of God to you? Please read or listen to Isaiah 55 and 56.

COMMENTS

Which of those verses do you think was the verse I referred to?

Was it in 56:7? *"For my house shall be called a* house *of prayer for all peoples."*

Or was it in chapter 55, maybe verse 3? *"Incline your ear, and come to me; hear, that your soul may live."*

Or was it 55:6? *"Seek the Lord while he may be found; call upon him while he is near."*

Or, maybe, 55:12? *"For you shall go out in joy and be led forth in peace; the mountains and the hills before you shall break forth into singing, and all the trees of the field shall clap their hands."*

Or maybe it was 55:8-9? *"For my thoughts are not your thoughts, neither are your ways my ways, declares the Lord. For as the heavens are higher than the earth, so are my ways higher than your ways and my thoughts than your thoughts."*

All those are wonderful verses of scripture; very encouraging. But none of those was the passage I was thinking about. It is 55:10-11:

For as the rain and the snow come down from heaven and do not return there but water the earth, making it bring forth and sprout, giving seed to the sower and bread to the eater, so shall my word be that goes out from my mouth; it shall not return to me empty, but it shall accomplish that which I purpose, and shall succeed in the thing for which I sent it.

Isaiah 55:11 has meant so much to me in my life. I have a personal mission statement. I developed it many years ago after working with many businesses and companies to develop their mission statements. I believe people can have a mission statement too. So I worked on one and came up with this: I am a man of His Word. That is my personal mission statement; to be a man of His Word. So, for me, verses like Isaiah 55:11 mean so much. Again, the verse says, *"So shall my word be that goes out from my mouth; it shall not return to me empty, but it shall accomplish that which I purpose, and shall succeed in the thing for which I sent it."*

Or as I memorized it, *"So shall my word be that goeth forth out of my mouth: it shall not return unto me void, but it shall accomplish that which I please, and it shall prosper in the thing whereto I sent it"* (KJV). It is a guarantee of the power of God's Word in my life and in yours. God's Word will never return void. It always accomplishes exactly what He sends it for. And God's Word always succeeds. That is worth pondering today.

> **So shall my word be that goeth forth out of my mouth: it shall not return unto me void, but it shall accomplish that which I please, and it shall prosper in the thing whereto I sent it.**
>
> **Isa. 55:11**

DIGGING DEEPER

Does the Word of God mean that to you? Does it mean so much to you that you want to spend time in His Word every day? I have and I will continue to do so. Not because it is a duty. Not because it is an obligation. Not because Christians should. No. Because this verse reminds me it will never return void, and it will always accomplish exactly what He pleases in my life. It reminds me of Hebrews 4:12, *"For the word of God is living and active, sharper than any two-edged sword, piercing to the division of soul and of spirit, of joints and of marrow, and discerning the thoughts and intentions of the heart."*

When I think about the power of the Word of God, I am reminded of these kinds of verses. It is living, active, sharp. It pierces my soul and my spirit. I want it to do that every day of my life. I need to read the Word of God. I want the Word of God. I want it to pierce between my soul and my spirit each and every day. I hope you do too.

Together, let's stay close to the Word of God. Let's commit to spend time each and every day in God's Word. Let's be sure to never use the excuse, "I was too busy in my life," to spend time in the Word of God.

The verse right before 55:11 reminds us, by an illustration, rain and snow water the earth. The earth sprouts with seeds and bread, sustenance for our physical lives. Then God says that same thing about his Word and our spiritual lives. It waters our spiritual lives. It brings forth seed. It brings forth food for our spiritual being.

Prayer

May God bless you as you spend time in His Word. Amen.

MY THOUGHTS

ISAIAH 57 AND 58

If and Then

Today brings us to Isaiah 57 and 58. Do you believe God is conditional or unconditional? Please read or listen to Isaiah 57 and 58.

COMMENTS

In my personal Bible reading journal in 1991, I did not write very much, "Isaiah 58: Fasting."

Ten years later, in 2001, I wrote, "There is a lot of 'if, if/then, then' in the Bible. If we do this, then God will do this. 'Ifs' are easy. If we obey, then God will bless. If we choose not to obey, God then allows the natural course of disobedience to take place. It's true of individuals as well as people groups, nations."

> For I will not contend forever, nor will I always be angry.
>
> Isa. 57:16

Another ten years later, in 2011, I wrote, "Though we rebel, walk away from God, He says, *'For I will not contend forever, nor will I always be angry'* (57:16). We backslide, but He will heal, and lead, and restore, according to 57:17-18. God sees through our religious hypocrisy, referring to 58:2-4. Obedience to God in His ways brings blessings, according to 58:8-14."

Then I did that "if/then" thing again in my journal. I do believe there are a lot of "if/thens" in the Bible. In fact, once I tried to find them all. I tried to do a message on all the "ifs" God wants us to do. And *if* we do them, then all the *thens* He will do. I have never given that message, but there are many "ifs and thens" in the Bible.

Isaiah 58 gives us a demonstration of some of them. First, he talks about the proper way to fast. Obviously, he was not pleased with the way the Jews were fasting. He says in verse 3, you fast to *"seek your own pleasure."* He says in verse 4, *"Fasting like yours this day will not make your voice to be heard on high."* In verses 6 and 7, he declares how they should be fasting. That is the "if," *if* you fast right, "then." The *then* is in verses 8 and 9:

> *Then shall your light break forth like the dawn, and your healing shall spring up speedily; your righteousness shall go before you; the glory of the Lord shall be your rear guard. Then you shall call, and the Lord will answer; you shall cry, and he will say, "Here I am."*

There are more "ifs" and "thens" in the closing of the chapter. Verse 9 continues, *"If you take away the yoke from your midst."* Verse 10 says, *"if you pour yourself out for the hungry."* Verse 13 says, *"If you turn back your foot from the Sabbath . . . if you honor it."*

These are examples of the conditions of God's blessings. It is the "ifs" in the Bible. But as we follow the "ifs" in the Bible, we can receive the blessing because the "then" occurs in verse 14, *"then you shall take delight in the Lord, and I will make you ride on the heights of the earth; I will feed you with the heritage of Jacob your father, for the mouth of the Lord has spoken."*

DIGGING DEEPER

Isaiah 58 is an example of the "ifs" and "thens" in the Bible. What "if" or "then" are you facing right now? God's Word may be convicting you to do certain things.

That is the "if." *If* you do these things, *then* God will bless you, *then* God will hear you, *then* God will provide for you.

Are you wrestling with an "if" today? What is God asking you to do? What condition is He asking you to change in your life, the "if"? Every time He puts an "if" out there in our lives, that "if" will release a blessing from Him. So today, find the "if." What is God asking you to do, that "if"? Obey in the Lord and *then* watch Him bless you.

Prayer

Father, we thank You for the "ifs" and "thens" in the Bible. We thank You through the Word You remind us what conditions You want from our own lives, the "ifs." When we do the "ifs," You will always release the blessings, the "thens."

Thank You for the conviction of the "ifs" in our lives. We look forward to the blessings You will release as we strive to obey You and Your Word. You will receive all the glory. And we give You the praise. In the name of Jesus, amen.

MY THOUGHTS

ISAIAH 59 AND 60

Where Has Truth Gone?

Today, we are in Isaiah 59 and 60. There is evil and oppression on earth and in our lives. We get the good, the bad, and the ugly each day. Do you focus on the bad and the ugly, or on the good? Please read or listen to Isaiah 59 and 60.

COMMENTS

My personal Bible reading journal entry in 1991, about these chapters, said, "God wants to save us, but sin separates us." Then I wrote, "The wealth of nations. I wonder if Adam Smith got his title from the Word of God?"

In 2001, concerning these chapters, I wrote, "God will prevail. He will shine in darkness. He is our hope."

In 2011, I wrote, "God is not limited, period. And He can save anyone anywhere. Any separation, any distance from God is our fault, not His." Then I wrote, "Where has truth gone?" Then, "God's Word will be preserved and passed on to generation to generation. God also preserves Israel from generation to generation. Nations and kingdoms who oppose Israel will not stand." I quoted 60:18, *"you shall call your walls Salvation, and your gates Praise."* Referring to chapter 60:19, I wrote, *"'The sun* (and the moon) *shall be no more . . . but the Lord will be your everlasting light, and your God will be your glory.'* O, for that day."

DIGGING DEEPER

Isaiah 59:14-15 say, *"Justice is turned back, and righteousness stands far away: for truth has stumbled in the public squares, and uprightness cannot enter. Truth is lacking."*

> Justice is turned back, and righteousness stands far away: for truth has stumbled in the public squares, and uprightness cannot enter. Truth is lacking.
>
> Isa. 59:14-15

As I write this, it is hard to find truth in the media, in business, in politics, in education, and even in churches. As we move farther from the Word of God, our moral compass disappears and with it, truth. It is hard to know who we can believe today.

One place we can still find truth is in the Bible. Jesus says, *"I am the way, and the truth, and the life. No one comes to the Father except through me"* (John 14:6). The Bible also tells us, *"and you will know the truth, and the truth will set you free"* (John 8:32). Stay in God's Word and be free in Jesus and His truth.

Prayer

Lord, we thank You that Your hand is not shortened. You can save anyone, anywhere, anytime. But if there is a separation between me and You, it is my fault, not Yours. You long to save everyone. Your prayer is that none would perish, but all would come to saving faith in Jesus Christ.

We thank You that Your hand will reach down and save us if we cry out to You. We also thank You, Lord, for Your covenant You remind us of in these chapters; Your Spirit is upon us, and the words You put in our mouths shall not depart from us. We are to pass on Your words to our offspring and their offspring for this time and forevermore.

We thank You, Lord, for Your prophetic Word, *"The sun shall be no more your light by day, nor for brightness shall the moon give you light; but the Lord* (You alone) *will be your everlasting light, and . . . God* (You) *will be your* (our) *glory"* (60:19). Father, we long for those days. Come quickly, Lord Jesus. Come quickly. We pray in Your name. Amen.

MY THOUGHTS

What Jesus Read from Isaiah

Today, we are in Isaiah 61 and 62. We know what we are reading is true because Jesus actually read from the scroll of Isaiah in the New Testament. If Jesus reads from it, it must be true. So, can you believe all of Isaiah is prophetic and either has come true, or will? Please read or listen to Isaiah 61 and 62.

COMMENTS

In my personal Bible reading journal of 1991, I wrote concerning Isaiah 61, "Proclaim liberty. Proclaim the favorable year of the Lord."

In 2001, I read these chapters with other chapters, but did not have any specific entries concerning these two chapters.

In 2011, I wrote, "Jesus reads 61:1-2 in a synagogue and declares He fulfills Isaiah's words." Then I wrote, "I pray for a double portion as referred to in 61:5-7. Bless me that I might bless You."

Let's look at the words that open chapter 61 of the Book of Isaiah, the words that Jesus read when He opened pages of scripture in a synagogue:

The Spirit of the Lord God is upon me, because the Lord has anointed me to bring good news to the poor; he has sent me to bind up the brokenhearted, to proclaim liberty to the captives, and the opening of the prison to those who are bound; to proclaim the year of the Lord's favor (vv. 1-2).

There, Jesus stopped reading, right in the middle of a sentence. The rest of that sentence says, *"and the day of vengeance of our God; to comfort all who mourn."* The sentence

> The Spirit of the Lord God is upon me, because the Lord has anointed me.
>
> Isa. 61:1

continued. Why did Jesus stop there? These passages are prophetic. The Book of Isaiah is prophetic. It is prophecy. In Jesus' first coming, He fulfilled the verses He read, but He stopped at this particular place, *"and the day of vengeance of our God; to comfort all who mourn,"* because that is the second coming of Jesus. Jesus only read the part about which He was fulfilling when He was here on earth as He read that portion of Isaiah. Amazing, He stopped right in mid-sentence.

I had the privilege of visiting the synagogue where Jesus read these words. I actually stood there, in Israel, and read the very passage we are reading right now, as Jesus read it in that very synagogue. By the way, it is not a megachurch. It is a very small place. But to read the very words Jesus read in that place was a powerful experience for me.

In my journal, I also refer to the double portion offered in 61:5-7. That, again, is the second time Jesus comes:

> *Strangers shall stand and tend your flocks; foreigners shall be your plowmen and vinedressers; but you shall be called the priests of the Lord; they shall speak of you as the ministers of our God; you shall eat the wealth of the nations, and in their glory you shall boast. Instead of your shame there shall be a double portion; instead of dishonor they shall rejoice in their lot; therefore in their land they shall possess a double portion; they shall have everlasting joy.*

Those are for days to come; the second time Jesus returns to the earth. But I said in my journal, I would like to have a double portion of Your blessing today, Lord.

Would you too?

In Isaiah 62, the Lord reminds us Jerusalem will be here in the end:

For Zion's sake I will not keep silent, and for Jerusalem's sake I will not be quiet, until her righteousness goes forth as brightness, and her salvation as a burning torch. The nations shall see your righteousness, and all the kings your glory, and you shall be called by a new name that the mouth of the Lord will give (62:1-2).

On to verses 6 and 7:

On your walls, O Jerusalem, I have set watchmen; all the day and all the night they shall never be silent. You who put the Lord in remembrance, take no rest, and give him no rest until he establishes Jerusalem and makes it a praise in the earth.

Isaiah says, Jesus came. Jesus proclaimed those words Himself. And Jesus will come again. Isaiah also proclaims Jerusalem is where Jesus will come and where He will reign on earth. We can shout the Hallelujah. Isaiah's prophecies will come to pass.

DIGGING DEEPER

Are you ready? Are you ready for the day of the Lord? Are you ready spiritually? If the day of the Lord came today, would you be ready to be captured up in the arms of your Savior, Jesus? If not, might I encourage you to have a little prayer time with the Lord before this day is over.

Prayer

Lord, we thank You for prophecy. We thank You that You read, You verified, the Book of Isaiah when You were here on earth by reading these very passages we just read today. Those verses came true as You read them. You said, *"Today this Scripture has been fulfilled in your hearing"* (Luke 4:21).

The other prophetic words of these chapters will also come true. We look to the day, Lord, when You come again. We look to the day when You reign from Jerusalem here on earth. Until then Lord, continue to instruct us in Your Word. Continue to teach us how to live until You come again. And in that day, we will greatly rejoice and give You all the praise. Come, Lord Jesus. Come quickly. Amen.

MY THOUGHTS

ISAIAH 63 AND 64

A Potter and Clay

Today brings us to Isaiah 63 and 64. God is the potter; we are the clay. Are you still moldable? Please read or listen to Isaiah 63 and 64.

COMMENTS

In 1991, after reading these chapters (NASB), I wrote primarily about Isaiah 64, "Our righteousness is as filthy rags and all of us wither like a leaf. It's fall. The leaves have lost their life and are withering. They blow off trees only to be raked up and discarded." Then I wrote, *"We are the clay, and You our potter"* (64:8).

In 2001, ten years later, I wrote, "We sin. We need to be saved. You are my Father, I am clay. You are the potter; I am the work of Your hand. Put me back on the potter's wheel and mold me, shape me anew."

In 2011, another ten years later, I wrote, "He is *'mighty to save'* (63:1). *'He became their Savior'* (63:8). *'He redeemed them; he lifted them up and carried them all the days of old. But they rebelled and grieved His Holy Spirit'* (63:9-10). Referring to 63:17, does God make us wander and harden our hearts? I think not. He lets us follow our own rebellious ways, lifting His hand of grace, protecting us, as we pursue our own desires. We are all sinners, unclean before a Holy God. Yet, He is our Father, we are the work of Your hand."

In Isaiah 64:5-7, the Lord reminds us:

Behold, you were angry, and we sinned; in our sins we have been a long time, and shall we be saved? We have all become like one who is unclean, and all our righteous deeds are like a polluted garment. We all fade like a leaf, and our iniquities, like the wind, take us away. There is no one who calls upon your name, who rouses himself to take hold of you; for you have hidden your face from us, and have made us melt in the hand of our iniquities.

No matter how we slice it, that is our lot in life. That is who we are. We have been in our sins a long time. We are unclean. We are like a polluted garment. Though we focus so much on our lives, it is like a leaf off of a tree. We bud to life, we blow in the wind, we finally crumble up and die. But there is hope. Isaiah 64:8, *"But now, O Lord, you are our Father; we are the clay, and you are our potter; we are all the work of your hand."*

> **But now, O Lord, you are our Father; we are the clay, and you are our potter; we are all the work of your hand.**
>
> Isa. 64:8

DIGGING DEEPER

What is our practical application from these chapters today? First, to realize regardless of what we think of ourselves, we are sinners. We may not like to be reminded of that, but the Word of God reminds us of it over and over. It is our natural condition. Today, can you admit you are a sinner?

Next, can you jump back on the potter's wheel? Can we humble ourselves enough to say, "Lord, I need You to mold me and shape me into something different than I really am"? We are like clay, and fortunately, God has those big hands that can and will shape us into more godliness, more Christlikeness. But we need to be willing. Will you do it? Will you jump back up on the potter's wheel and let Him put His hands around you and shape you and mold you into what He wants you to be?

Prayer

Lord, we are reminded in this passage, we are sinners. We are caught in our sins. But we are also reminded You are mighty to save. We thank You that You sent Jesus to save us from our sinfulness.

And Lord, we thank You that You invite us to be molded and shaped by You. Today, may we be willing to be back on the potter's wheel with Your loving hands shaping us as You see fit. When You do, Lord, help us be of service to You that You might receive the glory for how You shape our lives. In Jesus' name. Amen.

MY THOUGHTS

ISAIAH 65 AND 66

Hell or Heaven, Your Choice

Today, we finish the Book of Isaiah, chapters 65 and 66. As most of the Bible, Isaiah offers us the choice of hell or heaven. Have you made your choice? If not, make it today. Please read or listen to Isaiah 65 and 66.

COMMENTS

In 1991, I finished the Book of Isaiah with these words, "Finally finished Isaiah. It's a hard book to understand. Need to know history and geography to relate to this prophet. I look forward to Jeremiah. Isaiah does say there will be a new earth, one where God reigns. I look forward to that day."

In 2001, I wrapped up Isaiah with these words, "Finally completed Isaiah. Not a happy book. God continues to reach out to us. Thank You for reaching for me."

In 2011, I finished Isaiah with these words, "God reaches down to us. He rejects those who reject Him and protects those who follow Him. There will be a new heaven and a new earth." Then I quoted, *"But this is the one to whom I will look: he who is humble and contrite in spirit and trembles at my word"* (66:2). "Again, all do not go to heaven, referring to 66:15-16, *'and those slain by the Lord shall be many'"* (66:16).

We finish the themes of Isaiah with some of the verses in these chapters:

I was ready to be sought by those who did not ask for me; I was ready to be found by those who did not seek me (65:1).

I will destine you to the sword . . . because, when I called, you did not answer; when I spoke, you did not listen, but you did what was evil in my eyes and chose what I did not delight in (65:12).

That is the message of the Bible. Over and over and over, God says, "I am here and I am willing to have relationship with you, but you reject Me. You do not want a relationship with Me, and I will not force Myself upon you."

> For behold, I create new heavens and a new earth, and the former things shall not be remembered or come into mind.
>
> Isa. 65:17

In 65:17, the Lord reminds us, *"For behold, I create new heavens and a new earth, and the former things shall not be remembered or come into mind."* There will come a day, as verse 25 says, *"The wolf and the lamb shall graze together; the lion shall eat straw like the ox."* Yes, there will be a new heaven and a new earth and there will be peace here on earth.

In 66:1, God reminds us of who He is, *"Thus says the Lord: 'Heaven is my throne, and the earth is my footstool'."* He reminds us in verse 18, *"the time is coming to gather all nations and tongues. And they shall come and shall see my glory."*

DIGGING DEEPER

We journeyed through the Book of Isaiah, all sixty-six chapters, in thirty-one days. We were reminded sin separates us from God, but God longs to put His arms around us. It is our choice. He calls for us. He waits for us. Will you respond?

Some of us will experience that new heaven and that new earth because we gave our lives over to Jesus. Some of us will suffer His wrath as He declares in 66:15-16:

For behold, the Lord will come in fire, and his chariots like the whirlwind, to render his anger in fury, and his rebuke with flames of fire. For by fire will the Lord enter into judgment, and by his sword, with all flesh; and those slain by the Lord shall be many.

The book closes with this warning, *"And they shall go out and look on the dead bodies of the men who have rebelled against me. For their worm shall not die, their fire shall not be quenched, and they shall be an abhorrence to all flesh"* (66:24).

Yes, there is heaven. And yes, there is hell. We do not hear much preaching about fire and brimstone, and heaven and hell anymore. But Isaiah makes it clear. There is a choice. What choice have you made? Where will you spend eternity? Heaven or hell?

Prayer

Lord, we read or hear Your Word so we can get this reality. We may not like it, but You speak truth into our hearts. Through the Book of Isaiah, You have made the choice clear, once again. Help us, Lord, to choose life. To choose You. To choose to spend eternity with You in heaven through Your son, Jesus Christ, our Lord and Savior. Open Your arms to anyone reading this devotion today who wants to make a choice for You.

You reminded us earlier, Your arm is not short, and You are mighty to save. Praise the name of the Lord, who made heaven and earth. Praise the Father, the Son, and the Holy Spirit. Praise God from whom all blessings flow. Praise You, all creatures here below. In Jesus' name, we pray it. Amen.

MY THOUGHTS

THIRTY-ONE DAYS IN JEREMIAH

JEREMIAH 1

Jeremiah's Impact on The Ezra Project

Today, we begin the fifty-two chapters of the Book of Jeremiah. We will look at my English Standard Version Study Bible book introduction to learn more about the Book of Jeremiah. It is attributed to the Prophet Jeremiah and his scribe Baruch. Jeremiah was called to be a prophet in 627 B.C. and served over forty years. He was called as a youth, became a priest, and lived in an area of Israel allotted to the tribe of Benjamin. He lived close enough to Jerusalem to understand its people, their worship, and their daily habits. Yet he was far enough away from Jerusalem that he was not afraid to criticize what he saw there.

Jeremiah had a difficult life. His messages of repentance were not well received. His hometown plotted against him, and he suffered much persecution during his forty-year ministry. At God's command, he never married. Though his ministry spanned four decades, he apparently had only two converts. He is known as the weeping prophet, for weeping over the condition of Israel. He became a prophet during the reign of Josiah, the last faithful king of Judah's history. Other prophets of his day were Nahum, Habakkuk, and Zephaniah.

He was called to speak to the people of Jerusalem during the revival under King Josiah and continued this prophetic ministry through the fall of Jerusalem to the Babylonians. His task was to hammer home the message that the fall of Jerusalem was not God's fault, rather, because of Judah's unfaithfulness to God and listening to false prophets. The theme of the Book of Jeremiah is God's judgement on breaking His covenant, as well as His displeasure with sin.

In his book, Jeremiah asks people over one hundred times to turn around or repent. He also illustrates God's determination to restore people and establish new covenants. Jeremiah was a biblical theologian. He used truths found in Genesis, Exodus, Leviticus, Numbers, Deuteronomy, Hosea, and Psalms. He gave plenty of advice on what pleases God and what does not.

Though rejected by neighbors, family, and friends, this book teaches acceptance by God as far more important. We will learn man's heart is desperately wicked, but we will also see God loves with an everlasting love. Please read or listen to the nineteen verses of Jeremiah 1.

COMMENTS

To help us through the Book of Jeremiah, I selected three of my personal Bible reading journals. I picked the first one in 1991, the second one from 2004, and the third one from 2016. There are thirteen years between 1991 and 2004 and twelve years between 2004 and 2016. So, these journals will reflect various ages and stages of my life.

We will cover the fifty-two chapters of the Book of Jeremiah in thirty-one days. Some days, we will look at one chapter. Some days, it will be two. Let's begin our look at Jeremiah 1 from my journal from 1991, when I was thirty-six years old.

In 1991, I read Jeremiah 1 and 2 on the same day and wrote concerning verses 4-9 of chapter 1, "I hope they are my words, too. I have always wanted to be a speaker for God. Lord, stretch out Your hand and touch my mouth and put Your words in my mouth for You." Stepping aside from the journals for a moment, friends, that was 1991. I was thirty-six years old. I was not a speaker for God at that time, but you can see the desire of my heart was there.

In 2004, I was forty-nine years old when I read Jeremiah 1-3 on the same day and wrote in my journal, "Jeremiah was chosen and appointed by God, referring to

1:5, 9. We too have a task to perform from God. In the womb, He programmed me as well. We should seek His purpose for our lives and do it. Finding out does not guarantee success as we define it. Jeremiah was not successful in the world's eyes, but he sure was in God's eyes."

> We should seek His purpose for our lives and do it.

I wrote an interesting prayer after reading Jeremiah 1-3 that day. "Your purpose for my life. If it's what I'm doing, provide resources to accomplish it. If it's not what I'm doing, help me be willing to change." That ended my journal entry from 2004, so let's jump to 2016 when I was sixty-one years old.

In 2016, I read Jeremiah 1 on April 1st, which is a significant date of the Ezra Project. It is our anniversary date. It was our fourteenth anniversary on April 1, 2016, and I read Jeremiah 1. You are going to be amazed at what happened that day! Let's look at the journal.

I wrote, "Jeremiah started under the last good king of Israel, Josiah, and ended with the demise of Israel under Babylonian captivity. He understood he was appointed a prophet by God before he was even born. Was I destined to be president of The Gideons International in 2020 before I was even born? Though he was a youth, God put His Word in Jeremiah's mouth. God watches over His Word to perform it. Judgment is coming to Israel because, *They have made offerings to other gods and worshiped the works of their own hands'* (v. 16). Jeremiah is to dress himself for work, say everything God puts in his mouth, and stand rock solid. God will make him invisible if he does. Wow!"

After reading Jeremiah 1 that day, I began to pray and wrote my prayers in my journal, "Thanking God for this powerful passage. Praying for its application in my life. Thanking God for fourteen years of Ezra Project, His favor, His faithfulness. Saying I wanted March to be the month of discovery for the new direction of Ezra remembering I met with American Bible Society, Biblica, two pastor forums groups and no clear direction. Sought the Word."

In the middle of my praying, He asked me to read the passage again. I did and began to pray more, but God wanted quiet. Like Jeremiah, He asked me, "What do you see, Allen?" Nothing was clear to me. I saw a vibration back and forth, like some of old and some of new. He said, "You will do both."

Again, He asked, "What do you see, Allen?" I saw earbuds, wires around people's necks. "Yes, Lord, I see it." "Record daily Bible readings with your journal entries. People listening to their daily Bible reading every day, everywhere (can be translated into other languages). A new app, subscriptions to pay for it. Doing this will free me up for Gideon leadership. More flexibility. Now I see a recording studio. All this fulfilling my passion. I'm enthusiastic. It has high impact. The answer to all my needs, sustainable beyond me, on and on. On April 1st, the anniversary, Ezra 2.0. Board meeting today. I wanted to have the new direction by this day to announce, celebrate, but I had nothing. Now I have it directly from God! Hallelujah!"

DIGGING DEEPER

Yes, that was my journal entry on April 1, 2016, the fourteenth anniversary of the Ezra Project. God gave me our new direction. We had been ministering primarily by speaking in churches for fourteen years and the Lord led us to consider recreating the Ezra Project. I wrote in my journal, I had thought about it, visited various organizations, had pastor focus groups, but had nothing.

We spent months in prayer and seeking the Lord on this. As I mentioned in my journal, I hoped to have something to offer the board on the anniversary date and the board meeting that day and I had nothing until that morning. In my daily quiet time, the Lord opened Jeremiah 1 to my heart. That passage changed everything for the Ezra Project.

I took the message to the board meeting that afternoon. They got excited with tears in their eyes and said, "This new mission, this new direction, fulfills our purpose. Even Ezra himself read the Word to the people." So on that day, the board approved pursuing this new direction, but we had no idea what to do. I am not a techie so for me to record podcasts or create an app was incredibly unbelievable to me. But God guided our steps all along the way. The product became ADDBIBLE, Audio Daily Devotions.

Like Jeremiah, we obeyed the voice of the Lord. God watched over His Word to perform it through the Ezra Project and ADDBIBLE. Today, ADDBIBLE is played in countries and cities across the globe. To God be the glory for the practical application of His Word.

Jeremiah 1 transformed the ministry of the Ezra Project. I hope it has a transforming impact in your own life. God had a plan for Jeremiah. God had a plan for the Ezra Project. God has a plan for your life. Let's pray.

Prayer

Father, we thank You for the power of Your Word. We thank You that before You formed us in the womb, You knew us and You knew what our purpose was on this earth. We thank You for creating us, putting breath in our bodies, and giving us a purpose for life.

Today, may we take some time to pursue the purpose You have made us for. Show us, Lord, what You had in mind when You formed us in our mother's womb. Then Lord, give us the courage to pursue it. For thine is the kingdom, the power, and the glory forever. Amen.

MY THOUGHTS

JEREMIAH 2

Marriage

I was at a marriage retreat one year, when reading the second chapter of Jeremiah. Have you ever attended a marriage retreat? Should you? Please read or listen to the thirty-seven verses of Jeremiah 2.

COMMENTS

Today, we will go backwards in my journals, starting with 2016, going to 2004, then to 1991. Let's begin with my journal from 2016. I read Jeremiah 2 and 3 on the same day. Concerning Jeremiah 2, I wrote, "After his calling in chapter 1, Jeremiah gets right after it. And does he ever! At first, Israel followed the Lord like a new bride with her husband. But quickly, they *defiled my land . . . transgressed against me* (vv. 7-8). Israel changed its god, according to verse 11. Things go from blessing to curse. *'Have you not brought this upon yourself by forsaking the Lord your God'* (v. 17). *'The fear of me is not in you'* (v. 19). Jeremiah uses prostitution as his example of Israel. They have left their husband and went whoring after idols, false gods. Yet when trouble comes, they cry out to God for help, but God says, 'Are you kidding me? Go get help from your self-made gods in your time of trouble.'" That ends my journal entry for 2016, where Jeremiah uses marriage and prostitution to make his point about God's relationship with Israel.

In 2004, I read Jeremiah 1-3 on the same day, and did not have any notes concerning this chapter.

In 1991, I read Jeremiah 1 and 2 on the same day and only made notes concerning chapter 1. I also noted I was at a marriage retreat. Terry and I were thirty-six years old at the time. I made a bunch of notes in my Bible reading journal about the marriage retreat. I think you will find them interesting. So from Jeremiah 2, we will talk about marriage a little bit today.

From the marriage retreat, I wrote, "Three kinds of marriage: 1) am I happy? 2) are we happy? 3) is God pleased with our marriage?" What kind of marriage do you have? Are you happy? Are we happy? Is God pleased with your marriage?

> **What kind of marriage do you have? Are you happy? Are we happy? Is God pleased with your marriage?**

The next section of my notes has to do with problems of marriages, "First of all, isolation. We will not talk about our marriage. We'll talk about jobs, kids, but 'How is your marriage?' No way. The second problem is our models of marriage. We seem to bring into marriage the behaviors we watched in the marriages of our parents. And often, whether we like that behavior or not, we seem to be repeating the same things in our own marriages." One point from the marriage retreat was, "Get to know God so well your behavior becomes like Him rather than the marriages of your parents."

Another answer to this issue was, "See life as an adventure, not a struggle." Is your marriage an adventure or a struggle? The next point I wrote down was: "How to build distinctively Christian marriages." An idea here was, "Self-ism. How to overcome our natural state of selfishness? Jesus says, 'Be different.'"

The next point was, "Don't follow a cultural version of marriage. Follow a biblical perspective of marriage. Marriage was created not for our own lives and happiness, but that God can perform and be glorified in relationships. While we love one another, we can be discipled through marriage." Is that how you look at your marriage? Is it a place where God can perform His work between you and your spouse?

Another point of how to build a distinctively Christian marriage was, "Love in such a way the world will know." And we got to the issue of communication.

"Communicating too directly with each other can cause problems. So temper your communication with each other based on biblical principles."

The last issue covered was conflict. Woah! Do you have any conflict in your marriage? What I wrote down from the marriage retreat was: "Two different people can resolve conflict by communicating. There is room for differences. Two distinctively different people need to be whole together, not halves." I do not profess to be a marriage counselor, but you can see at thirty-six years old Terry and I were investing in our marriage by going to a marriage retreat, a *Christian* marriage retreat.

DIGGING DEEPER

Jeremiah 2 is about a marriage relationship, God, the husband and His people, His bride. In verses 2 and 3, He says, *"I remember the devotion of your youth, your love as a bride. Israel was holy to the Lord."* But then God asks, *"What wrong did your fathers find in me that they went far from me?"* (v. 5).

Israel broke its marriage relationship with God. Do not do that in your own marriage. If you are married and you are in love, hug your husband or your wife today, give your spouse a kiss on the cheek and say, "I love you." If you are not happily married today, but still married, think about attending a Christian marriage retreat. Invest in your marriage. God is certainly going to invest in Israel throughout the Book of Jeremiah. I encourage you to do the same. Invest in your marriage.

Prayer

Father, throughout the Bible You use the marriage relationship as an illustration. You always remain faithful. We often do not. So let's transfer this illustration in Jeremiah 2 to our marriages today. May we remain faithful in our marriages, as You remain faithful to us.

Thank You for allowing us to be the bride of Christ. Someday, we will enjoy the marriage supper of the Lamb. But until then, Lord, intervene in our own marriages. Bless our marriages. Help us remain faithful to one another in a loving relationship as You have always done with us. Thank You for loving us. In Your precious name, we pray. Amen.

MY THOUGHTS

JEREMIAH 3

Whoring Around

In Jeremiah 3, God likens Israel to a whore. Pretty harsh, right? Have you been faithful to God your whole walk with Him, or have you left Him for another, or something else? Have you played the whore? Please read or listen to the twenty-five verses of Jeremiah 3.

COMMENTS

We will go backwards in my journals, once again starting in 2016 and go back to 2004 and 1991. In 2016, I read Jeremiah 2 and 3 on the same day. Concerning chapter 3, I wrote, "By playing the whore they polluted their land, according to verse 2. And God's blessings are withheld. Judah does the same thing. Even so, God begs them to come back, return, repent. God is merciful, forgiving, and He would bless again."

In 2004, I read Jeremiah 1-3 (NASB) on the same day, and I did not make any notes on chapter 3. In 1991, I read Jeremiah 3 and 4 on the same day. Concerning chapter 3, I wrote, "As harlots, we turn back to the Lord and God opens His arms and hugs us, declaring, *'I will not look upon you in anger. For I am gracious . . . I will not be angry forever. Only acknowledge your iniquity.'*"

In Jeremiah 3, God uses the illustration of marriage, once again, for His relationship with Israel. Let's look at the first couple of verses:

If a man divorces his wife and she goes from him and becomes another man's wife, will he return to her? Would not that land be greatly polluted? You have played the whore with many lovers; and would you return to me? declares the LORD (vv. 1-2).

Jeremiah is accusing Israel of walking away from the relationship with God. Let's go back to 2:19, *"Your evil will chastise you, and your apostasy will reprove you. Know and see that it is evil and bitter for you to forsake the Lord your God; the fear of me is not in you."* Jeremiah 2:22 says, *"Though you wash yourself with lye and use much soap, the stain of your guilt is still before me, declares the Lord God."* And 2:35 says, *"you say, 'I am innocent; surely his anger has turned from me.' Behold, I will bring you to judgment for saying, 'I have not sinned.'"*

Those verses in chapter 2 set us up for chapter 3:1, *"You have played the whore with many lovers; and would you return to me? declares the Lord."* Verses 2 and 3 reiterate the point, *"You have polluted the land with your vile whoredom . . . yet you have the forehead of a whore; you refuse to be ashamed."*

Verses 6-8 continue the case:

The Lord said to me in the days of King Josiah: "Have you seen what she did, that faithless one, Israel, how she went up on every high hill and under every green tree, and there played the whore?" And I thought, "After she has done all this she will return to me," but she did not return, and her treacherous sister Judah saw it. She saw that for all the adulteries of that faithless one, Israel, I had sent her away with a decree of divorce. Yet her treacherous sister Judah did not fear, but she too went and played the whore.

> **God would not be pleased with us today, either, if we traded our relationship with Him for some idol or something more important than Him in our lives today.**

The whoredom being described is walking away from the relationship with God and worshiping idols from the nations surrounding Israel. And God is not pleased.

He is not pleased with the tribes of Israel, and He is not pleased with the tribe of Judah. God would not be pleased with us today, either, if we traded our relationship with Him for some idol or something more important than Him in our lives today.

But, praise God, He is a forgiving God. In spite of all that has been done against them, He says:

Go, and proclaim these words toward the north, and say, "Return, faithless Israel, declares the Lord. I will not look on you in anger, for I am merciful, declares the Lord; I will not be angry forever. Only acknowledge your guilt, that you rebelled against the Lord your God" (vv. 12-13).

With God, there is always hope, *"And I will give you shepherds after my own heart, who will feed you with knowledge and understanding"* (v. 15). And verse 17, *"At that time Jerusalem shall be called the throne of the Lord, and all nations shall gather to it, to the presence of the Lord in Jerusalem."* Though Israel and Judah have sinned, God holds out His hand of forgiveness. Aren't you glad He does that for you and me today?

DIGGING DEEPER

How do we apply Jeremiah 3 to our lives? Is there anything between you and your relationship with God today? Is there a thing, is there a person, is there anything between you and your relationship with the Lord? If so, you are like Israel, whoring around. Our application today is to stop that behavior and seek the Lord's forgiveness. It is what the Lord wants; acknowledge your guilt, that you rebelled against the Lord your God.

The chapter closes with their admission of guilt, *"For we have sinned against the Lord our God, we and our fathers, from our youth even to this day, and we have not obeyed the voice of the Lord our God"* (v. 25). Maybe you need to offer a prayer like that, even now.

Prayer

Father, we are thankful for the stark reality of Jeremiah 3. You want relationship with us. You do not want any competition. When we go outside our relationship with You, You are angry, and yet You say, "If you would just come back to Me, I will forgive you." Thank You, Almighty God, for Your forgiveness.

Reach out Your hand to us today. Forgive us if we have gone outside our relationship with You. As You promised in Jeremiah 3, feed us also with knowledge and understanding so we can walk worthy in Your sight. We ask it, in Jesus' name. Amen.

MY THOUGHTS

JEREMIAH 4 AND 5

Return to Me

Today, we will cover Jeremiah 4 and 5. God begs Israel to return to Him. They do not; will you? Please read or listen to the sixty-two verses in these two combined chapters 4 and 5 of the Book of Jeremiah.

COMMENTS

Due to the length of the reading today, I will go through my journals very quickly. In 1991, on Jeremiah 4 (NASB), I wrote, "God begs us to come back to Him. Like a husband whose bride has been unfaithful, who has chased another man, but God calls us back, asks us to repent and welcomes us back to His love." I quoted verse 18, *"Your ways and your deeds have brought these things to you. This is your evil. How bitter! How it has touched your heart!"*

In 2004, concerning Jeremiah 4 and 5 (NASB), I wrote, "Jeremiah really lays it on! He begs Israel to turn from its wicked ways and come back to God. He outlines terrible judgment. Why? How can a good God do this? It's not God, it's us. *'Because of the evil in your deeds'* (4:4). *'Your ways and your deeds have brought these things to you'* (4:18). They rejected God and His Word. We bring judgment upon ourselves."

In 2016, concerning Jeremiah 4 and 5, I wrote, "God wants Israel to return to Him. He wants us to return to Him. But they didn't and we don't either. He warns of judgment. They don't care. We don't, either. Whose fault is it? Theirs and ours. *'Wash your heart from evil'* (4:14). *'Your ways and your deeds have brought this upon you'* (4:18). *'For my people are foolish; they know me not; they are stupid children; they have no understanding. They are "wise"—in doing evil! But how to do good they know not'* (4:22). Even in all that, God has mercy. *'For thus says the Lord, "The whole land shall be a desolation; yet I will not make a full end"'* (4:27). God blessed and blesses, but we don't honor Him, according to verses 7 and 9 of chapter 5."

> They rejected God and His Word. We bring judgment upon ourselves.

"We think God owes us and will not punish us. *'He will do nothing: no disaster will come upon us'* (5:12). He wouldn't hurt me. He has to love me. We are the same. Haven't learned much because we ignore His Word."

DIGGING DEEPER

The reading of the scripture and my journal entries make it pretty clear what chapters 4 and 5 of Jeremiah are all about. To sum it up, let's look at 5:19, *"And when your people say, 'Why has the Lord our God done all these things to us?' you shall say to them, 'As you have forsaken me and served foreign gods in your land, so you shall serve foreigners in a land that is not yours.'"*

Jeremiah 5:22-23, *"Do you not fear me? declares the Lord. Do you not tremble before me? . . . But this people has a stubborn and rebellious heart; they have turned aside and gone away."*

Prayer

Lord, turn our hearts back to You. That is the cry of Jeremiah. It is the cry of Jeremiah 4 and 5 to us today. Turn our hearts back to You. In Jesus' name, we ask it. Amen.

MY THOUGHTS

JEREMIAH 6

We Bring Judgment Upon Ourselves

Jeremiah 6 explains God does not cause pending judgment. Do you ask, "Why would God let this happen?" Find out in this chapter. Please read or listen to the thirty verses of Jeremiah 6.

COMMENTS

In 1991, when I was thirty-six years old, I read Jeremiah 5-7 on the same day, and I made no notes in my journal. Thirteen years later in 2004, I was forty-nine years old. I read Jeremiah 4-6 together on the same day, and I just wrote, "They rejected God and His Word. We bring judgment upon ourselves."

In 2016, twelve more years later and at sixty-one years old, I read Jeremiah 6 on one day, and wrote, "Warning! Warning! Disaster is coming! Why? *'There is nothing but oppression within her. As a well keeps its water fresh, so she keeps fresh her evil'* (vv. 6-7). *'The word of the Lord is to them an object of scorn; they take no pleasure in it'* (v. 10). *'Everyone is greedy for unjust gain'* (v. 13). *'They have not paid attention to my words'* (v. 19). Therefore, there will be disaster upon this people, *'terror is on every side'* (v. 25). *'For the Lord has rejected them'*" (v. 30).

In chapter 6, Jeremiah warns the people judgment is on the way. Verses 6-7, *"This is the city that must be punished; there is nothing but oppression within her. As a well keeps its water fresh, so she keeps fresh her evil."* At the end of verse 10 and on into verse 11, the Word of God says, *"the word of the Lord is to them an object of scorn; they take no pleasure in it. Therefore I am full of the wrath of the Lord; I am weary of holding it in."* Verses 15-19 make the case:

> *Were they ashamed when they committed abomination? No, they were not at all ashamed; they did not know how to blush . . .*

> *Thus says the Lord: "Stand by the roads, and look, and ask for the ancient paths, where the good way is; and walk in it, and find rest for your souls. But they said, 'We will not walk in it.' I set watchmen over you, saying, 'Pay attention to the sound of the trumpet!' But they said, 'We will not pay attention'"* (vv. 15-17).

So for all those reasons God pronounces His judgement:

> **The same warnings Jeremiah gave to his people apply to us today.**

Therefore hear, O nations, and know, O congregation, what will happen to them. Hear, O earth; behold, I am bringing disaster upon this people, the fruit of their devices, because they have not paid attention to my words; and as for my law, they have rejected it (v. 19).

And what is the judgment that is going to take place? Jeremiah tells them:

> *Thus says the Lord: "Behold, a people is coming from the north country, a great nation is stirring from the farthest parts of the earth. They lay hold on bow and javelin; they are cruel and have no mercy; the sound of them is like the roaring sea; they ride on horses, set in array as a man for battle, against you, O daughter of Zion!"* (vv. 22-23).

Jeremiah is describing the nation of Babylon that is going to come and destroy the city of Jerusalem.

DIGGING DEEPER

What do we gain from warnings like this Jeremiah is giving his people? The same warnings Jeremiah gave to his people apply to us today. The Word of God reminds us the Lord is the same yesterday, today, and forever. We need to have ears to hear the warnings Jeremiah is making. And we need the courage to correct our behavior before it is too late.

Prayer

Lord, we see through these chapters the things that displease You. The things we do that You are not happy with. Yet we know from Your Word, You are a God of forgiveness, You are a God of the second chance. Holy Spirit, help us repent of our behavior that is not biblical, that is not pleasing in Your sight. And Lord, give us the strength and the courage to correct our behavior because You love us and we love You. Help us, Lord, walk in Your ways. We ask it, in Your name. Amen.

THE MESSAGE OF JEREMIAH

I encourage you to share *Day by Day Through the Bible* with a family member or a friend. The warnings of Jeremiah need to be heard across our world today. They need to be heard in your community, in your church, in your family.

Ask people to study *The Writings of the Major Prophets*. Your friends and your family can go to ezraproject.net and get the book there, or they can go to online bookstores where *The Writings of the Major Prophets* can be found. All of us can spread the Word. I thank you for doing so.

MY THOUGHTS

JEREMIAH 7 AND 8

Amend Your Ways

Today, we will cover Jeremiah 7 and 8. The charges against Israel mount up until God will not even hear the prayers of Jeremiah. Does God hear your prayers? Please read the thirty-four verses in Jeremiah 7 and the twenty-two verses in Jeremiah 8.

COMMENTS

Because of the length of the reading, I will summarize my journals very quickly. Beginning with 1991, I wrote, "God's judgment comes upon those who reject Him. He has given us standards to live by through His Word, yet we go our own way, causing us problems."

In 2004, I wrote, "Jeremiah is instructed not to pray for Judah. How far do we have to go before God will not even listen to our prayers for people anymore?" Then I wrote, "We look like they did. Lies, not truth, prevail in the land."

And in 2016, I wrote, "Going to church does not make us Christians. Jeremiah is standing at the temple doors denouncing those who enter as hypocrites. God has had enough. He will not even hear Jeremiah's prayer for people anymore. God asks for obedience, but we refuse.

He continually sends messengers, prophets with the message, but we will not hear. No one listens to Jeremiah either. Truth perishes when we will not hear God.

> **Truth perishes when we will not hear God.**

People turn away from God. They hold fast to deceit; they refuse to return. Everyone turns to his own course. They have rejected the Word of God therefore, God will punish."

DIGGING DEEPER

To avoid God's punishment, what does Jeremiah and the Lord instruct us to do today? *"Amend your ways and your deeds, and I will let you dwell in this place"* (7:3). Secondly, *"Obey my voice, and I will be your God, and you shall be my people. And walk in all the way that I command you, that it may be well with you"* (7:23). I would rather do those things than suffer the wrath and the punishment of God. How about you?

Prayer

Lord, keep me from getting so far gone that You will not even hear my prayers anymore. Help me, Lord. Keep me from being stubborn and rebellious towards You or Your Word. Keep me from turning to my own course and rejecting Yours.

Forgive me, Lord, if I have grieved You. By reading the warnings of Jeremiah, Lord, I am hearing Your Word. I am coming back to You. Open Your arms, Father and receive me. Forgive me as I confess my unfaithfulness to You. Once again Lord, wrap Your arms around me. Hold me close. I love You. Amen.

MY THOUGHTS

JEREMIAH 9 AND 10

Course Correction

Today brings us to Jeremiah 9 and 10. God tries over and over to get our attention. He has high standards. Is He trying to get your attention? Please read or listen to the twenty-six verses of Jeremiah 9 and the twenty-five verses of Jeremiah 10.

COMMENTS

In 1991, I referred to a few verses in my journal. First, I looked at Jeremiah 9:13-16:

And the Lord says: "Because they have forsaken my law that I set before them, and have not obeyed my voice or walked in accord with it, but have stubbornly followed their own hearts and have gone after the Baals, as their fathers taught them. Therefore thus says the Lord of hosts, the God of Israel: Behold, I will feed this people with bitter food, and give them poisonous water to drink. I will scatter them among the nations whom neither they nor their fathers have known, and I will send the sword after them, until I have consumed them."

Most of us have been taught good things come from the Father. But here we see God feed people with bitter food, poisonous water, and consume them with the sword in battle. Few are suffering so today.

If you feel oppressed or depressed, maybe it is because you have been disobedient to the Lord. Maybe you sense an oppressive hand from God on your life right now. If so, come back to the Lord. That is why He does this. He may apply a little pressure on your life once in a while to get you to return to Him. If so, remember Romans 8:28 says, *"all things work together for good to those who love God, to those who are the called according to His purpose"* (NKJV).

> **If you feel oppressed or depressed, maybe it is because you have been disobedient to the Lord.**

In my journal, I wrote, "Advice," referring to 9:23-24, *"Thus says the Lord: 'Let not the wise man boast in his wisdom, let not the mighty man boast in his might, let not the rich man boast in his riches, but let him who boasts boast in this, that he understands and knows me, that I am the Lord who practices steadfast love, justice, and righteousness in the earth. For in these things I delight,' declares the Lord."*

These verses remind us whether it is wisdom, might, or riches, they all come from the Lord, therefore, we have no claim to boast.

The last verses I referred to in 1991, were Jeremiah 10:23-24:

> *I know, O Lord, that the way of man is not in himself, that it is not in man who walks to direct his steps. Correct me, O Lord, but in justice; not in your anger, lest you bring me to nothing.*

DIGGING DEEPER

You may think you are walking out your own life, but the verse above tells me it is not so, *"that it is not in man who walks to direct his steps"* (10:23). If your walk is a little uphill or your path may not be very straight, it may be because God is trying to correct your steps. Submit to Him today so He does not have to do it in anger, but in justice. Thank You, Lord, for intervening in our walk in this life.

Prayer

Lord, we bow our hearts humbly before You, after reading these chapters in Jeremiah today. We learned if we are suffering, if we were oppressed, if our course is not straight, it may be because You are trying to get our attention.

The words of Jeremiah stung the people of Jerusalem. They are stinging us as well as we hear the words and apply them to our own lives. We learned, Lord, You have high standards. We are reminded in these chapters today there is none like You, O Lord. You are great and Your name is great in might. You are the true God, the Living God, the Everlasting King. You made the earth by Your power. You establish the world by Your wisdom. You stretched out the heavens. Thank You for reminding us there is none like You.

Forgive us for our boast in our wisdom, our might, or in our riches. After this passage, Lord, we set all that aside, and we only boast in knowing You, the one who practices steadfast love, justice, and righteousness in the earth. You are the mighty King, Master of everything. We boast in You. Amen.

MY THOUGHTS

Stay the Course

J eremiah chapter 11 reminds Israel of God's covenant. He expects us to keep it, as we expect Him to keep it. Are you? Please read or listen to the twenty-three verses of Jeremiah 11.

COMMENTS

In 1991, I read Jeremiah chapters 11-13 on the same day. Concerning chapter 11, I wrote, "God wants us to listen to Him, referring to verses 4 and 8."

Stepping aside from the journal entry for the moment, let's look at verses 4 and 8. Verse 4 says, *"Listen to my voice, and do all that I command you. So shall you be my people, and I will be your God."* Verse 8 says, *"Yet they did not obey or incline their ear, but everyone walked in the stubbornness of his evil heart. Therefore I brought upon them all the words of this covenant, which I commanded them to do, but they did not."*

Back to my 1991 journal. I referred to verse 11 saying, "He brings disaster upon those who refuse to listen and worship other gods." Next, I referred to verse 14, "He tells us not to pray for certain people."

Let's step aside from the journal again and look at those specific verses. Verse 11, *"Therefore, thus says the Lord, Behold, I am bringing disaster upon them that they cannot escape. Though they cry to me, I will not listen to them."* On to verse 14, *"Therefore do not pray for this people, or lift up a cry or prayer on their behalf, for I will not listen when they call to me in the time of their trouble."* That would be disastrous. When we cry out to the Lord, He turns a deaf ear toward us. O God, may that never happen to me.

In 2004, I read Jeremiah 10-13 (NASB) on the same day and wrote concerning those chapters, "Jeremiah continually points the people back to God. He ridicules idol worship and begs people to come back to the one true God." I quoted, *"I know, O Lord, that a man's way is not in himself, Nor is it in a man who walks to direct his steps. Correct me, O Lord, but with justice; Not with Your anger, or You will bring me to nothing"* (10:23-24). "Praise God for mercy or I would be nothing."

At times, I refer to prayers in my journals. On that day, I wrote, "Can God trust me to stay the course?" Can He trust you to stay the course?

Part of staying the course means we need to be able to be corrected by the Lord. In that regard, verse 20 says, *"But, O Lord of hosts, who judges righteously, who tests the heart and the mind."* To stay the course, we have to allow the Lord to test our heart and our mind. If God tested your heart and your mind today, how would you measure up? Can God trust you to stay the course?

> ## Can God trust you to stay the course?

Moving on to my journal in 2016, I wrote, "God almost begs us to listen to Him, but He won't make us listen. Yet, we won't because *"everyone walked in the stubbornness of his evil heart"* (v. 8). Finally, God judges, even His own people, because He is just. Therefore, there comes a point where He will not listen to their cry for help anymore.

"Even prophets, or God's messengers, are not safe. God reveals a plot against Jeremiah from his hometown. God protects and delivers Jeremiah, as He promised He would when He called him back in chapter 1. Standing for God against culture, family, friends, has never been easy. Won't be easy now, either."

DIGGING DEEPER

Why does the Lord say in Jeremiah 11, He will bring disaster upon his own people? Verses 9-11 explain it clearly:

Again the Lord said to me, "A conspiracy exists among the men of Judah and the inhabitants of Jerusalem. They have turned back to the iniquities of their forefathers, who refused to hear my words. They have gone after other gods to serve them. The house of Israel and the house of Judah have broken my covenant that I made with their fathers. Therefore, thus says the Lord, Behold, I am bringing disaster upon them that they cannot escape. Though they cry to me, I will not listen to them."

God has a covenant with us. Are you keeping it or are you breaking it? His covenant is clearly expressed in His Word. Have you turned your back on His covenant? Have you refused to hear His Words? Have you gone after other gods to serve them? Have you broken your covenant with your God? Let's pray.

Prayer

Father, thank You for revealing Your covenant in Your Word. Thank You for instructing us as to what You want from us in this thing called life. As we read Your Word, reveal Your truth to us. And as we hear Your Word, Your covenant, help us make a commitment to You and You alone.

Forgive us, Lord, where we have disobeyed. Forgive us where we have walked away from Your Word. Forgive us if we place another god before You, some idol in our own lives. Through Jeremiah, You are warning us. We heed Your warning today.

We thank You that You are a loving, forgiving God and You will open Your arms to us if we will just cry out to You before it is too late. Hear our cry, O Lord. Restore to us the joy of Your salvation. In Jesus' name, we ask it. Amen.

MY THOUGHTS

JEREMIAH 12 AND 13

Why Do the Wicked Prosper?

J eremiah 12 and 13 are more of God's complaint against Israel. Does God have a complaint against you? Please read or listen to the seventeen verses of Jeremiah 12 and the twenty-seven verses of Jeremiah 13.

COMMENTS

In 1991, concerning Jeremiah 12 and 13, I wrote in my personal Bible reading journal, "Hypocrisy. Thou art near to their lips but far from their minds. But Thou knowest me, O Lord. Thou see-est me and Thou dost examine my heart's attitude toward all, referring to 12:3." Concerning 12:15, I wrote, "He is a God of compassion." Onto chapter 13, "Refuse to listen, walk in stubbornness of heart, go after other gods, become worthless in God's eyes." About 13:11, "What God wants: My people for praise and glory. Listen." I continued, "God is God. He wants a people to love Him, listen to him, obey Him, worship Him, love Him, give Him glory. God help me be so."

> We question God, plead our case before Him, and wonder why He doesn't do what we want or think He should.

Skipping over 2004, and jumping to 2016, I wrote, "Jeremiah is not the only one who complains to God. We all do. We question God, plead our case before Him, and wonder why He doesn't do what we want or think He should. God never answered Job, but He gives Jeremiah an answer in 12:5-17. He is fair and just. He judges His heritage, Israel and Judah, and every other nation that will not listen to him."

I continued to write, "Pride separates us from God, causing us evil for being unwilling to listen to God. God gets mad, angry at us. Yes, even His own people. Repent. Jeremiah wants us to turn and give glory to God, but they and we do not."

DIGGING DEEPER

In 12:1, Jeremiah pleads his case before the Lord, *"Righteous are you, O Lord, when I complain to you; yet I would plead my case before you. Why does the way of the wicked prosper?"*

God answers Jeremiah in verses 5 through the rest of chapter 12. So, why do the wicked prosper? Let's look at verses 7-8:

I have forsaken my house; I have abandoned my heritage; I have given the beloved of my soul into the hands of her enemies . . . My heritage (Israel and Jerusalem) *has become to me like a lion in the forest; she has lifted up her voice against me; therefore I hate her.*

Why do the wicked prosper? Because God allows them to. He uses the wicked to judge Israel, Judah, and us. Why do the wicked prosper? Let's look at verse 14-17:

Thus says the Lord concerning all my evil neighbors who touch the heritage that I have given my people Israel to inherit: "Behold, I will pluck them up from their land, and I will pluck up the house of Judah from among them. And after

I have plucked them up, I will again have compassion on them, and I will bring them again each to his heritage and each to his land. And it shall come to pass, if they will diligently learn the ways of my people, to swear by my name, 'As the Lord lives,' even as they taught my people to swear by Baal, then they shall be built up in the midst of my people. But if any nation will not listen, then I will utterly pluck it up and destroy it, declares the Lord."

Why do the wicked prosper? Because the Lord allows it. He used nations around Israel to judge Israel. Then He says, "I will restore Israel, and I could restore those nations that I have used for my purposes, if they listen to me. But, if they do not, I will destroy them as well."

Prayer

Lord, we pray You would never need to use the wicked to discipline us. Place a hedge of protection around us, O God.

Help me keep my eyes focused on You so You would never have to raise up wickedness around me to get me back in step with You. Keep me in the palm of Your hand, Lord. Put a hedge of protection around my life. I ask, in the name of Jesus. Amen.

MY THOUGHTS

Do Prophets Lie?

Today, we will cover another two chapters in the Book of Jeremiah, chapters 14 and 15. God does not let up on His people. Are there times when you wonder what God is doing in your life? Please read or listen to the twenty-two verses in Jeremiah 14 and the twenty-one verses of Jeremiah 15.

COMMENTS

In Jeremiah 14, a drought comes upon the land. The people are desperate, so they cry out to the Lord, *"Though our iniquities testify against us, act, O Lord, for your name's sake; for our backslidings are many; we have sinned against you"* (14:7). What is God's response? *"The Lord said to me: 'Do not pray for the welfare of this people. Though they fast, I will not hear their cry, and though they offer burnt offering and grain offering, I will not accept them. But I will consume them by the sword, by famine, and by pestilence'"* (14:11-12).

But then Jeremiah says to the Lord, "That's not what the people are hearing from the other prophets." And what does God say? *"The prophets are prophesying lies in my name. I did not send them, nor did I command them or speak to them. They are prophesying to you a lying vision, worthless divination, and the deceit of their own minds"* (14:14).

And, by the way, these were supposedly prophets of God. Passages like these remind us to be careful about the pastors, shepherds, or priests we sit under. Are they biblical teachers or are they teaching us lying visions, worthless divination, and the deceit of their own minds?

> **Passages like these remind us to be careful about the pastors, shepherds, or priests we sit under.**

The people continue to cry out to God:

> *We acknowledge our wickedness, O Lord, and the iniquity of our fathers, for we have sinned against you. Do not spurn us, for your name's sake; do not dishonor your glorious throne; remember and do not break your covenant with us* (14:20-21).

Their plea falls on deaf ears as we turn to Jeremiah 15:1, *"Then the Lord said to me, 'Though Moses and Samuel stood before me, yet my heart would not turn toward this people. Send them out of my sight, and let them go!'"* This time, though they cry out to God, God is not going to listen, *"You have rejected me, declares the Lord; you keep going backward"* (15:6). May that never be said of anyone of us. Do not continue to reject the Lord. Do not keep walking backwards away from God.

Here in chapter 15, Jeremiah is the lone voice crying in the wilderness warning the people and no one is paying attention. So Jeremiah complains to the Lord in 15:10, *"Woe is me, my mother, that you bore me, a man of strife and contention to the whole land!"* He continues, *"O Lord, you know; remember me and visit me, and take vengeance for me on my persecutors"* (15:15).

Then Jeremiah reminds God of his calling all the way back in Jeremiah 1, with 15:16-18:

> *Your words were found, and I ate them, and your words became to me a joy and the delight of my heart, for I am called by your name, O Lord, God of hosts. I did not sit in the company of revelers, nor did I rejoice; I sat alone, because your hand was upon me, for you had filled me with indignation. Why is my pain unceasing, my wound incurable, refusing to be healed? Will you be to me like a deceitful brook, like waters that fail?*

And God once again answers Jeremiah's complaint:

Therefore thus says the Lord: "If you return, I will restore you, and you shall stand before me. If you utter what is precious, and not what is worthless, you shall be as my mouth. They shall turn to you, but you shall not turn to them. And I will make you to this people a fortified wall of bronze; they will fight against you, but they shall not prevail over you, for I am with you to save you and deliver you, declares the Lord. I will deliver you out of the hand of the wicked, and redeem you from the grasp of the ruthless" (15:19-21).

DIGGING DEEPER

For Jeremiah, life was not easy. Maybe life is not easy for you either. Maybe you find yourself complaining to God like Jeremiah did. If so, hear the Word of the Lord today:

If you return, I will restore you, and you shall stand before me . . . they will fight against you, but they shall not prevail over you, for I am with you to save you and deliver you (15:19-20).

Prayer

To God be the glory. Amen.

MY THOUGHTS

Conditions of Service

Jeremiah 16 lays out some of the conditions God required of Jeremiah, His prophet. They were not easy. Has God called you? Do you question some of the conditions of your calling? Please read or listen to the twenty-one verses of Jeremiah 16.

COMMENTS

According to my personal Bible reading journal in 1991, I read Jeremiah14-16 (NASB) on the same day, and related to chapter 16, quoted verse 17, *"For my eyes are on all their ways; they are not hidden from My face, nor is their iniquity concealed from My eyes."*

Yes, God is watching. He sees everything we do. We may be able to hide our actions from others, but we cannot hide anything from the Lord. Again, the verse says, *"For my eyes are on all their ways, they are not hidden from My face, nor is their iniquity concealed from My eyes."*

Onto my journal from 2004. Again, I read Jeremiah 14-16 (NASB) on the same day. I am going to read my notes on all three chapters. "Why harsh judgement? Because their forefathers sinned, followed other gods, worshipped them, and did not keep His Law. And they themselves did evil, walking in *'the stubbornness of his own . . . heart, without listening to Me'* (16:12). *'You keep going backward. So I will stretch out My hand against you and destroy you'* (15:6). We blame God for His judgment, but it's our fault."

Let's step aside from the journal a moment and look at 16:10-12. I asked the question in my journal why such harsh judgement and God gives us the answer:

And when you tell this people all these words, and they say to you, "Why has the Lord pronounced all this great evil against us? What is our iniquity? What is the sin that we have committed against the Lord our God?" then you shall say to them: "Because your fathers have forsaken me, declares the Lord, and have gone after other gods and have served and worshiped them, and have forsaken me and have not kept my law, and because you have done worse than your fathers, for behold, every one of you follows his stubborn, evil will, refusing to listen to me."

He finishes by saying, *"I will show you no favor"* (v. 13). Why did God judge them and why does God judge us? Measure your behavior against what we just read.

Let's go on to my journal from 2016, "What kind of life did God ask from Jeremiah? No wife, no kids, no attending funerals, marriages, or celebrations. He must have been a pretty lonely guy. But he professes, *'O Lord, my strength and my stronghold, my refuge in the day of trouble'* (v. 19). What has God called me to do? What is the price he asked me to pay?" I continued, "And the people ask, *'Why has the Lord pronounced all this great evil against us?'* (v. 10). Because we worship idols, forsake God, don't keep His Law, and we follow our stubborn, evil will."

I continued, "Finally, *'I will show you no favor'* (v. 13). I love God's favor and never want to be without it. After God drives Israel out of the Promised Land for a season, He will bring them back because though we stray, He keeps His covenant promise, referring to verse 15."

DIGGING DEEPER

In Jeremiah 1, God called Jeremiah to be a prophet. He said in chapter 1:4-5, *"Now the word of the Lord came to me, saying, 'Before I formed you in the womb I knew you, and before you were born I consecrated you; I appointed you a prophet to the nations.'"* And the Lord reminds Jeremiah, *"Then the Lord put out his hand and touched my mouth. And the Lord said to me, 'Behold, I have put my words in your mouth'"* (1:9). In 1:17-19, God prepares Jeremiah for this mission of being a prophet:

> *But you, dress yourself for work; arise, and say to them everything that I command you. Do not be dismayed by them, lest I dismay you before them. And I, behold, I make you this day a fortified city, an iron pillar, and bronze walls, against the whole land, against the kings of Judah, its officials, its priests, and the people of the land. They will fight against you, but they shall not prevail against you, for I am with you, declares the Lord, to deliver you.*

In Jeremiah's calling as a prophet, the Lord said it was not going to be easy for him. Here, in chapter 16, are some other conditions of Jeremiah the prophet, *"You shall not take a wife, nor shall you have sons or daughters in this place"* (16:2). To be a prophet for God, Jeremiah was not allowed to marry or have children.

In 16:5, He says to Jeremiah, *"Do not enter the house of mourning, or go to lament or grieve for them."* Jeremiah could not go to funerals. In 16:8, He says, *"You shall not go into the house of feasting to sit with them, to eat and drink."* Jeremiah could not go celebrate with the people. That is why I mentioned in one of my journals, Jeremiah might have been a very lonely man.

Do you think about what God has you sojourning on this earth for?

God required those things of Jeremiah to make him an example to the people he was speaking to. What has God asked from you? Like Jeremiah, before God formed you in your mother's womb, He knew you and He purposed you. Do you realize that? Do you think about what God has you sojourning on this earth for? Have you taken time in your life to even discover what God may have placed you here for? What does God want out of your life? Like Jeremiah, has He placed some conditions of service around your life?

Maybe you do not have everything you want. Maybe your experiences have not been exactly what you hope they would be. Maybe you do not have those things because your life is like Jeremiah. God has asked you to give up some things to serve Him. Maybe you need to see your life from God's perspective and not your own. Let's pray.

Prayer

Father, as we read chapter 16 of the Book of Jeremiah, it may seem a little tough to us. You required much from Jeremiah. What are You requiring of us today?

Lord, You formed me in my mother's womb. You purposed me, just like You did Jeremiah. Holy Spirit, reveal that purpose for my life. Strengthen me to walk in that purpose for You regardless of what You require of me. Reveal Your will and give me the courage to pursue it. In Your name, we ask it. Amen.

MY THOUGHTS

JEREMIAH 17 AND 18

Desperately Wicked

Today, we will look at two chapters in the Book of Jeremiah, chapters 17 and 18. There are total of fifty verses in these two chapters. Are you basically good, or basically evil? Do you trust in the Lord or in man? Please read or listen to Jeremiah 17 and 18.

COMMENTS

Due to the length of today's reading, I will only use my journal from 2016. I wrote, "The simple contrast. *'Cursed is the man who trusts in man and makes flesh his strength, whose heart turns away from the Lord'* (17:5). *'Blessed is the man who trusts in the Lord, whose trust is the Lord'* (17:7). Life boils down to this: Trust in man or trust in the Lord. Cursed or blessed. Our choice. Our heart is deceitful and desperately wicked, our natural sinful condition, according to verse 9. And God searches our wicked hearts and tests our minds for reward according to our deeds. Is it fair that God knows our hearts are desperately wicked and tests us anyway?"

I continued, "But God can heal and save. And He does. Jeremiah's heart is being turned by God. At first, he defended his people. He wanted to pray for them. Now he agrees with God. They are guilty and deserve destruction, referring to 17:16-18." I continued to write, "Honor the Sabbath. They didn't, nor do we. There are consequences to disobedience, then and now, according to 17:27."

I wrote more, "Object lessons: the potter and the clay. God is our maker, so He has the right to shape us the way He wants. Our problem is God calls us to return to Him, *"amend your ways and your deeds." But they say, "That is in vain! We will follow our own plans, and will every one act according to the stubbornness of his evil heart"* (18:11-12). No one listened to Jeremiah. Few listen to God's messages today."

DIGGING DEEPER

In Jeremiah 17, God gives us the very clear contrast of life. *"Cursed is the man who trusts in man and makes flesh his strength, whose heart turns away from the Lord"* (17:5). The contrast is, *"Blessed is the man who trusts in the Lord, whose trust is the Lord"* (17:7). Yet, He tells us the condition we are born into, *"The heart is deceitful above all things, and desperately sick; who can understand it?"* (17:9). Yet, He says, *"I the Lord search the heart and test the mind, to give every man according to his ways, according to the fruit of his deeds"* (17:10).

Jeremiah 17:9 is one of those verses I refer to often, my heart is desperately wicked; therefore, I need something between my heart and my day and that is the Word of God. I want to put the Word of God between my heart and my day every day. I hope you do too.

> My heart is desperately wicked; therefore, I need something between my heart and my day and that is the Word of God.

Chapter 18 is that great story about the potter and the clay. The Lord takes Jeremiah down to a potter who is shaping a pot:

And the vessel he was making of clay was spoiled in the potter's hand, and he reworked it into another vessel, as it seemed good to the potter to do.

Then the word of the Lord came to me: "O house of Israel, can I not do with you as this potter has done? declares the Lord. Behold, like the clay in the potter's hand, so are you in my hand O house of Israel" (18:4-6).

Yes, God is shaping us. His hands are shaping us. He can start over with us if we just let Him.

We finish with Jeremiah 18:11-12:

Thus says the Lord, Behold, I am shaping disaster against you and devising a plan against you. Return, every one from his evil way, and amend your ways and your deeds.

But they say, "That is in vain! We will follow our own plans, and will every one act according to the stubbornness of his evil heart."

They did not listen to Jeremiah, and they did not listen to God, rather they said, *"Come, let us make plots against Jeremiah . . . Come, let us strike him with the tongue, and let us not pay attention to any of his words"* (18:18).

Prayer

Lord, we are like them. We are clay. We are in Your hands. You are the potter. Please mold us and shape us so we can be pleasing in Your sight. Though our hearts are desperately wicked, Lord, help us. Forgive us when we follow our own plans in the stubbornness of our own evil hearts. May these chapters remind us to resubmit ourselves to You. So let it be written, so let it be done. Amen.

MY THOUGHTS

When the Going Gets Tough

Today brings us to Jeremiah 19 and 20. Chapter 19 has fifteen verses and chapter 20 has eighteen verses. Jeremiah wants to quit; being a prophet is too hard. Is it tough for you right now? Do you want to quit? Please read or listen to Jeremiah 19 and 20.

COMMENTS

In 1991, I read Jeremiah 20-22 (NASB) on the same day. I wrote concerning 20:12, *"Yet, O LORD of hosts, you who test the righteous, who see the mind and the heart."*

Thirteen years later, in 2004, I read Jeremiah 17-20 on the same day, and wrote, "Life of a prophet was rough. He proclaimed bad news. Finally, was beaten and put in jail. He complains to God as a laughingstock, everyone mocks. Sometimes, it's pretty rough doing God's will. But if he didn't proclaim God's message, it became a burning fire in his heart, and he gets weary of holding it in. Maintain faithfulness to God's calling."

Another twelve years later, in 2016, I wrote concerning Jeremiah 19 and 20, "God has Jeremiah demonstrate the coming destruction of Jerusalem by breaking a potter's vessel before elders and priests. The priests had enough, so they beat Jeremiah and put him in jail. Upon his release, he clearly proclaims they will be destroyed and taken off into Babylon. Then he complains to God. He is tired of being mocked for doing what God has called him to do. Yet, he can't stop. The call of God on a life does not mean it will be easy. Jeremiah curses the day he was born. My own ebb and flow of my calling is natural. I try not to complain about

> The call of God on a life does not mean it will be easy.

what God has called me to do, but I murmur from time to time. Forgive me. My hope is in You."

Then I prayed and wrote this about my prayer, "Forgive me for whining about the challenge of leadership You have placed before me. Strengthen me. Shape me to stand for You."

DIGGING DEEPER

In Chapter 20, the Prophet Jeremiah gets beaten and put in jail. In verses 7-8, it looks like Jeremiah has had enough. He says to the Lord:

I have become a laughingstock all the day; everyone mocks me. For whenever I speak, I cry out, I shout, "Violence and destruction!" For the word of the Lord has become for me a reproach and derision all day long.

But Jeremiah cannot stop preaching. *"If I say, 'I will not mention him, or speak any more in his name,' there is in my heart as it were a burning fire shut up in my bones, and I am weary with holding it in, and I cannot'"* (20:9). Why? Because, remember Jeremiah's calling in chapter 1:

Before I formed you in the womb I knew you, and before you were born I consecrated you; I appointed you a prophet to the nations (1:5).

Then the Lord put out his hand and touched my mouth. And the Lord said to me, "Behold, I have put my words in your mouth" (1:9).

When the Word of God is in your heart, when you have a calling on your life, regardless of what you suffer, you cannot not stop. That is where we find Jeremiah in chapter 20. He wants to quit but he cannot because he knows he is called of the Lord.

I hope God has a call on your life. I hope you are doing all you can to be obedient to that call, even when it gets really, really tough. It got tough for Jeremiah. It may be getting tough, or it may be very tough for you right now. But like Jeremiah, remember your calling. Stand firm in the Lord. May your heart burn with the passion of God's will for your life.

Prayer

Father, we bow humbly before You. We think about Jeremiah and how tough it got. And we think about our own lives. It may be tough serving You in our workplace, in our family, among our friends. But Lord, help us. Burn that passion again in our hearts to stand firm for You. Blessed be the name of the Lord who fashioned us in my mother's womb. Help us remain faithful to our callings. In Your name, we ask it. Amen.

MY THOUGHTS

JEREMIAH 21 AND 22

Never Leave or Forsake Us?

Jeremiah 21 and 22 are about God forsaking His own people, Israel. Do you think God will never leave you or forsake you? Please read or listen to the fourteen verses of Jeremiah 21 and the thirty verses of Jeremiah 22.

COMMENTS

When reading Jeremiah 21 and 22 in 2016, I wrote in my personal Bible reading journal, "Ouch! These are words that came to Jeremiah from the Lord! They are harsh, unmerciful, devastating. *'I myself will fight against you with outstretched hand and strong arm, in anger and in fury and in great wrath'* (21:5). Why do Christians say universally that He will never leave me nor forsake me? That may have been a promise to Joshua, but it is clearly not universal to all people. *'For I have set my face against this city for harm and not for good, declares the Lord'* (21:10). Babylon is used by God to take down Jerusalem, Judah, kings, and His people. Why? Because they have forsaken the covenant of the Lord their God and worshipped other gods and served them. Sounds like the USA today."

DIGGING DEEPER

Let's look at "forsaking" for a moment. In Joshua 1:5, the Lord does say to Joshua, *"No man shall be able to stand before you all the days of your life. Just as I was with Moses, so I will be with you. I will not leave you or forsake you."* Somehow, Christians take, "I will never leave you nor forsake you" and say that is always the case in their own lives.

I do not believe it because of passages like we are reading in Jeremiah. Throughout the Old Testament, God certainly forsakes His people. He says in Jeremiah 21:5, *"I myself will fight against you with outstretched hand and strong arm, in anger and in fury and in great wrath."* If that is not enough, let's go on to verse 6, *"And I will strike down the inhabitants of this city, both man and beast. They shall die of a great pestilence."*

Do I need to keep going? Verse 7:

Afterward, declares the Lord, I will give Zedekiah king of Judah and his servants and the people in this city who survive the pestilence, sword, and famine into the hand of Nebuchadnezzar king of Babylon and into the hand of their enemies, into the hand of those who seek their lives. He shall strike them down with the edge of the sword. He shall not pity them or spare them or have compassion.

> There may be too many Christians who think they can get away with living a lifestyle however they want, thinking God will never forsake them because He "has" to forgive them.

Jumping down to verse 10, the Word of God says, *"For I have set my face against this city for harm and not for good, declares the Lord."* I do not know what your definition is of forsaking, but it sure does sound like God is forsaking people right here. So, as Christians, I think we need to be very careful when we say, "God will never leave me nor forsake me."

We have heard and read over and over in Jeremiah, God wants our obedience. He wants our allegiance, and when we do not do so, He very likely will forsake us. We probably ought to go one step farther. If God said He will never forsake anybody, then why do people go to hell?

O, I certainly believe God is a God of love. He would that none would perish, and all would come to saving faith in Him. He admonishes us over and over to love Him, obey Him, keep His commandments, walk with Him. But if we do not, there are plenty of places in scripture where He forsakes us.

There may be too many Christians who think they can get away with living a lifestyle however they want, thinking God will never forsake them because He "has" to forgive them. Friends, that is cheap grace. It dishonors what Jesus Christ did on the cross of Calvary for us.

Here in Jeremiah 22:8-9, the Word of God says, *"And many nations will pass by this city, and every man will say to his neighbor, 'Why has the Lord dealt thus with this great city?' And they will answer, 'Because they have forsaken the covenant of the Lord their God and worshiped other gods and served them.'"* When it comes to forsaking, we are guilty.

Prayer

Lord, forgive us for forsaking You. Forgive us for believing You will never forsake us. Help us understand Your true biblical principles. Though You are a God of great patience, of great love, of great mercy, and of great grace, Your patience runs out on us. It ran out on Your own people here in the Book of Jeremiah and You judged them. It too can wear out on us and You will forsake us and judge us.

To be sure You will never forsake us, Lord, it is easy: obey You, keep Your commandments, love You, walk with You all the days of our lives. Holy Spirit, help us get a right understanding of You through the power of Your Word. We ask it, in Jesus' name. Amen.

MY THOUGHTS

JEREMIAH 23 AND 24

Warnings to Preachers

Jeremiah 23 and 24 contain warnings to shepherds, pastors, and preachers. Does your pastor preach the Word of God? Please read or listen to the combined fifty verses of Jeremiah 23 and 24.

COMMENTS

In 1991, I read Jeremiah 23 and 24 together and wrote in my personal Bible reading journal, "It is dangerous to be a pastor, a shepherd of God's flock. There is no room

> **Without God's Word, man perverts truth.**

for fake preaching or leading people astray or dreaming without the basis of the Word of God. Without God's Word, man perverts truth."

Continuing that same theme, jumping to 2016, I read Jeremiah 23 and 24 on the same day and wrote, "I doubt if many preachers use chapter 23 as their text. God lights up shepherds, priests, prophets who are not true to His Word. So much of preaching today is like visions of their own minds; not from the mouth of the Lord."

Then I quoted, *"It shall be well with you'; and to everyone who stubbornly follows his own heart, they say, 'No disaster shall come upon you'* (23:17). Feel-good sermons, prosperity gospel, stories, but not preaching and teaching God's Word." Then I quoted

Jeremiah 23:18, "Who is getting his message from the Lord? *'Who has paid attention to his word and listened?'* God prefers not dreams of men, but preaching My Word faithfully, according to verse 28. God raise up preachers who will preach Your Word."

DIGGING DEEPER

God's warnings are very clear in these chapters to the shepherds, the priests, the pastors who lead our flocks today. *"Woe to the shepherds who destroy and scatter the sheep of my pasture"* (23:1).

Jeremiah 23:16-18 and 29 say:

Thus says the Lord of hosts: "Do not listen to the words of the prophets who prophesy to you, filling you with vain hopes. They speak visions of their own minds, not from the mouth of the Lord. They say continually to those who despise the word of the Lord, 'It shall be well with you'; and to everyone who stubbornly follows his own heart, they say, 'No disaster shall come upon you.'"

For who among them has stood in the council of the Lord to see and to hear his word, or who has paid attention to his word and listened?

Is not my word like fire, declares the Lord, and like a hammer that breaks the rock in pieces?

The application from today's message may be, go to a Bible teaching, Bible preaching church.

Prayer

Father, we pray Your blessings upon the pastors and the priests that teach Your Word faithfully. We need to be under the teaching of Your Word. Raise up shepherds who will be faithful to Your Word. We ask it, in Jesus' name. Amen.

MY THOUGHTS

JEREMIAH 25 AND 26

Can You Change the Plans of God?

Today, we reach the halfway point of the Book of Jeremiah. It is a pivotal point in the Book of Jeremiah, as God instructs Jeremiah not to hold back His Word. His life is threatened for his obedience to God. Will the people listen? If so, God may change His mind. Can we change the plans of God? Please read or listen to the thirty-eight verses in Jeremiah 25 and the twenty-four verses in Jeremiah 26.

COMMENTS

Today, we will look at my journal entries from 1991 and 2016. From 1991, "Jeremiah faces death as a prophet of God, but God reserves the right to change His mind if the people will amend their ways and deeds. God is ever patient, but He also carries through on His promises of punishment for sin and disobedience. If He didn't, why would anyone ever obey?"

From 2016, "For twenty-three years now, Jeremiah has shared the Word of the Lord, *'but you have not listened'* (25:3). Maybe nothing has happened yet. Jeremiah has proclaimed warnings and pending destruction, but nothing has come to pass, so why listen? God is patient. He warns us over and over until finally He does act. God calls Nebuchadnezzar, King of Babylon, a pagan, His servant. God will use him to destroy Israel or Judah. After seventy years, God will judge Babylon for destroying Judah. All nations are subject to God's sovereignty. Jeremiah stands in the court of the temple and speaks to those coming to worship. They want to kill him. People want the Word of God silenced, especially religious leaders. Jeremiah does not back down. He stands in the face of death for God and His Word. And God preserves him."

DIGGING DEEPER

In Jeremiah 26:2, God instructs Jeremiah to, *"Stand in the court of the Lord's house, and speak to all the cities of Judah that come to worship in the house of the Lord all the words that I command you to speak to them; do not hold back a word."* Verse 3 is our focus, *"It may be they will listen, and every one turn from his evil way, that I may relent of the disaster that I intend to do to them because of their evil deeds."*

"It may be they will listen" draws my attention. Does God not know if they will listen or not? Do we have a choice to listen to God or not? He can respond to listening or

Does God not know if they will listen or not?

not listening, *"I may relent of the disaster that I intend to do."* He has a plan of disaster, but might He change His plan based on their response to Jeremiah's message?

God's desire is they listen, but He does not force them to. We have choice. He gives us options, *"listen, and every one turn from his evil way."* If we do, God acts one way. He *"relents."* Amazing! However, *"If you will not listen to me, to walk in my law that I have set before you, and to listen to the words of my servants the prophets whom I send to you urgently, though you have not listened, then I will make this house like Shiloh, and I will make this city a curse for all the nations of the earth"* (26:4-6). If we do not, God acts another way. He judges, curses, and destroys.

It sure looks to me like our sovereign God, who knows everything, all the time, keeps His options open based on whether we listen or not. Are you listening? Do you listen to God through His Word? Do you heed His warnings? Do you respond to His consistent appeals to turn from our wicked ways and come back to Him? He gives us the choice. Amazing!

Prayer

Father, may we turn our ears to You. Speak to us through Your Word, speak to us through Your Prophet Jeremiah, speak to us with Your small, still voice in our inner being. As You do, open our ears to listen to You.

Father, may we also be steadfast, immovable, always abounding in the work of the Lord, knowing in the Lord, our labor is not in vain. Thank You for preserving Jeremiah. Preserve us too as we stand for You. Amen.

MY THOUGHTS

JEREMIAH 27

Who Do You Listen To?

In Jeremiah 27, will kings listen to their own counselors or the Prophet Jeremiah? Who do you listen to, the words of men, or the Word of God? Please read or listen to the twenty-two verses of Jeremiah 27.

COMMENTS

I will only refer to my 2016 journal in this devotion. I wrote concerning Jeremiah 27, "God is sovereign over all nations. He decides the fate of Edom, Moab, Ammon, Tyre, Sidon, Israel, Babylon. And Nebuchadnezzar was God's servant. Jeremiah alone is telling the truth. Everyone else is lying. How would you like to carry that message?"

In Jeremiah 27, God asks Jeremiah to act out another prophetic message. Verse 2 says, *"Thus the Lord said to me: 'Make yourself straps and yoke-bars, and put them on your neck.'"* My English Standard Version Study Bible footnote on that verse says, "Yokes were made of wooden bars affixed to the animal by leather thongs" (p. 1422).

Do you have a visual picture of Jeremiah walking through the town with yoke bars and straps? You can just see Jeremiah, with a yoke bar hanging around his neck, speaking to the king of Edom, the king of Moab, the king of sons of Ammon, the king of Tyre, the king of Sidon, and the king of Jerusalem. What a picture we have, once again, of the Prophet Jeremiah. Here is the message he delivers to those kings,

"It is I who by my great power and my outstretched arm have made the earth, with the men and animals that are on the earth, and I give it to whomever it seems right to me. Now I have given all these lands into the hand of Nebuchadnezzar, the king of Babylon" (vv. 5-6).

I guess that would have been a pretty difficult message for those kings to hear. But if they did not quite get it, Jeremiah goes on, *"But if any nation or kingdom will not serve this Nebuchadnezzar king of Babylon, and put its neck under the yoke of the king of Babylon, I will punish that nation with the sword, with famine, and with pestilence, declares the Lord, until I have consumed it by his hand"* (v. 8). Jeremiah is saying, you have no hope. You must surrender to this king of Babylon, and if you do not, God is going to destroy you anyway.

He goes on to say, *"So do not listen to your prophets, your diviners, your dreamers, your fortune-tellers, or your sorcerers, who are saying to you, 'You shall not serve the king of Babylon.' For it is a lie that they are prophesying to you, with the result that you will be removed far from your land, and I will drive you out, and you will perish"* (vv. 9-10).

DIGGING DEEPER

The question for those kings is the same question you and I have today. Who are we going to believe? Are they going to believe their counselors, their advisors? Or are they going to believe the voice of the prophet of Almighty God?

It is easy for us to listen to the words of men rather than the Word of God.

We have the same challenge today. There are many voices speaking into our ears. But there is only one voice, like Jeremiah, a true prophet of God, speaking into our hearts. It is easy for us to listen to the words of men rather than the Word of God.

Prayer

Lord, help us be discerning people. Help us understand Your Word over the words of men. You say in the New Testament, Your sheep hear Your voice. May we hear Your voice and Your voice alone. Holy Spirit, help us tune out the noise of the world so we can hear the truth of Your Word.

Like in Jeremiah's day, when we listen to You, we will be preserved. But if we do not listen to You, we could be destroyed or we could perish. Holy Spirit, lead us into all truth and away from the lies of this world. We ask it, in the name of Jesus. Amen.

MY THOUGHTS

JEREMIAH 28 AND 29

God Has Plans for You

Today, we are in Jeremiah 28 and 29. In the middle of despair, God has plans for a future and a hope. Do you believe God has plans for you? Please read or listen to the seventeen verses in Jeremiah 28 and the thirty-two verses in Jeremiah 29.

COMMENTS

In 1991, when reading the Book of Jeremiah, I read Jeremiah 27-30 on the same day. I referred to one of those great, famous verses in Jeremiah, 29:11, *"For I know the plans that I have for you,' declares the Lord, 'plans for welfare and not for calamity to give you a future and a hope'"* (NASB).

I have not referred to my journal in 2004 for the last few devotions because I was reading the Bible chronologically, and in the middle of Jeremiah it started jumping around in other books like Kings and Chronicles and some of the other prophets. So let's look at my journal entry from 2016.

In 2016, I read Jeremiah 28 and 29 on the same day, and wrote in my journal, "Be careful what we say. Hananiah is a false prophet. Though he may have looked good preaching in the house of the Lord, he was lying. Too many are preaching lies today in the house of worship. Israel was to remain in captivity in Babylon for seventy years, not two years according to Hananiah. 29:11, often quoted, should be remembered in its setting: exile, hopelessness, frustration. Yes, in desperate situations, God responds when we call upon Him. Seek Him with all of our heart." I finished my journal entry by writing, "Be careful who we listen to."

> **Too many are preaching lies today in the house of worship.**

Back in Jeremiah 23, we were warned about false shepherds, false prophets, speaking their own words and their own visions and not the words of the Lord. Here in chapter 28, we see another example, a false prophet, Hananiah. He was even so bold as to remove the yoke bars from Jeremiah's neck. Let's pick up the story in 28:10-11, *"Then the prophet Hananiah took the yoke-bars from the neck of Jeremiah the prophet and broke them. And Hananiah spoke in the presence of all the people, saying, 'Thus says the Lord: Even so will I break the yoke of Nebuchadnezzar king of Babylon from the neck of all the nations within two years.'"*

Notice Jeremiah does not even respond. He just walks away. Sometime later, Jeremiah hears from the Lord about that incident. God says to Jeremiah, *"Go, tell Hananiah, 'Thus says the Lord: You have broken wooden bars, but you have made in their place bars of iron'"* (28:13).

After that Jeremiah did respond to Hananiah:

And Jeremiah the prophet said to the prophet Hananiah, "Listen, Hananiah, the Lord has not sent you, and you have made this people trust in a lie. Therefore thus says the Lord: 'Behold, I will remove you from the face of the earth. This year you shall die, because you have uttered rebellion against the Lord.'"

In that same year, in the seventh month, the prophet Hananiah died (vv. 15-17).

The lesson here is very clear, once again. Be careful who we listen to, even if they are in the house of the Lord, even if they claim to be a prophet from the Lord.

DIGGING DEEPER

Let's close with that great, famous verse in chapter 29. Let's put the verse in context. Jeremiah has been prophesying for all these chapters that Israel would be carted off into captivity in Babylon. Let's look at 29:1, *"These are the words of the letter that Jeremiah the prophet sent from Jerusalem to the surviving elders of the exiles, and to the priests, the prophets, and all the people, whom Nebuchadnezzar had taken into exile from Jerusalem to Babylon."*

Though nothing happened for years, finally what Jeremiah prophesied occurred. He remains in Jerusalem, but the people have been carted off to Babylon, and he is writing them a letter of encouragement. He says in his letter:

> *For thus says the Lord: When seventy years are completed for Babylon, I will visit you, and I will fulfill to you my promise and bring you back to this place. For I know the plans I have for you, declares the Lord, plans for welfare and not for evil, to give you a future and a hope. Then you will call upon me and come and pray to me, and I will hear you. You will seek me and find me, when you seek me with all your heart. I will be found by you, declares the Lord, and I will restore your fortunes and gather you from all the nations and all the places where I have driven you, declares the Lord, and I will bring you back to the place from which I sent you into exile* (vv. 10-14).

What a promise, what a hope; a God we can also depend on today. His anger is for a moment, but His mercy is for a lifetime. Yes, you may be suffering under the wrath of God at the moment, but friends, there is hope. He is a God of restoration. Let's pray.

Prayer

Lord, we thank You that You have plans for us like You did for the people of Israel. We thank You that Your plans are for welfare and not evil. We thank You that You will give us a future and a hope. We thank You that You said if we call on You, You will hear us once again. And if we seek You, we will find You, if we seek You with all our heart. Lord, we do just that today. We seek You with all our heart. Restore us to the joy of our salvation and we will give You the praise. In Jesus' name, amen.

MY THOUGHTS

JEREMIAII 30 AND 31

A God of Restoration

In Jeremiah 30 and 31, we are reminded He is a God of restoration. Have you strayed, been disobedient, need to come back? Please read or listen to the twenty-four verses in Jeremiah 30 and the forty verses in Jeremiah 31.

COMMENTS

Due to the length of the reading today, I will not use my journals but just summarize some of the great encouragement we read or heard in these chapters after so much judgment and destruction in the first several chapters of Jeremiah. Praise God He is a God of restoration:

For behold, days are coming, declares the Lord, when I will restore the fortunes of my people, Israel and Judah, says the Lord, and I will bring them back to the land that I gave to their fathers, and they shall take possession of it (30:3).

For I am with you to save you, declares the Lord (30:11).

I have loved you with an everlasting love; therefore I have continued my faithfulness to you (31:3).

Wow! Thank You, Lord, for Your everlasting love to us.

There is hope for your future, declares the Lord (31:17).

And there is hope for our future, as well, *"Behold, the days are coming, declares the Lord, when I will make a new covenant with the house of Israel and the house of Judah"* (31:31).

Jumping down to 31:33-34, one of those great passages of Jeremiah:

I will put my law within them, and I will write it on their hearts. And I will be their God, and they shall be my people. And no longer shall each one teach his neighbor and each his brother, saying, "Know the Lord," for they shall all know me, from the least of them to the greatest, declares the Lord. For I will forgive their iniquity, and I will remember their sin no more.

DIGGING DEEPER

Praise God He is a God of restoration even though He is a God of judgment. He was very upset with His own people, Israel. You may think He is, or has been, very upset with you. But hear the encouragement in

> **He is a God of restoration even though He is a God of judgment.**

these chapters for Israel and you. He loves you enough to restore, save, continue His everlasting love and faithfulness to you, and give you hope! He is ready to make a new covenant with you if you come back to Him. Will you?

Prayer

Hallelujah, Lord! We thank You for Your everlasting love. The fact that You will renew Your covenant with us. You will remember our sins no more. We come back to You! We give You praise and thanks. In Jesus' name, amen.

MY THOUGHTS

JEREMIAH 32 AND 33

Acting on Faith

Today, we will cover Jeremiah 32 and 33. They are long chapters. Why are we covering two long chapters in one day? Because I did not think you wanted to spend fifty-two days in the Book of Jeremiah, so we consolidated the fifty-two chapters into thirty-one days.

Jeremiah is asked to buy a "bridge to nowhere" in chapter 32. He obeys God in a publicly embarrassing transaction. Do you act on faith in public? Please read or listen to the forty-four verses of Jeremiah 32 and the twenty-six verses of Jeremiah 33.

COMMENTS

I will refer to only one journal entry and that is 2016, "Jeremiah's prayer. I love to read the prayers of the heroes of the Bible. They talk to God like we get to, and God answered them. I hope He answers me. We are all like the children of Israel with our sin nature like theirs. We do nothing but evil, provoke God to anger, we turn our back on God, resist Him, and do not listen or receive His instruction. We worship idols and we kill our babies (abortion).

> We are all like the children of Israel with our sin nature like theirs.

"Yet, *'Just as I have brought all this great disaster upon this people, so I will bring upon them all the good that I promise them'* (32:42). God keeps His promises despite our disobedience. Even in the midst of the battle, God begs us to call out to Him because God forgives. He will also prosper Jerusalem once again. He will honor His covenant with David and raise up a Messiah. As day and night come out at their appointed times, that alone should remind us of God's covenant with Israel, Judah, and David. Powerful."

DIGGING DEEPER

God uses another illustration with Jeremiah to demonstrate His prophetic word will come true. He tells Jeremiah to buy a field near Jerusalem, though the city is going to be burned with fire. Jeremiah obeys the voice of God and consummates the transaction in public. Those witnessing must have thought he was a fool. But Jeremiah acted on the Word of his God, not the impressions of men. He believed God would restore Jerusalem, and the field would be worth more tomorrow than today, *"Houses and fields and vineyards shall again be bought in this land"* (32:15).

How do you respond when God tests your faith? Are you sure enough you hear God, you act accordingly, even at the risk of embarrassment before family and friends? Jeremiah trusted God's voice and acted accordingly; I pray we can too.

Prayer

Lord, Your Word is powerful. Yes, You will judge. Yes, You will punish. But, yes, You are a God of restoration and a covenant-promise keeper. Thank You for the promise of restoration in my life as well. Please make Your voice clear to us and give us courage to act out in public what we hear in private from You. To God be the glory. Amen.

MY THOUGHTS

JEREMIAH 34

The Word of the Lord Came to Jeremiah

Today, we will cover just one chapter, Jeremiah 34, and it is only twenty-two verses. We are reminded the Word of the Lord came to Jeremiah. That is what he writes. We are reading God's Word. Do you cherish the fact you can read words from the lips of God? Please read or listen to Jeremiah 34.

COMMENTS

With only one chapter, we can get back to my journals. In 1991, I read Jeremiah 33-35 on the same day, three chapters, like I did on other days through the Book of Jeremiah. I wrote about chapters 33 and 35, but I did not write anything about chapter 34.

In 2004, I was reading the Bible chronologically. In the middle of Jeremiah, I read other passages out of Kings and Chronicles and sometimes other prophets. I looked around a few pages of my journal where I was reading Jeremiah but did not find any notes on chapter 34; but I encourage you to read the Bible chronologically someday. It is a very exciting and different way to read the scriptures. If you are interested in doing so, visit our website ezraproject.net and get yourself a Chronological Bible Reading Journal as it has the readings laid out chronologically.

On to 2016, where I read Jeremiah 34 on one day, and wrote, *"'The Word that came to Jeremiah from the Lord'* (v. 1). Over and over Jeremiah speaks what he hears from God." Then I wrote, "Jerusalem is going to lose to Babylon." I continued to write, "Another example of disobedience: not freeing Hebrew slaves after six years."

I mentioned in my journal over and over and over we hear what Jeremiah hears from the Lord. 34:1 says, *"The word that came to Jeremiah from the Lord."* Verse 2 says, *"Thus says the Lord."* Verse 8 says, *"The word that came to Jeremiah from the Lord."* Verse 12, *"The word of the Lord came to Jeremiah from the Lord."* Verse 17, *"Therefore, thus says the Lord."* I repeat that because it is important to realize the Bible comes from the Lord.

Jeremiah wrote down what he heard from the Lord. And he hears some pretty clear instructions from the Lord, *"Thus says the Lord: Behold, I am giving this city into the hand of the king of Babylon, and he shall burn it with fire. You shall not escape from his hand but shall surely be captured and delivered into his hand"* (vv. 2-3).

Through Jeremiah, God tells Jerusalem exactly what is going to happen, and it did. That is why Jeremiah is a prophet: because the things he said came true. We read about some false prophets earlier in Jeremiah. The things they said never came true. That is how you know the difference between a true prophet and a false prophet; things must come true.

I also mentioned in my journal, the Hebrews were violating the law by enslaving fellow Hebrews and not releasing them after six years of servitude. The only reason they did so here was to fight Babylon, then they re-enslave them, violating God's law.

We need to go back to Exodus to see where God was giving the Hebrews the law and he says in Exodus 21:2, *"When you buy a Hebrew slave, he shall serve six years, and in the seventh he shall go out free, for nothing."* That is the provision of the law they are violating

> **If you think you are going to get away with something, you are not. God is watching.**

here. One thing I get out of this is God is watching. He watches them release the slaves and then He watches them re-enslave them:

You recently repented and did what was right in my eyes by proclaiming liberty, each to his neighbor, and you made a covenant before me in the house that is called by my name, but then you turned around and profaned my name when each of you took back his male and female slaves, whom you had set free according to their desire, and you brought them into subjection to be your slaves (vv. 15-16).

Like He watched them, He watches us. He watches our activity. If you think you are going to get away with something, you are not. God is watching.

DIGGING DEEPER

How do we apply what we read today to our lives? First, we realize, "Thus saith the Lord." The words we are reading are God's words. Next, we realize God knows the future. He knew the future of Jerusalem. He knows your future as well. Lastly, God is watching us. He watches us daily. Are you abiding by His Word? Avoid God's judgment, avoid God's punishment, by living according to the Word of God. Let's pray.

Prayer

Father, we thank You that You spoke through the Prophet Jeremiah, not only to the Jews of that day, but to us today. May we hear the Word of the Lord. You did all You could to keep the people from falling. You warned them over and over. As we read Jeremiah, You warn us over and over. May Your words not go through one ear and out the other. May they land in our hearts. We ask it, in Jesus' name, amen.

CHALLENGE

Friends, I know Jeremiah might be a tough book, but I hope you will share it with someone else. All of us need the whole counsel of God. We cannot pick and choose the passages of scripture we want to read. We need to hear all of the Word of God. I encourage you to share *Day by Day Through the Bible* with some of your friends and your family. We all know people who need to hear more from the Word of God. Share *Day by Day* today. God bless you. Amen.

MY THOUGHTS

JEREMIAH 35 AND 36

A King Burns the Book of Jeremiah

Today, we will cover two more chapters of the Book of Jeremiah, chapters 35 and 36. The King of Judah throws the pages of Jeremiah's scroll into a fire, so how do we have this book today? Are you glad we do? Please read or listen to the nineteen verses of Jeremiah 35 and the thirty-two verses of Jeremiah 36.

COMMENTS

In my journal in 2016, concerning these two chapters, I wrote, "An example of obedience. A family whose father said, *'drink no wine'* (35:14), a simple thing to discard, this family obeyed. All of them. So obedience to a father over drinking wine could be kept, but the children of Israel could not keep God the Father's commandments."

> Some people fear when hearing God's Word, others laugh at what God says.

I continued, "God instructs Jeremiah to, *'Take a scroll and write on it all the words that I have spoken'* (36:2). Jeremiah dictates to Baruch all the words of the Lord that He had spoken to him. Jeremiah is banned from going to the house of the Lord, so he sends Baruch to read the scroll. Some people fear when hearing God's Word, others laugh at what God says. The king burned the scroll. How do I respond to God's Word? God tells Jeremiah to write it all again."

In chapter 35, Jeremiah uses a simple illustration from the Lord to demonstrate how easy it would have been for Israel to fulfill God's Word. He uses the example of a father who tells his family not to drink wine. And they obeyed. Verses 14-15 of chapter 35 make the point of the illustration:

The command that Jonadab the son of Rechab gave to his sons, to drink no wine, has been kept, and they drink none to this day, for they have obeyed their father's command. I have spoken to you persistently, but you have not listened to me. I have sent to you all my servants the prophets, sending them persistently, saying, "Turn now every one of you from his evil way, and amend your deeds, and do not go after other gods to serve them, and then you shall dwell in the land that I gave to you and your fathers." But you did not incline your ear or listen to me.

To us, it should be as easy as that. Sometimes our fathers give us instruction and we are to obey them. Our heavenly Father has given us instruction too, and we are to obey those instructions like we do our earthly fathers.

DIGGING DEEPER

Why do we have the Book of Jeremiah today? Because God instructed Jeremiah to write down everything He said. *"Take a scroll and write on it all the words that I have spoken to you against Israel and Judah and all the nations, from the day I spoke to you, from the days of Josiah until today"* (36:2).

Yes, God instructed Jeremiah to write this book. Yes, it was burned, but Jeremiah and Baruck rewrote it:

Now after the king had burned the scroll with the words that Baruch wrote at Jeremiah's dictation, the word of the Lord came to Jeremiah: "Take another scroll and write on it all the former words that were in the first scroll" (36:27-28).

Then Jeremiah took another scroll and gave it to Baruch the scribe, the son of Neriah, who wrote on it at the dictation of Jeremiah all the words of the scroll that Jehoiakim king of Judah had burned in the fire. And many similar words were added to them (36:32).

We have the Book of Jeremiah; we have the Word of God because God wanted us to have it. Let's pray.

Prayer

Father, we thank You our fathers gave us simple instructions and we obeyed them. You, heavenly Father, give us instructions as well and we are expected to obey them. Lord, help us hear Your words and be willing to obey.

And Lord, we thank You that You have preserved Your Word for generations. We thank You we have the Word of the Lord today. Hallelujah! Thank You for preserving Your Word. Amen.

MY THOUGHTS

Kill Him!

In chapters 37 and 38 of the Book of Jeremiah, Jeremiah is accused of desertion, imprisoned, and some want him dead. Do you think you have it tough serving the Lord? Please read or listen to the twenty-one verses of Jeremiah 37 and the twenty-eight verses of Jeremiah 38.

COMMENTS

In 2016, concerning these chapters, I wrote, "Stay the course. Jeremiah never weakens his message. He doesn't bow to pressure. He stays consistent no matter who he's talking to or what it may cost him. This is at least the second time he is beaten and imprisoned. Understandably, the officials want him put to death because his words over and over would weaken the resolve of the people to fight. Often truth is not popular, and it hurts. He gets a private audience with the king and doesn't back down. As promised, God spares Jeremiah again."

Do you think doing God's will in your life is easy? It was not very easy on Jeremiah. In chapter 37, Jeremiah is accused of desertion. He is beaten and put in prison. The king requests his presence from the dungeon. He *questions him secretly . . . 'Is there any word from the Lord?'"* (37:17). Jeremiah says, *"There is . . . You shall be delivered into the hand of the king of Babylon"* (37:17). Jeremiah does not back down. He cannot. He has the words of the Lord in him.

At the end of chapter 37, the king spares Jeremiah from going back to somebody Jeremiah thought would kill him. So Jeremiah remained in the court of the guard.

Those officials hear Jeremiah, and they say he is discouraging the city. They too want to put Jeremiah to death. They cast him into the cistern and Jeremiah sinks into the mud. How low can it get when you are serving the Lord?

> **How low can it get when you are serving the Lord?**

A foreigner, an Ethiopian, comes and pleads to the king to save Jeremiah's life. The king allows Jeremiah to be raised from the pit. The king is desperate again, so he sends for Jeremiah. Jeremiah gives him the same message. Jerusalem is going to fall to the Babylonians.

Jeremiah 38 ends with these words, *"And Jeremiah remained in the court of the guard until the day that Jerusalem was taken"* (38:28). Jeremiah never backed down from speaking God's truth.

DIGGING DEEPER

What kind of pressure are you under? Is your faith ridiculed by your friends or members of your family or your co-workers? If so, do you get quiet before them, or do you stand bold and proclaim the truth of your God?

Prayer

Lord, embolden us. Let us learn from Jeremiah to stand for Your truth. Even when his life was on the line, he did not compromise. Again Lord, embolden us to stand up for our Christian faith even when those around us ridicule us.

Back in Jeremiah 1, you said, *"They will fight against you, but they shall not prevail against you, for I am with you, declares the Lord, to deliver you"* (1:19). Be with us, Lord, and deliver us too from those who ridicule us for our faith in You. Strengthen us. In Your name, we pray. Amen.

MY THOUGHTS

JEREMIAH 39 AND 40

The Fall of Jerusalem

Today, we read or listen to the fall of Jerusalem. Have you pushed God too far? Will He never leave you or forsake you? Please read or listen to the thirty-four verses of both Jeremiah 39 and 40.

COMMENTS

In 1991, I read Jeremiah 36-39 on the same day. Concerning chapter 39, I wrote, "Jerusalem falls, as Jeremiah prophesied, because they would not repent or turn from their own ways. Such will probably be true of the USA."

We skip 2004, when I was reading the Bible chronologically, and we move to my journal in 2016. "It happens just like Jeremiah had said. Babylon takes down Jerusalem in chapter 39. As Jeremiah said, King Zedekiah is spared but his eyes are put out. Many are taken to Babylon in exile, but some are left as a remnant in Jerusalem. God's will is done; even the enemy knows it. Jeremiah is spared, like God said he would be. Jeremiah stays among the people. A sad reading."

DIGGING DEEPER

What can we learn from the Book of Jeremiah? God warns us over and over and over to repent, to come back to Him. If we do not, He will punish. He gave Israel every chance, yet they refused to turn back to God. Through the Book of Jeremiah, are you heeding the warnings of God to come back to Him, to be fully committed to Him?

If there was no punishment for disobedience, why would anybody obey?

I said once before in these devotions, if there was no punishment for disobedience, why would anybody obey? If you are suffering, maybe it is the Lord trying to get your attention to come back to Him. But look at how God treats Jeremiah. Even as the city is burned and falls around him, even though people are taken off into exile, Jeremiah is spared. Even the enemy king, Nebuchadnezzar, knew of Jeremiah. *"Nebuchadnezzar king of Babylon gave command concerning Jeremiah . . . 'Take him, look after him well, and do him no harm, but deal with him as he tells you'"* (39:11-12).

That is what can happen if you stand with the Lord. He gives you favor even with your enemies. Jeremiah chooses to stay. He does not go to Babylon. He stays with the people, *"Jeremiah . . . lived with him among the people who were left in the land"* (40:6).

I said in my journal, it is a sad reading. Yes, it is sad when God warns us over and over and over and we do not listen. Do not let that happen in your life. Heed the words of the Lord. Trust in God against all odds. Learn the lesson from Jeremiah's life. He stayed true to the Lord. He never backed down. He never gave up. Though beaten, imprisoned, and thrown into a pit, Jeremiah stayed true to His God. Can you?

Prayer

Almighty God, these chapters break our hearts. But we read them thousands of years later to admonish us and to encourage us. Holy Spirit, help us stand for You. Help us trust in You like Jeremiah did. Deliver us from the enemies around us like You did Jeremiah. To God be the glory. Amen.

MY THOUGHTS

JEREMIAH 41 AND 42

Now We Will Listen

After Jerusalem fell and most Jews were carried off to Babylon, the remnant is ready to listen to Jeremiah in Jeremiah 41 and 42. Are you the same? After enough bad happens, are you finally ready to listen to God? Please read or listen to the forty verses of Jeremiah 41 and 42.

COMMENTS

> He leaves a flicker of light in our lives to fan and bring back the flame.

In 1991, I read Jeremiah 40-42 on the same day, and wrote, "God keeps a remnant in Judah. He always keeps a few to start over with. Or He leaves a flicker of light in our lives to fan and bring back the flame. Thanks be to God. He won't snuff me out completely for disobedience. He keeps giving Israel a chance to obey and be blessed. Help me, Jesus, obey and receive Your blessing."

In 2016, I read these two chapters on the same day and wrote, "Unsettled. Most of Israel was taken captive to Babylon and a remnant remained in Jerusalem. But now their governor is murdered, and most of them are being taken away. God intervenes again to save them and they are returned. They want to know from Jeremiah what to do next. They promise to obey the Lord whether it's good or bad. Will they really obey the Lord or fail like the others of Israel that are now given into captivity in Babylon because of their disobedience?"

We will find out how the people respond to the prophecy of Jeremiah in the next chapter.

DIGGING DEEPER

It is interesting after the murder of the appointed Governor Gedaliah, the people are nervous again about what they are supposed to do. What is their future? Amazingly, they come to Jeremiah and ask him what he thinks. These are the same people that would not listen to him before. This time they promise Jeremiah they are going to listen to what he says. *"Then they said to Jeremiah, 'May the Lord be a true and faithful witness against us if we do not act according to all the word with which the Lord your God sends you to us. Whether it is good or bad, we will obey the voice of the Lord our God to whom we are sending you, that it may be well with us when we obey the voice of the Lord our God'"* (42:5-6).

Ha! We shall see! Jeremiah hears from the Lord after ten days and he shares what he hears with the people: stay in the land and be blessed. *"Do not go to Egypt"* (42:19). Tomorrow, in Jeremiah 43, we will see what the people do.

Prayer

Lord, as much as we hate to admit it, we are like these people. You try to get our attention over and over and over. We will not listen. We live our own lives the way we want and things do not go well. Then we say to someone, "Pray for me, and this time I will listen to whatever the Lord tells me," when we should have listened in the first place.

O Lord, forgive us. If that has been our pattern in the past, this time, this time, this time we will listen to You. May it be so as we see the lessons from Jeremiah apply to our lives. This time Lord, help us be true to Your Word. Amen.

MY THOUGHTS

JEREMIAH 43

Praying Without Listening

Today, we will cover Jeremiah 43, a continuation of where we left off yesterday, in Jeremiah 42. Have you ever asked someone to pray for you, then refused to listen to them? Have you prayed to God but refused to obey His answer? Please read or listen to the thirteen verses of Jeremiah 43.

COMMENTS

Amazing. Absolutely amazing. Once again, these people will not do what they hear from Jeremiah. They will not obey the Word of the Lord. Let's turn to my journals.

In 1991, I read Jeremiah 43-45 on the same day and concerning this chapter wrote, "People accuse Jeremiah of lying. They absolutely disobey God."

I found a journal entry in 2004. I was reading Jeremiah with a couple of other books chronologically and read Jeremiah 40-44 on a certain day and wrote about this part of the reading, "Absolute willful disobedience. The remnant of Judah asks Jeremiah to intercede for them, promising to do everything Jeremiah hears from God. Ten days later, God speaks to Jeremiah. He proclaims it to those who asked and they accuse him of lying and refuse to obey."

Turning to 2016, I read Jeremiah 43 on one day and wrote, "Why ask, if we won't listen? In chapter 42, Johanan pleads with Jeremiah to go to the Lord and ask Him what to do and says they will do whatever God reveals to him. Not really. What they wanted was God to rubber-stamp what they wanted to do and were going to do anyway, go to Egypt. Often we pray the same, not really for God to show us what His will is, rather for Him to approve what we want, and what we want to do. Because they did not hear what they wanted to hear from Jeremiah or the Lord, they did not obey the voice of the Lord. They took the remnant left that did not go to Babylon to Egypt including Jeremiah."

DIGGING DEEPER

The application from Jeremiah 43 may be, how is your prayer life? How do you go to the Lord? Do you really go with an open heart and an open mind to hear from the Lord? Or do you go, like these people, with an agenda in mind, seeing if God will rubber-stamp what you want to do anyway?

These people did not say to Jeremiah they were thinking about going to Egypt. God revealed it to him. Once again, Jeremiah is bold enough to give the truth from God to the people though it is not what the people wanted to hear.

> **When you pray, are you willing to hear what you do not want to hear from the Lord?**

When you pray, are you willing to hear what you do not want to hear from the Lord? When you ask other people to pray, do you really want to hear from them? Are you willing to listen to the counsel of others in a decision you want to make? If not, why ask other people to pray for you?

Recently, Terry and I had a decision to make. We thought the decision we had to make was a blessing from the Lord. The day I called the person to tell him of our decision, God intervened. With that person, God gave us lots of new information.

Were we to go on with the decision we thought we made or were we to listen to the new information.

I absolutely believe God prevented me from making that decision that day. I shared the new information with Terry. O yeah, we had prayed about the previous decision, but we needed to pray more. And we decided to visit with some other people about the choices we had to make.

We got wise Christian counsel from a couple of different people. Did we go to them to basically rubber-stamp the decision we wanted to make? I hope not, and I do not think so. In fact, with one person I asked, "Have I given you slanted information so it appears you only can give us council one direction?" She said, "No." Through this process, we reversed the decision we originally made.

In other words, we did not go to the Lord and ask Him to rubber-stamp a decision we thought we wanted to make. As best we could, we remained open to the Lord in our prayer, and He redirected our decision. We will not know the results of that decision for several years, but we pray we took the right steps. We prayed about it. We went to make the decision. We believe God prevented us from making it. We got new information. We went and got wise counsel from our Christian friends and people who are knowledgeable about the decision we needed to make, and we changed our decision.

So let's go back to where we started. How is your prayer life? Do you take things to the Lord to really get His input? Or do you take things just to get His rubber-stamp? May we learn from the examples of scripture how to conduct our own lives.

Here in Jeremiah, we see a poor example of people who wanted someone to pray for them, but they already had what they wanted to do in mind. God is not going to bless them, and He might not bless us either when we go to Him that way.

Prayer

Lord, through Your Word we pray we could learn how to pray more effectively, more appropriately, to You. Remind us, Lord, prayer is not just us talking to You, it is allowing You to speak to us. Because we spend time in Your Word, might You change our prayers toward You. We ask it, in Your name. Amen.

MY THOUGHTS

JEREMIAH 44 AND 45

We Will Not Listen to You!

Today brings us to Jeremiah 44 and 45. Off to Egypt they go because they would not listen to Jeremiah or the Lord. Where are you headed? Please read or listen to the thirty-five verses of these two chapters.

COMMENTS

In 1991, I read Jeremiah 43-45 on the same day. Concerning these chapters, I wrote, "Flat rejection of the message of God. They are blind to the one true God. They think their idol worship brought their good fortune. Help me, Lord, know where my blessings come from."

In 2004, I read Jeremiah 40-44 on the same day. Concerning these chapters, I wrote, "The women defy Jeremiah, saying they will continue to offer sacrifices to the queen of heaven. Absolute defiance."

In 2016, I read Jeremiah 44 and 45 together, and wrote, "Even after all they saw in Jerusalem, those who went to Egypt worshipped idols. When Jeremiah confronts them, they flat-out say, *we will not listen to you*' (44:16). Women will offer to the queen of heaven with their husbands' approval. So God judges them like the others. They too will die, be consumed. Baruch, Jeremiah's scribe, will be spared for his faithfulness."

It is hard to believe, after all these people have been through, they still would be so stubborn against the Word of the Lord? They still believe their idol worship gave them prosperity. They obviously have no regard for Jeremiah, the prophet of God, and yet you would think they could see everything Jeremiah said has come to pass.

> **The enemy of this world blinds our eyes to the things of God.**

Yes, the enemy of this world blinds our eyes to the things of God. But, once again, God's mercy and grace are on display in these chapters. Particularly in Jeremiah 45 about Baruch. The faithfulness of Baruch, Jeremiah's scribe, is observed by the Lord and will be rewarded. In 45:5, the message to Baruch is this, *"And do you seek great things for yourself? Seek them not, for behold, I am bringing disaster upon all flesh, declares the Lord. But I will give you your life as a prize of war in all places to which you may go."*

DIGGING DEEPER

Is God asking you the same question today? Are you seeking great things for yourself, or are you willing to follow the Lord? Disaster then and now comes upon those who will not follow. But those who are faithful, God will give the prize of life. Spare your life. Remain faithful to God.

Prayer

Father, forgive us if we have defiantly disobeyed You. We seek Your forgiveness so we do not go so far You cannot forgive us anymore. Jesus, You went to the cross for our sins. The prize of life, eternal life, is there for us, but we must reach for it in You. Thank You for providing a way of escape. I reach for it today. I confess my sins and thank You that You are faithful and just to forgive all my sins and cleanse me from all unrighteousness. I reach to the cross today. As I do, forgive me and give me the prize of eternal life, and I will give You all the praise and thanks. Amen.

MY THOUGHTS

JEREMIAH 46 AND 47

The Protector Becomes the Victim

Today, we are in Jeremiah 46 and 47. We are on the last lap of finishing the fifty-two chapters of Jeremiah. Israel flees to Egypt for protection, but God will turn them over to Babylon too. Who do you look to for your protection? Please read or listen to the thirty-five verses of Jeremiah 46 and 47.

COMMENTS

In 1991, when I was thirty-six years old, I read Jeremiah 46-48 (NASB) on the same day and wrote in my journal, "Jeremiah prophesies judgment on various countries. Why is God after them? *'Vengeance . . . avenge Himself on his foes'* (46:10). *'The time of punishment'''* (46:21).

In 2004, I was forty-nine years old, and read Jeremiah 46 and 47 on the same day. I was reading the Bible chronologically, so I also read 2 Kings and 2 Chronicles and various other passages and made no notes on these two chapters.

In 2016, at sixty-one years old, I read Jeremiah 46 and 47 on the same day and wrote, "Egypt is next in God's judgment. They too will fall to Babylon. Historical records should prove this happened. God will still protect Israel through it all, *'I will discipline you in just measure, and I will by no means leave you unpunished'* (46:28). Protection, preservation, yes, with discipline and punishment. That's God."

DIGGING DEEPER

The next few chapters of the Book of Jeremiah turn God's face toward the nations that have harassed Israel. We start here, in chapter 46, with God's judgment on Egypt. Though Israel went to Egypt for protection against Jeremiah's advice, Jeremiah, also in Egypt, now proclaims God's judgment against the nation of Egypt where they are located. In 46:13, the Word of God says, *"The word that the Lord spoke to Jeremiah the prophet about the coming of Nebuchadnezzar king of Babylon to strike the land of Egypt."*

As Babylon came and destroyed the city of Jerusalem, they will also come and destroy the capital city of Egypt, which was Memphis. *"A beautiful heifer is Egypt, but a biting fly from the north has come upon her"* (46:20). What an interesting description of the great and mighty Egypt as this biting fly, Babylon, comes to destroy her.

In the same chapter, verses 25-26 say, *"The Lord of hosts, the God of Israel, said: 'Behold, I am bringing punishment upon Amon of Thebes, and Pharaoh and Egypt and her gods and her kings, upon Pharaoh and those who trust in him. I will deliver them into the hand of those who seek their life, into the hand of Nebuchadnezzar king of Babylon and his officers.'"*

Verse 27 starts with "but," and I am glad there are so many "buts" in scripture. Let's read the "but" in 46:27, *"But fear not, O Jacob my servant, nor be dismayed, O Israel,*

> **I am glad there are so many "buts" in scripture.**

for behold, I will save you from far away." Continuing down to verse 28, *"I will make a full end of all the nations to which I have driven you, but of you I will not make a full end. I will discipline you in just measure, and I will by no means leave you unpunished."*

Despite the impending destruction of the protector, Egypt, Israel will be saved once again. That, friends, is God's mercy. That is His grace. Over and over, He saves His people. Aren't you glad that same mercy, that same grace, is extended to us even in our consistent disobedience? Praise God for His mercy and grace.

Prayer

Father, as we read these chapters in scripture, we understand You judge the nations, which means You judge all peoples on the earth. You use nations like You used Babylon to destroy Egypt, and You are going to use Babylon to destroy other nations that have come against Israel. Then, You will destroy Babylon itself. But Your people will last forever.

As we utter this prayer to You today, Israel still exists. Jews are in Israel and across this world. Your Word is true. You are a covenant keeper, and we thank You. May we turn our hearts toward You as You continue to turn Your heart toward us. In the name of Jesus, we pray. Amen.

MY THOUGHTS

JEREMIAH 48 AND 49

I Will Restore

Today, we are in Jeremiah 48 and 49. These are long chapters on judgment of nations other than Israel. Throughout Israel's history, the nation interacted with neighboring nations. Sometimes God used them for good, sometimes they turned on Israel. Who do you interact with? Who do you depend on? Please read or listen to the forty-seven verses of Jeremiah 48 and the thirty-nine verses of Jeremiah 49.

COMMENTS

Those are some long readings about the judgment of God upon the nations. I will not go through my journals but only make brief comments. After most of these very horrific judgments, we hear the Lord say:

Yet I will restore the fortunes of Moab in the latter days, declares the Lord (48:47).

But afterward I will restore the fortunes of the Ammonites, declares the Lord (49:6).

But in the latter days I will restore the fortunes of Elam, declares the Lord (49:39).

Yes, friends, God is a God of judgment, but He is also a God of restoration.

DIGGING DEEPER

Who are your friends? Who do you depend on? Have they let you down? It may be friends, or family, or your job, or your church. Eventually, you find they are not dependable; you get hurt and you look for comfort elsewhere. Yes, we need friends, family, jobs, and church, but we need to depend on the Lord. Israel would not listen to their God, nor His prophet. They looked to others often in their history. Sometimes, God used other nations for Israel's good; sometimes, other nations betrayed Israel.

Stay on the right side of God by staying obedient to Him and His Word.

God eventually rights all wrongs; He judges nations and people. Stay on the right side of God by staying obedient to Him and His Word. Depend on God for protection, for provision, and for deliverance. Why go through the pain of judgment and restoration? Stay the course in the Lord.

Prayer

Father, we thank You that You are true to Your Word. We must obey or we can be judged. It is evident in the Book of Jeremiah. But we also thank You that You are a God of love and restoration. You are the God of the second chance. If any of us have blown it and need a second chance from You today, be the God of restoration in our lives. We ask it, in Jesus' name. Amen.

MY THOUGHTS

JEREMIAH 50 AND 51

Know Any Babylonians Today?

Today, we are in day thirty of our thirty-one-day journey through the Book of Jeremiah. We cover chapters 50 and 51, long chapters, once again. Jeremiah prophesies the great world power that just conquered Israel and Egypt will fall. Do you know any Babylonians today? Please read or listen to the forty-eight verses of Jeremiah 50 and the sixty-four verses of Jeremiah 51.

COMMENTS

> There are no Babylonians today, but there are Egyptians and Jews. God's Word is true.

I will only read my journal entry from 2016 concerning these two chapters. "Leadership matters. *'My people have been lost sheep. Their shepherds have led them astray'* (50:6). Yet they will be restored, returned to the Promised Land, according to 50:19-20. Babylon was used by God to punish Israel, but they too will be overtaken by God and destroyed. God is in control over nations, referring to 51:15. Babylon will be so completely destroyed nothing will dwell in it, *'and it shall be desolate forever'* (51:62). Did it happen? Yes, destroyed by the Medes and the Persians. There are no Babylonians today, but there are Egyptians and Jews. God's Word is true."

DIGGING DEEPER

Babylon was a great world power in Jeremiah's day. It was located in central-south Mesopotamia, part of ancient Persia, which is present day Iraq and Syria. Jeremiah says this great kingdom will fall, which occurred in 539 B.C. when Persia conquered Babylon. Not only does it fall by the hand of God, it would become like Sodom and Gomorrah and never rise again. It has not.

Israel was a divided nation consisting of Judah and the northern tribes known as Israel. When Babylon fell, Judah and Israel were to be reunited, *"In those days the house of Judah shall join the house of Israel, and together they shall come from the land of the north to the land that I gave your fathers for a heritage"* (3:18). Did it happen? Yes, Israel returned to the Promised Land, and miraculously resides there today, thousands of years later.

The great world power, Babylon, is gone forever, yet the tiny nation of Israel lives forever. Why? God's sovereignty over nations and peoples. We read about it in Jeremiah and other parts of the Bible, and it comes true every time! God's Word is true, believable, and predictable. Believe it. Praise the Lord!

Prayer

Father, please bless us for staying in Your Word, for showing us how You raise and destroy nations according to Your purposes. Babylon is no more, yet Israel remains to this day. That is the power of Your Word. That is the power of Almighty God. We give You the praise and the honor. Amen.

MY THOUGHTS

JEREMIAH 52

Jerusalem Destroyed

Today, we conclude our journey through the Book of Jeremiah with the last chapter, chapter 52. If God allowed the destruction of His Promised Land, His temple He instructed to be built, and the people called by His name, do you really think He will never leave you or forsake you? Please read or listen to the thirty-four verses of Jeremiah 52.

COMMENTS

As we end the Book of Jeremiah, we will refer to my journal entries one last time.

In 1991, I summarized the end of Jeremiah this way, "Israel carried away into exile. Jerusalem destroyed. The temple burned; artifacts removed. A sad day of judgment, indeed. But the Lord is a God of recompense. He will fully repay." I concluded, "Those who don't believe God will punish sin and disobedience have not read Jeremiah."

> Those who don't believe God will punish sin and disobedience have not read Jeremiah.

In 2004, I finished the Book of Jeremiah, but it was hard for me to find the journal entry because I was reading the Bible in chronological order. I found I read portions of Ezekiel, Daniel, 2 Kings, Psalms, and Jeremiah 52 on the same day, but wrote mostly about Daniel 4 and nothing about Jeremiah 52.

In 2016, I wrote, "In summary, the book ends with a brief recap of the demise of Israel at the hands of the Babylonians. As Jeremiah prophesied, Jerusalem falls to Babylon. The temple is destroyed, the walls are broken down, and people are exiled to Babylon. A sad ending to God's people."

I wrote a prayer as I finished the Book of Jeremiah, "May I never let God down so much He needs to punish me like He did His own people, His own family, the Jews. Help me stay in the palm of Your hand, love You, and serve You all the days of my life."

DIGGING DEEPER

Let's finish Jeremiah from where we began on that first day as we looked at the beginning of the Book of Jeremiah. We learned Jeremiah was called as a youth, became a priest, and lived in an area of Israel allotted to the tribe of Benjamin.

As we saw, he had a difficult life. His messages of repentance were not well received. He personally suffered much persecution during his forty-year ministry. At God's command, he never married. And though his ministry spanned four decades, he apparently had only two converts.

His task was to hammer home the message that the fall of Jerusalem was not God's fault, but because of Judah's unfaithfulness to God and listening to false prophets. The theme of this book was God's judgment on breaking His covenants as well as His displeasure with sin.

In this book, Jeremiah asked people over one hundred times to turn around or repent. We saw over and over God's judgment on sin and disobedience. But we also saw God extend His hand of mercy, forgiveness, and restoration over and over to the people of Israel.

I will conclude with the journal entry I concluded Jeremiah with in 1991, "Those who don't believe God will punish sin and disobedience have not read Jeremiah."

Prayer

Father, we thank You for the Book of Jeremiah. We thank You for the Prophet Jeremiah. Through his life, we are reminded the call of God on our lives may not be easy. But, by walking with Jeremiah through his forty years of life, we saw Your truth and Your promise extended over and over.

You said You put the words in his mouth and You would protect him and You did. You can do the same for us. Might we be challenged to get out of our Christian comfort zones, get in tune with what You purposed for us from our mother's womb, and get about Your business for You. Judgment is coming. Like Jeremiah, will we stand in the gap for You? Use us, Lord, to build Your kingdom here on earth. Amen.

MY THOUGHTS

FIVE DAYS IN LAMENTATION

LAMENTATIONS 1

The Lonely City

Today, we begin the Book of Lamentations. Lamentations is the sequel to the Book of Jeremiah. Both books focus on one event, the destruction of Jerusalem. The Book of Jeremiah predicts the fall of Jerusalem; the Book of Lamentations reflects on it.

Jerusalem fell to the Babylonians in 587 B.C. Lamentations was written around 586-583 B.C. Most scholars name Jeremiah as its author. However, the book itself does not identify an author. The theme of the Book of Lamentations is belief in God's mercy and faithfulness as the key to a restored relationship with God. Hope, not despair, is the final word in Lamentations.

Lamentations was most likely written to be prayed or sung in worship services devoted to asking God's forgiveness and seeking restoration to a covenant relationship with God. It is a collection of five laments or melancholy dirges for a ruined society. They regularly include a description of the problem, protests of innocence, a plea for help, a statement of faith, and a pledge of sacrifice when the situation changes.

Lamentations is a graphic reminder sin has consequences, and continuous rebellion against God is an invitation to personal disaster. It balances God's characteristics of punishment of sin with compassion at the same time.

The Book of Lamentations is five chapters, and we will cover it a chapter a day. Please read or listen to the twenty-two verses of Lamentations 1.

COMMENTS

To help us through the Book of Lamentations, I selected three of my personal Bible reading journals. One from 1997, when I read the Old Testament; one from 2009, when I also read the Old Testament; and one from 2014, when I read the Bible chronologically.

In 1997, I read Lamentations 1 and 2 (NKJV) on the same day, and wrote concerning chapter 1, *"She did not consider her destiny; therefore her collapse was awesome'* (v. 9). Jeremiah stayed in Jerusalem after Babylon destroyed it and took the Jews captive. He predicted it, warned the people, cried out to them, and for them, but they would not listen. He saw it coming, saw it happen, and now laments its aftermath."

> **God's judgment came to pass. It was devastating, harsh, and anguishing.**

In 2009, I also read Lamentations 1 and 2 on the same day. Concerning chapter 1, I wrote, "Heartbroken. Jeremiah had warned Judah for years. They would not turn from their wicked ways nor repent. Finally, God's judgment came to pass. It was devastating, harsh, and anguishing. Jeremiah lived through it. He wept for his nation, his city, his temple. All destroyed by sin, stubbornness, disobedience."

In 2014, I read the Bible chronologically, so I read passages out of 2 Kings, Jeremiah, and also Lamentations 1-3, all on the same day and wrote in my journal, "Israel has fallen. Jeremiah is taken to Babylon, but Nebuchadnezzar treats him well. He chooses to go back to Jerusalem, the lonely, burned, besieged city."

If Jeremiah is the author, and many think he is, he laments over the fall of Jerusalem. In 1:1, he says, *"How lonely sits the city that was full of people!"* The inhabitants of the city were taken captive to Babylon. Only a remnant remains, *"Judah has gone into exile because of affliction and hard servitude"* (v. 3). Verse 8 reminds us why, *"Jerusalem sinned grievously; therefore she became filthy"* and Jeremiah weeps for his beloved city, *"For these things I weep; my eyes flow with tears; for a comforter is far from me"* (v. 16). Yet Jeremiah knows God is right about this judgment, *"The Lord is in the right, for I have rebelled against his word"* (v. 18).

Jerusalem has fallen because of sin and rebellion. Jeremiah has warned the people over and over God's judgment was imminent. Now it has come to pass.

DIGGING DEEPER

What is the application of Lamentations in your life today? Have you had a casual relationship with God over the years? Has He tried to get your attention over and over, but have you been interested more in your own life than His life for you? Maybe you too are on the slippery slope of judgment by God.

Throughout the Book of Jeremiah, God appealed to the people to come back to Him, "Return to Me and I will return to you." You also have that chance today. If you, like Jerusalem, continue down the path of sin and rebellion, God will judge. Why do that? Why not return to the Lord today?

Prayer

Father, we pray for any today who are in rebellion or continual sin before You to stop, turn around, repent, and receive the grace and mercy of You, a loving and forgiving God. You gave Jerusalem the chance and they rejected it. May we not reject Your open hand and Your open arm today. May we return to You before it is too late for us.

We thank You for Your grace, Your mercy, and Your love. But we also see in Lamentations, You are also a God of judgment. It is our choice; receive Your mercy, grace, and love, or suffer Your judgment. May we return to You today and You return to us. We ask it, in Jesus' holy and precious name. Amen.

MY THOUGHTS

LAMENTATIONS 2

What God's Judgment Looks Like

Lamentations 2 contains harsh descriptions of God's eventual judgment. Yes, He is a God of love; but He also is a God of judgment. Judgment comes by not following God and His commandments, as Israel experienced. How are you doing with basking in God's love and following His commandments? Please read or listen to the twenty-two verses of Lamentations 2.

COMMENTS

In 1997, I read Lamentations 1 and 2 (NKJV) on the same day. I referred to my journal entry yesterday, but it is worth referring to again today, *"She did not consider her destiny; therefore her collapse was awesome"* (1:9). I went on to write, "Jeremiah stayed in Jerusalem after Babylon destroyed it and took the Jews captive. What a sad sight. He predicted it, warned the people, cried out to them and for them, but they would not listen. He saw it coming, saw it happen, and now laments its aftermath."

In 2009, like in 1997, I read Lamentations 1 and 2 (NASB) on the same day. Concerning chapter 2, I wrote *"'The law is no more. Also, her prophets find No vision from the Lord'* (v. 9). *'My terrors on every side; And there was no one who escaped or survived In the day of the Lord's anger'* (v. 22). Do we really think God will treat the USA any different than he did Judah?"

In 2014, I read the Bible chronologically, so I read other passages on the day I read Lamentations 1-3. Concerning chapter 2, I wrote, *"The Lord has done what he purposed: he has carried out his word"* (v. 17).

> I hope by reading
> Lamentations 2, you
> never want to face the
> judgment of God.

I hope by reading Lamentations 2, you never want to face the judgment of God. In this chapter, it is descriptive and difficult:

He has cast down from heaven to earth the splendor of Israel . . .

The Lord has swallowed up without mercy all the habitations of Jacob; in his wrath he has broken down the strongholds of the daughter of Judah . . .

He has cut down in fierce anger all the might of Israel . . .

He has killed all who were delightful in our eyes . . . he has poured out his fury like fire (vv. 1-4).

The Lord has scorned his altar, disowned his sanctuary . . .

He stretched out the measuring line; he did not restrain his hand from destroying (vv. 7-8).

That is God's judgment. The effect on His people is devastating:

The law is no more, and her prophets find no vision from the Lord.

The elders of the daughter of Zion sit on the ground in silence; they have thrown dust on their heads and put on sackcloth . . .

My eyes are spent with weeping; my stomach churns; my bile is poured out to the ground because of the destruction of the daughter of my people, because infants and babies faint in the streets of the city (vv. 9-11).

The testimony of God's judgment is known to everybody:

All who pass along the way clap their hands at you; they hiss and wag their heads at the daughter of Jerusalem: "Is this the city that was called the perfection of beauty, the joy of all the earth?"

All your enemies rail against you; they hiss, they gnash their teeth . . .

The Lord has done what he purposed; he has carried out his word (vv. 15-17).

Lamentations 2 is very, very sad, but God had warned Israel over and over through the prophets. If God had continued to warn and not completed His judgment, who would ever pay attention to His warnings again?

DIGGING DEEPER

What is our application from Lamentations 2? To understand God is a God of love, mercy, and grace; but He also runs out of patience, and He will judge. Has he been trying to warn you? Are you listening?

My hope and prayer is through Lamentations chapter 2, you will heed the warnings God has been giving you, so you will not have to face the judgment described in this chapter. We pray like they did:

Arise, cry out in the night, at the beginning of the night watches!
Pour out your heart like water before the presence of the Lord!
Lift your hands to him for the lives of your children, who faint for hunger at the head of every street (v. 19).

Yes, cry out to the Lord in the night. Yes, pour out your heart like water before the presence of the Lord. Yes, lift your hands to Him, confess your sin, your disobedience, your selfish concern for your own life, and turn from those ways. Turn back to the Lord. Turn back the judgment of God in your own life.

Prayer

Almighty God, sear in our hearts the seriousness of which You take life. May we understand from books like Lamentations, from chapters like these, You have created us, therefore, we owe everything to You. In the name of Jesus, we pray. Amen.

MY THOUGHTS

LAMENTATIONS 3

Great Is Thy Faithfulness!

Lamentations 3 reminds us, in the midst of judgment, pain, and suffering, God is faithful. Are you suffering, in pain, or under God's judgment? Please read or listen to the sixty-six verses of Lamentations 3.

COMMENTS

In 1997, I read Lamentations 3-5 (NKJV) together on the same day, and concerning chapter 3 wrote, "In the desert of despair, Jeremiah finds hope, *'Through the Lord's mercies we are not consumed, Because His compassions fail not. They are new every morning; Great is Your faithfulness'*" (vv. 22-23). I went on to quote verses 39 and 48, *"'Why should a living man complain, A man for the punishment of his sins?'* (v. 39). *'My eyes overflow with rivers of water For the destruction of the daughter of my people'*" (v. 48).

In 2009, I did the same, reading Lamentations 3-5 on the same day. I wrote about chapter 3, "The other side of blessing: to be under the judgment of a Holy God. No hope, referring to verse 18; yet spiritual

> The other side of blessing: to be under the judgment of a Holy God.

hope, according to verses 21-24; in grief, compassion thanks to verse 32; no answers to prayer, referring to verse 8 and verse 44; yet we can cry out according to verses 55-56."

In 2014, when reading the Bible chronologically, I read Lamentations 1-3 with various other passages on the same day. Concerning chapter 3, I wrote, "He does not willingly afflict or grieve the children of men, referring to verse 33. Judgment is our fault, not His. He always holds out hope, verses 22-26 and 31-33."

Here in Lamentations 3, in the middle of the Book of Lamentations, the dirge or the lament continues, but there is hope once again revealed in this chapter. First, the dirge or the lament:

Though I call and cry for help, he shuts out my prayer (v. 8)

I have forgotten what happiness is (v. 17)

Why should a living man complain, a man, about the punishment of his sins (v. 39)

But now the hope of chapter 3:

The steadfast love of the Lord never ceases; his mercies never come to an end; they are new every morning; great is your faithfulness. "The Lord is my portion," says my soul, "therefore I will hope in him."

The Lord is good to those who wait for him, to the soul who seeks him. It is good that one should wait quietly for the salvation of the Lord (vv. 22-26).

For the Lord will not cast off forever, but, though he cause grief, he will have compassion according to the abundance of his steadfast love; for he does not afflict from his heart or grieve the children of men (vv. 31-33).

Let us test and examine our ways, and return to the Lord! Let us lift up our hearts and hands to God in heaven (vv. 40-41).

You have taken up my cause, O Lord; you have redeemed my life (v. 58).

You may remember in the introduction of Lamentations that this book was most likely written to be prayed or sung in worship services. How many of us have sung verses 22-23? *"The steadfast love of the Lord never ceases; his mercies never come to an end; they are new every morning; great is your faithfulness."*

Many of us have sung Great Is Thy Faithfulness. So in the midst of pain and suffering, in the book of Lamentations, there is hope. God is a God of hope.

DIGGING DEEPER

If you think God has shut out your prayer, if you have forgotten what happiness is, might you test and examine your ways and return to the Lord. Lift up your hearts and your hands to the God in heaven. Might you gain great strength and great hope from these verses once again, *"The steadfast love of the Lord never ceases; his mercies never come to an end; they are new every morning; great is your faithfulness. 'The Lord is my portion,' says my soul, 'therefore I will hope in him'"* (vv. 22-24).

Prayer

Father, we thank You for the hope found in the Book of Lamentations. The promise You are good to those who wait for You. The promise You will return to those who return to You. The promise Your steadfast love never ceases, and great is Your faithfulness to us. We give You praise, and we give You thanks for You and You alone have taken up the cause of our lives. You have redeemed our lives. We give You the praise and the glory. In Your name, we pray. Amen.

MY THOUGHTS

LAMENTATIONS 4

The Lord Gave Full Vent to His Wrath

L amentations 4 describes Jerusalem after its fall to the Babylonians. It is not a pretty picture. Do you believe God judges? Please read or listen to the twenty-two verses of Lamentations 4.

COMMENTS

In 1997, I read Lamentations 3-5, but did not make any notes on chapter 4. The same is the case in 2009.

In 2014, reading the Bible chronologically, I read Lamentations 4 and 5 on the same day with the Book of Obadiah. I wrote in my journal, "Jerusalem, God's Holy City, is devastated. Women eat their own children to survive, referring to verse 10. *'The Lord gave full vent to his wrath'* (v. 11). If He did it then to the Promised Land, His chosen people, why do we not think he will do it again?"

Lamentations 4 returns to the laments of chapters 1 and 2. The writer compares the judgment of Jerusalem to the judgment of Sodom, *"For the chastisement of the daughter of my people has been greater than the punishment of Sodom, which was overthrown in a moment, and no hands were wrung for her"* (v. 6).

Things become so desperate in the Holy City of Jerusalem that:

The hands of compassionate women have boiled their own children; they became their food during the destruction of the daughter of my people.

The Lord gave full vent to his wrath; he poured out his hot anger, and he kindled a fire in Zion that consumed its foundations (vv. 10-11).

During the siege by Babylon in the City of Jerusalem, things became very desperate. Part of the reason for the fall of Jerusalem was because of unfaithful priests:

This was for the sins of her prophets and the iniquities of her priests, who shed in the midst of her the blood of the righteous.

They wandered, blind, through the streets; they were so defiled with blood that no one was able to touch their garments (vv. 13-14).

The Lord himself has scattered them; he will regard them no more; no honor was shown to the priests, no favor to the elders (v. 16).

DIGGING DEEPER

The religious leaders of that day were leading the people astray. Is that happening in our day? In the midst of the siege of the Babylonians, the Jews continue to look for help from somewhere or someone other than the Lord, *"Our eyes failed, ever watching vainly for help; in our watching we watched for a nation which could not save"* (v. 17).

> When the battle rages around you, when you sense God's judgment, where do you look for help?

Primarily they look to Egypt, but they did not look to the Lord. How about you? When the battle rages around you, when you sense God's judgment, where do you look for help? Sometimes we look within ourselves.

Sometimes we look to our friends, maybe even our families. Most of the time, we look everywhere but where help can come from and that is from above.

Chapter 4 concludes with the completion of God's judgment and the destruction of Jerusalem, *"The punishment of your iniquity, O daughter of Zion, is accomplished"* (v. 22).

Lamentations is a painful book. Many Christians probably avoid even reading Lamentations, but we do not. We want to involve ourselves in the whole counsel of God, all the books of the Bible. By doing so, we get a well-rounded view of God Almighty. Thank You for walking through the Book of Lamentations. One chapter to go.

Prayer

Father, thank You for reminding us You are a God of judgment. You judged the people of Israel. You will also judge us. But You are also a God of restoration as we will learn in the final chapter of the Book of Lamentations. May You continue to bless all of us as we stay connected to Your Word. In Jesus' name, we pray. Amen.

MY THOUGHTS

LAMENTATIONS 5

Restoration

Today, we finish the Book of Lamentations with chapter 5. Jerusalem was destroyed under God's watchful eye, but there is hope. Do you need hope today? Please read or listen to the twenty-two verses of Lamentations 5.

COMMENTS

In 1997, I finished the Book of Lamentations by reading chapters 3-5 (NKJV) and wrote, "*The joy of our heart has ceased; Our dance has turned into mourning. The crown has fallen from our head. Woe to us, for we have sinned!*' (vv. 15-16). God's judgment is sure, fair, just, and complete. He will punish sin. He always has, but He also restores, raises up, grants mercy, pours out His love on the sinner. He doesn't expect the sinless life, He expects confession and repentance."

In 2009, I finished the Book of Lamentations in the same way reading Lamentations 3-5 (NASB) on one day. Concerning this chapter, I wrote, "*The joy of our hearts has ceased; Our dancing has been turned into mourning. The crown has fallen from our head; Woe to us, for we have sinned!*' (vv. 15-16). Our only way out, '*You, O Lord, rule forever . . . Restore us to You, O Lord, that we may be restored; Renew our days as of old*'" (vv. 19, 21).

In 2014, I read Lamentations 4 and 5 as I finished the book, also with Obadiah, as I was reading the Bible chronologically that year. I made notes on chapter 4, which I shared yesterday, but I did not make any notes on chapter 5. I did write a note concerning the end of chapter 4 and the judgment of Edom also contained in Obadiah, which relates to this last chapter of Lamentations, "Edom will face judgment after Jerusalem, but Israel will be restored and has been as promised by God. It exists today, but Edom does not."

Then I wrote a prayer in 2014, "Spare Your judgment on America for those of us still faithful, spreading Your gospel worldwide. For peace and protection of Israel." Thus ends my journal entries on the Book of Lamentations.

DIGGING DEEPER

The people of Jerusalem had taken God's blessings for granted. We do too. For example:

We must pay for the water we drink;
the wood we get must be bought.
Our pursuers are at our necks;
we are weary; we are given no rest (vv. 4-5).

We get our bread at the peril of our lives,
because of the sword in the wilderness.
Our skin is hot as an oven
with the burning heat of famine.
Women are raped in Zion,
young women in the towns of Judah.
Princes are hung up by their hands;
no respect is shown to the elders.
Young men are compelled to grind at the mill,
and boys stagger under loads of wood (vv. 9-13).

Life gets tough under the judgment of God. We too take all these things for granted today. We take water, food, and safety for granted, all of it provided under the watchful eye of God. O, how we forget. We, like Jerusalem, believe wealth now comes from our own hands. Our lifestyle is because of what we do. Our prosperity is because of our own making or because of our government.

> We, like Jerusalem, believe wealth now comes from our own hands.

Jerusalem found out differently. We can learn lessons from this chapter in the Book of Lamentations. Never, never, never take God's blessings for granted. May we understand the lessons in the Bible are not just written for days of old, they are written for our edification, for our use as we live our lives today.

Sometimes, as we read the Old Testament, we become critical of the Jews. We can wonder how they fell so far. How they did not see what the prophets were saying. How they disobeyed God's laws and were punished. But we are no different if we do not learn from what we read. Verses 15-16, *"The joy of our hearts has ceased; our dancing has been turned to mourning. The crown has fallen from our head; woe to us, for we have sinned!"*

We are the same. And if we take God's blessings for granted, we can suffer what we just read in the Book of Lamentations. But the Book of Lamentations does not end there. Aren't you glad for the "buts" in the Bible? The "But" is in verse 19, *"But you, O Lord, reign forever; your throne endures to all generations."* Verse 21 says, *"Restore us to yourself, O Lord, that we may be restored!"* It was their hope; it is our hope. God does reign forever.

We are dependent upon Him to restore Himself to us so we may be restored to Him. He did so at Calvary, at the cross. He made a way of restoration because the crown had fallen from our heads by our sin; there was no way back. But God, but God, provided a way of escape that we may have eternal life with Him. Our sins may be forgiven. We may be restored through the blood of Jesus. To God be the glory, the God of restoration.

At the beginning of Lamentations, we said Lamentations was the sequel to the Book of Jeremiah. Both books focused on the same event, the destruction of Jerusalem. The Book of Jeremiah predicted the fall. The Book of Lamentations reflected on it.

The Bible is the same. The Bible predicts our fall, reflects on it, but does not stop there. The New Testament gives us the answer. All of us, like Jerusalem, were destined for destruction, for all the same reasons: sin, disobedience, arrogance, disregard for God and His laws. But praise be to God. He is a God of restoration.

We said at the beginning, Lamentations is a graphic reminder sin has consequences, and continuous rebellion against God is an invitation for personal disaster. Yet, Lamentations balances God's character of punishment for sin with compassion at the same time. We leave Lamentations with hope, not despair. We thank You, Lord, You are a God of restoration, then and now.

Prayer

Father, lead us to the cross where You made the ultimate restoration for each and every one of us. Throughout history, You call Your people back to Yourself. Today, maybe You are calling some of us to come back to You. Meet us at the cross where You paid the penalty for sin, rebellion, arrogance, so we can have right relationship with You once again.

May we humble ourselves at the cross, confess our sins, seek Your forgiveness, and reach out our hand toward the restoration You provide. To God be the glory. Great things You have done. In Your name, we praise You and thank You. Amen.

MY THOUGHTS

FORTY-EIGHT DAYS IN EZEKIEL

EZEKIEL 1

The Heavens Were Opened

Today, we begin the Book of Ezekiel. We will look at my English Standard Version Study Bible book introduction so we can get familiar with this book. Ezekiel was a street preacher in Babylon for twenty-two years. Ezekiel is both the name of the prophet and the title of the book that records his messages. His name means "God strengthens."

He lived out his prophetic career among the community of the exiled Jews in Babylon. His first oracle is in 593 B.C., five years after the first group of exiles showed up in Babylon. He spoke to Jews forced from their homeland because they had broken faith with their God. His message was to restore God's glory to a people who had spurned Him. His message is unrelenting with language that seems hard and offensive.

Jeremiah was an older contemporary of Ezekiel. Ezekiel knew of Jeremiah's messages and actually developed some of his themes, but they probably did not know each other because Ezekiel was in Babylon for five years before he started preaching and Jeremiah was in Jerusalem. Ezekiel was deeply concerned about the holiness of God and with the sin of His people; their behavior which offended a holy God.

What are we going to see in the Book of Ezekiel? Let's look for the fact that the call of God may come in the midst of the greatest trials of life. We can also see what it takes to do what God asks even when it may not make sense at the time. We will also see the Valley of Dry Bones and hear God say about seventy times, *"They shall know that I am the Lord."* There are forty-eight chapters in Ezekiel, and we will take them one-a-day. Please read or listen to Ezekiel 1.

COMMENTS

To help us through the Book of Ezekiel, I selected three of my personal Bible reading journals. One from 1997, one from 2006, and one from 2016. Let's begin with 1997. I read Ezekiel 1-3 and wrote in my journal, "Very specifically, God called Ezekiel to be a prophet, a specific date, time, and place. I want the same clarity of calling for the Ezra Project. He specifically heard the voice of one speaking. I too want to hear God speak to me about this. The Spirit entered Ezekiel. I want the Spirit to enter me in this too. Help me be willing to go whether they hear or they refuse. Give me a scroll to eat, a message to deliver on Your Word. Decide who You will send me to. For Ezekiel, it was only his own people, Israel, not foreigners."

Stepping away from the journal for a moment, that was 1997. I was contemplating and praying about something like the Ezra Project, but it did not happen for another five years. The Ezra Project began in 2002. It is over twenty years old. God heard those prayers back in 1997, and He answered them. Hallelujah! Praise the Lord!

In 2006, I also read Ezekiel 1-3 on the same day and concerning chapter 1, wrote, "Ezekiel was in Babylon while Jeremiah was in Judah. God showed Ezekiel visions. Like Jeremiah, Ezekiel is called to be a prophet to a rebellious people."

In 2016, I read Ezekiel 1 on one day, and wrote, "Ezekiel is in exile in Babylon. He is a priest, and his name means 'God strengthens.' He spoke to those in exile who broke faith in God, thus removed from their land. He tried to restore God's glory in a people that spurned it. Ezekiel probably knew Jeremiah and his message. He said he saw visions of God. The first one is hard to understand, *'Wherever the spirit would go, they went'* (v. 12). The Spirit, or a spirit, was guiding the four living creatures and four wheels. The spirit of the living creatures was

> **Is the Spirit guiding me? Am I going where the Spirit goes?**

in the wheels. Is the Spirit guiding me? Am I going where the Spirit goes? Ezekiel sees the throne of God, fire and brightness all around. And he sees God in His glory. When he saw it, he fell on his face. We will too as every knee shall bow and every tongue confess that He is Lord."

Due to the length of the passage, my comments about Ezekiel 1 will be brief. We see in the first verse, he says, *"I was among the exiles,"* so he is writing this, and he refers to himself. He also said, *"I saw visions of God"* (v. 1). In verse 2, he gives a very specific day, month, and year. And in verse 3, Ezekiel says, and *"the word of the Lord came to Ezekiel the priest."* These comments are very important as we read any book in the Bible, especially the prophets, so we know they, and we, are hearing from the Lord.

DIGGING DEEPER

I am not going to try to describe what the wheels mean in chapter 1. What is more important is how does this apply to our lives? In that regard, I refer to a few verses, *"Wherever the spirit would go, they went"* (v. 12) and *"Wherever the spirit wanted to go, they went"* (v. 20). That is a great application in our own lives. Is that how we live? Where the Spirit wants to go, we go? I pray, from Ezekiel 1, we would be more sensitive to the leading and guiding of the Holy Spirit in our lives. How sensitive are you to the Holy Spirit on a daily basis, or on a regular basis? *"Wherever the spirit wanted to go, they went"* (v. 20).

Next, let's look at the final verse of this chapter, *"Such was the appearance of the likeness of the glory of the Lord. And when I saw it, I fell on my face, and I heard the voice of one speaking."* Ezekiel had a special privilege. He saw the glory of God. We too shall someday have an audience with God Almighty. As Ezekiel fell on his face before the Lord, I expect we will too. Philippines 2:10-11 remind us, *"every knee should bow, in heaven and on earth and under the earth, and every tongue confess that Jesus Christ is Lord, to the glory of God the Father."* Our second application is to think about our reverence for God Almighty. Do you see Him sitting on His throne high and lifted up? Take a moment after this devotion today to honor and glorify the Lord. Let's pray.

Prayer

Father, we thank You for the opening chapter of the Book of Ezekiel. We look forward to what You have in store for us. Thank You for the visions You gave to Your prophet, Ezekiel. Thank You for the opportunity to look into those visions centuries later. Thank You for the reminder, wherever the Spirit would go, they went. May we do likewise. Holy Spirit, guide and direct our steps.

And Lord, thank You for a glimpse into Your throne room from Ezekiel. Thank You for the glory of the Lord. May we fall on our face before You and then, may we hear Your voice. We ask it, in Jesus' name. Amen.

MY THOUGHTS

EZEKIEL 2

God Calling

Ezekiel 2 records the call of Ezekiel by the Lord Himself. Have you ever wanted to be called by God to do something for Him? If He did call, how would you respond? Please read or listen to this very short chapter, Ezekiel 2.

COMMENTS

In the devotion on Ezekiel 1, I mentioned the selection of three of my personal Bible reading journals to help us through this book. I was referring to my daily Bible reading journals for over thirty-five years. Each year, I write down some thoughts on the passages I read.

For Ezekiel, I selected a journal from 1997 when I just read the Old Testament, at forty-two years old. Then one from 2006, when I read the whole Bible in a year, and then one from 2016, when I read various books. In 2006, I was fifty-one years old, and in 2016, sixty-one years old; so three different decades of my life, and three different perspectives on the Book of Ezekiel.

Let's look at the journal from 1997. I read Ezekiel 1-3 on the same day. I referred to some of this in the devotion on chapter 1, but specifically relating to chapter 2, I wrote, "The Spirit entered Ezekiel. I want the Spirit to enter me in this too. Help me be willing to go whether they hear or whether they refuse. Give me a scroll to eat, a message to deliver on Your Word."

Ezekiel was being called by God. I was hoping to be called by God at the time. I was referring to the initial thoughts about starting the Ezra Project. In 1997, I was in the business community, so if I was going to do something like this, I needed the Spirit of God to enter me like the Spirit entered Ezekiel. I needed the Word of the Lord like Ezekiel needed the Word of the Lord. The Ezra Project did not start until 2002. But it is important for anyone who is starting a ministry or contemplating ministry to be sure of the call of God on your life. In this chapter, we see the call of God on Ezekiel's life. I was trying to find that call as well.

In 2006, nine years later, I also read Ezekiel 1-3, and concerning chapter 2, wrote, "Ezekiel is called to be a prophet to a rebellious people, whether they listen or not."

Twice in this brief chapter, the idea of whether they listen or not is referred to. First, in verse 5, *"And whether they hear or refuse to hear (for they are a rebellious house) they will know that a prophet has been among them."* God says it again to Ezekiel in verse 7, *"And you shall speak my words to them, whether they hear or refuse to hear, for they are a rebellious house."*

> **The call of God is not easy. Oftentimes, the mission God calls us to is tough and hard.**

The call of God is not easy. Oftentimes, the mission God calls us to is tough and hard. Here, God is calling Ezekiel to be a prophet, to speak His words to a people who are rebellious and may hear or not hear. That is a tough calling. When we contemplate the call of God, we want it to be successful. God's call on Ezekiel was a call of obedience, not necessarily success. People may or may not listen.

Ten years later, in 2016, at sixty-one years old, I read Ezekiel 2 and 3 on the same day, and related to chapter 2, wrote, "From the throne of God, Ezekiel hears Him speak. As He spoke, the Spirit entered Ezekiel, sent as a prophet to the people of Israel in captivity in Babylon. Ezekiel's job is to speak even if the audience is *'nations of rebels who have rebelled against me'* (v. 3), says the Lord, whether they hear or refuse to hear. Ezekiel consumes God's Word of lamentation, warning, and woe."

Let's take a look at Ezekiel 2. In chapter 1, the last verse said, *"Such was the appearance of the likeness of the glory of the Lord. And when I saw it, I fell on my face, and I heard the voice of one speaking."* Chapter 2 continues with what Ezekiel heard the One speaking. Remember, Ezekiel was on his face and the One speaking said, *"stand on your feet, and I will speak with you"* (v. 1). Verse 2 says, *"And as he spoke to me, the Spirit entered into me and set me on my feet, and I heard him speaking to me."* When the Spirit of the Lord entered Ezekiel, it stood him right up on his feet.

Verses 3-4 describe Ezekiel's mission, *"I send you to the people of Israel, to nations of rebels, who have rebelled against me. . . . I send you to them, and you shall say to them, 'Thus says the Lord God.'"* God is sending Ezekiel to a rebellious people. He wants them to know there is a prophet in their midst. Ezekiel is not to fear his audience, *"And you, son of man, be not afraid of them, nor be afraid of their words"* (v. 6). The Lord is strengthening Ezekiel for his mission.

The next scene is amazing. A hand reaches out to him with a scroll and gives the scroll to him to eat. Here is the first test for Ezekiel. Will he be rebellious like the house he is going to speak to, or will he have an obedient heart and do what he is instructed to, open his mouth and eat this scroll? Before he is asked to eat it, it is spread out before him. He sees its words of lamentation, mourning, and woe, probably not the message he was hoping to deliver to his people.

DIGGING DEEPER

We have to wait till the next chapter to see what Ezekiel does. But let's apply these words to our lives. Have you ever hoped to be called by God to do something for Him? Here, we are reading about a man being called by God. I have sought that myself, and I believe it has been granted to me. It might not have happened in 1997, but eventually it happened. As you pray for a call of God on your life, remember it may not be what you expect. Delivering messages of lamentation, mourning, and woe was probably not what Ezekiel was hoping for.

The next application is a step of obedience. The Spirit is asking Ezekiel to open his mouth and eat something. Will he obey or will he have the same attitude of the rebellious people around him? The same may be for you. When God knocks, will you answer? Do you have a heart of obedience?

Prayer

Father, we thank You for this chapter in Ezekiel, the call by You on Ezekiel's life. Many of us may want a similar calling. If so, might Your Spirit enter in. And, if so, when You test us with our first test of obedience, may we succeed, may we follow You.

Thank You for calling Ezekiel. If You are speaking to us, might we hear Your voice, might we stand to our feet, and might we listen and obey Your voice. Thank You for speaking to Ezekiel and thank You for speaking to us through Ezekiel today. In Jesus' name, amen.

MY THOUGHTS

EZEKIEL 3

Ezekiel and Allen

E zekiel 3 is the continuation of the call of God on Ezekiel's life as a watchman for Israel. Has God ever spoke directly to you from His Word? He has me. Please read or listen to Ezekiel 3.

COMMENTS

In 1997, I read Ezekiel 1-3 on the same day. Concerning chapter 3, I wrote, "Decide who You will send me to. For Ezekiel, it was only his own people, Israel, not foreigners."

In 2006, I also read Ezekiel 1-3 (NASB), and referred to this journal entry before, but want to share it all today as we finish these three chapters. "Ezekiel was in Babylon while Jeremiah was in Judah. God showed Ezekiel visions. Like Jeremiah, Ezekiel is called to be a prophet to a rebellious people, whether they listen or not. *'I will make your tongue stick to the roof of your mouth so that you will be mute . . . But when I speak to you, I will open your mouth and you will say to them, "Thus says the Lord God"'* (vv. 26-27). Another tough calling of God. Isaiah goes naked for three years. Jeremiah couldn't marry or have a family. Ezekiel, a mute speaking only God's words."

In 2016, I read Ezekiel 2 and 3 on the same day. Concerning chapter 3, I wrote, "He is sent to speak even though *'the house of Israel will not be willing to listen to you, for they are not willing to listen to me'* (v. 7). God toughens Ezekiel so he can proclaim boldly and face rejection. Ezekiel is transported out of the presence of the throne of God, back to reality in Babylon, according to verses 12-15. Overwhelmed by being in God's presence, he doesn't move for seven days! Ezekiel is made a watchman for the house of Israel. God requires him to speak, and, if he doesn't, he, not the people, is held accountable by God.

> The Spirit enters him but makes him mute, so God asks him to speak and then shuts his mouth.

"Again, in the presence of God's glory, Ezekiel falls on his face. Again, the Spirit enters him but makes him mute, so God asks him to speak and then shuts his mouth until *'I will open your mouth'* (v. 27). As I begin these Ezra podcasts, instructed to do so when reading Jeremiah 1, about his call to be a prophet, now my calling is more clear. God will put His Word and His Spirit in my mouth. I will *'Go, shut yourself within your house'* (v. 24) and *'I will open your mouth'* (v. 27). Thank You, Jesus."

That day was the day I was going to do my very first ADDBIBLE recording. I prayed after reading Ezekiel 3, and wrote, "Wow. Once again God speaks clearly, directly into my life circumstance, exactly concerning the Ezra podcasting. I needed direction and confidence. I knew You called me to do this April 1st through Jeremiah 1. Now it's time to roll, and You use Ezekiel to give me confidence. You are amazing."

As I step aside from the journals, what am I referring to? That was 2016. We had been doing the Ezra Project for fourteen years. Our primary mission the first fourteen years was to speak to God's people in His churches and challenge them to come back to daily Bible reading. In those fourteen years, I spoke in hundreds of churches before over 40,000 people and God moved about 60-65% to commit to daily Bible reading. But then God began to change things.

On April 1, 2016, I was reading Jeremiah 1 and sensed God's call to do something different. I sensed His call to create recordings, we later called ADDBIBLE. I went to my Ezra Project board meeting that very day and explained what I heard from the Lord in Jeremiah that morning. The board was in agreement, and we charted a new path.

That was on April 1st. This journal entry was August 2nd. It took four months to figure out what we were going to do and how we were going to do it, and August 2, 2016 was going to be my first attempt at recording. I set up a little studio in my home, but I can tell you, I was intimidated. The studio was in the basement. It seemed like a long staircase down to that studio. I did not want to go. I did not want to do it. I did not know how I was going to read a passage of scripture and comment and apply it to people's lives.

But, as I said in this journal entry, I knew God called me to do it back in April. Now, it was August, and I was hesitant. Then I read Ezekiel 3 and it applied directly to my circumstances. I remember reading, *"Go, shut yourself within your house"* (v. 24) and *"But when I speak with you, I will open your mouth, and you shall say to them, 'Thus says the Lord God'"* (v. 27). I was in my home. My studio was in my house. God Himself was telling me through Ezekiel 3, *"Go, shut yourself within your house"* (v. 24) and *"I will open your mouth"* (v. 27) on the very day I was going to do the first recording!

After my quiet time that morning, I had confidence! I was ready to go! I bounded down those steps into the studio in the basement and began to record ADDBIBLE. God kept His promise. For three years, I shut myself up within my house where my recording studio was, and He opened my mouth as I recorded over 950,000 words covering every chapter of every book in the Bible. To God be the glory, great things He has done.

DIGGING DEEPER

You can see friends; I believe the Word of God is applicable to my daily life. I could not have picked that chapter that day. But God knew exactly what I needed. He provided the confidence I needed in His Word that day because I am a daily Bible reader. He knows what is coming in your life as well. Give Him a chance by staying in the Word each and every day of your life. Again, to God be the glory. Great things He has done.

Prayer

Father, thank You for calling Ezekiel and putting Your words in his mouth, which we are enjoying today. Thank You for calling me to record ADDBIBLE podcasts on every book of the Bible and for putting Your words in my mouth as well. Thank You for reminding us, You are the same yesterday with Ezekiel, today with me, and forever with whomever You choose to use next. To God be the glory! In Jesus' name. Amen.

MY THOUGHTS

Street Theater

In Ezekiel 4, Ezekiel symbolizes the siege of Jerusalem. Want to be a prophet of God? Are you an actor? Please read or listen to Ezekiel 4.

COMMENTS

In 1997, at forty-two years old, I read Ezekiel 4-6 on the same day, and wrote concerning chapter 4, "Unbelievable! God instructed Ezekiel to lay on his left side for three hundred and ninety days! That's over a year! Then his right side for forty days and eat very little food cooked over cow dung! Dramatic demonstrations of judgment of Israel and spiritual uncleanliness."

Nine years later, in 2006, I also read Ezekiel 4-6 on the same day, and concerning chapter 4 wrote, "Lay on your left side for three hundred and ninety days, then on your right side for forty days for the iniquity of Israel and Judah. Cook your food over human dung. And by the way, Ezekiel, have a nice life as my people experience my judgment, anger, wrath, and raging rebukes."

In 2016, ten years later, I read Ezekiel 4 and 5 on the same day, and concerning chapter 4, wrote, "Ezekiel acts out messages from God. He lies on his left side for three hundred and ninety days, that's over a year, symbolizing God's punishment of Israel. Then another forty days on his right side for the punishment of Judah. He eats sparingly as part of the drama, cooking his food over cow's dung instead of human dung! What a concession from the Lord. The punishment of Israel and Judah is severe."

Let's take a look at Ezekiel 4. In the first three chapters of Ezekiel, Ezekiel is commissioned, equipped, and positioned. He now receives his first oracle from God. He is called upon to perform street theater; actions, rather than words, conveying divine messages. Most likely this performance was before the fall of Jerusalem. Ezekiel's message was pointing toward judgment. Like any prophet, the test comes when what he says or does comes true. Did it happen? Yes, a few years later, Jerusalem fell just like Ezekiel demonstrated.

We can see God's instructions in chapter 4, *"take a brick and lay it before you, and engrave on it a city, even Jerusalem"* (v. 1). Ezekiel builds a siege wall, casts up a mound, and puts battering rams up against this brick. No telling how big the brick was, but surely these people could see the demonstration Ezekiel was performing.

Then amazingly, God asks Ezekiel to lay on his side for three hundred and ninety days! According to my English Standard Version Study Bible footnote, three hundred and ninety days correspond to the period of exile, referring to page 1506. In other words, the time Israel spent away from the Promised Land.

> **Because Ezekiel raises an objection, God gives him a break. He says you can cook it over cow dung instead of human dung!**

After over a year of laying on his left side, God moves him to his right side. The forty days could have been a reminder of the years the nation of Israel spent in the wilderness because of their rebellion and disobedience.

In verse 9, we have a recipe for bread. Wheat, barley, beans, lentils, *"put them into a single vessel and make your bread from them."* One of your practical applications from Ezekiel 4 is make this bread! See what it tastes like. See if you could eat that bread for three hundred and ninety days. But do not forget to cook it over human dung or cow dung!

Ezekiel had no objections to what God instructed him to do until he was told to cook it over human dung. Let's look at my English Standard Version Study Bible footnote for an explanation. "Animal dung is common fuel, but Ezekiel, as a priest, regards food as holy and excrement as defiling" (p. 1508). Because Ezekiel raises an objection, God gives him a break. He says you can cook it over cow dung instead of human dung!

How is your recipe coming along with this bread you are going to eat for over a year? God is using Ezekiel in his street theater to show what is going to happen to Jerusalem and Judah, *"I will do this that they may lack bread and water, and look at one another in dismay, and rot away because of their punishment"* (v. 17).

In chapter 4, God called Ezekiel to be a street performer. He is not just to proclaim the message; he is to demonstrate the messages of God. Being called a prophet was oftentimes a very tough assignment.

DIGGING DEEPER

What is our practical application from Ezekiel 4? I hope you enjoy your bread! More importantly, I hope we understand the message. God warns them, and He warns us over and over, to obey His laws, His statutes, His commandments. But when we rebel, when we become disobedient, judgment, punishment, is right around the corner. It is virtually the same message from all of God's prophets.

So how are you living your life? Are you in tune with God's commandments, His statues, His laws? Or are you just living life your own way? You may not consider yourself rebellious or disobedient, but how does God see you? Hopefully, we learn from this demonstration from Ezekiel in chapter 4. God's punishment can be severe. To avoid it, heed His statutes, commandments, and rules as you live your life.

Prayer

Father, thank You for street theater demonstrations from Your prophet, Ezekiel. Though we are reminded of Your punishment through a chapter like this, we are also reminded of Your love for us.

Thank You for Your warnings, a demonstration of Your love. Thank You for warning us through Ezekiel 4. May we heed Your warnings and strive to live in a love relationship with You. May our actions be pleasing in Your sight. For it is in Your name, we pray. Amen.

MY THOUGHTS

EZEKIEL 5

God's Holy City Will Be Destroyed

Ezekiel 5 contains Ezekiel's prophecy that Jerusalem will be destroyed. If God destroys His Promised Land, His holy city, do you think you will be spared? Please read or listen to Ezekiel 5.

COMMENTS

Those are some pretty harsh words from the Lord. I said in the book introduction, Ezekiel's messages are sometimes unrelenting with language that seems hard and offensive. Ezekiel 5 demonstrates those characteristics. Let's see what I said about this chapter in my personal Bible reading journals over the years.

In 1997, I wrote, "Ezekiel shaves his head and beard to signify mourning, repentance, and humiliation. Famine will be so severe, fathers will eat their own sons and sons shall eat their fathers. God's judgment is just. He warned Israel over and over and over like a parent to a child saying, 'Do that one more time and I will'. Finally, He did. But He also leaves a remnant, a place to start over. God's judgment and grace are there at the same time."

My journal entry in 2006, nine years later, had to do with Ezekiel 4-6 and I already shared that entry.

Ten years later, in 2016, concerning chapter 5, I wrote, "Ezekiel shaves his head and beard, signs of shame and desertion. Ezekiel is doing all this in Babylon, not Israel or Jerusalem. They have already been virtually destroyed and taken into captivity. Why such harsh judgment? They rebelled against God, their wickedness, and they rejected God's rules and statutes, *'And because of all your abominations I will do with you what I have never yet done, and the like of which I will never do again'* (v. 9). God's punishment is beyond harsh. He withdraws. I think that's what God is doing in the USA today for the same reasons. He is withdrawing."

Let's take a look at Ezekiel 5. Once again, God instructs Ezekiel to demonstrate His judgment. This time he shaves his head and his beard. According to the law, priests were not to shave their hair or their beards. God uses this as a demonstration of desecration and shame.

The Lord says, *"This is Jerusalem. I have set her in the center of the nations, with countries all around her"* (v. 5). This was His Promised Land, His holy city, yet Jerusalem rebelled against God Himself. Doing wickedness more than any of the other nations around it. God is displeased, *"And because of all your abominations I will do with you what I have never yet done, and the like of which I will never do again"* (v. 9). Imagine the evilness or the desperation by fathers eating their sons and sons eating their own fathers. How harsh can God's judgment be?

> That is the harshest punishment God could ever do to any of us; withdraw His presence from us.

I mentioned in one of my journals, the aspect of withdrawing. Let's look at verse 11, *"Therefore, as I live, declares the Lord God, surely, because you have defiled my sanctuary with all your detestable things and with all your abominations, therefore I will withdraw."* That is the harshest punishment God could ever do to any of us; withdraw His presence from us.

Why would He? Why would He forsake His people, His Promised Land, His holy city? Verse 13, *"Thus shall my anger spend itself, and I will vent my fury upon them and satisfy myself. And they shall know that I am the Lord—that I have spoken in my jealousy—when I spend my fury upon them."* And verse 15, *"You shall be a reproach and a taunt, a warning and a horror, to the nations all around you, when I execute judgments on you in anger and fury, and with furious rebukes—I am the Lord."* As Christians, we spend a lot of time in the New Testament. Oftentimes, we forget this side of the character of God.

DIGGING DEEPER

What is our practical application as individuals and as a nation? As individuals, may we never provoke God to this level of anger. The same can be said as a country. May our moral failure never fall so far God's fury is unleashed. After this devotion, consider pondering for a few minutes how your behavior is before a Holy God. Is there anything you are doing that can cause God's fury to fly toward you? I hope not. Let's pray.

Prayer

Father, this is a tough chapter. It is hard to see Your judgment come down on Your own people, Your Promised Land, Your holy city. We understand, Lord, if You did not spare them, You will not spare us, either. But thank You for the forgiveness of sin. Your grace abounds even more. We reach for Your grace today. Forgive us, Lord, and restore right relationships with You. We ask it, in the name of Jesus. Amen.

MY THOUGHTS

EZEKIEL 6

Breaking God's Heart

In Ezekiel 6, Ezekiel is going to deal with idolatry. Are you fully committed to God alone, or are you breaking God's heart in idolatry? Please read or listen to Ezekiel 6.

COMMENTS

In 1997, I read Ezekiel 4-6 on the same day, and concerning chapter 6 wrote, "God's judgment, though severe, is just. He warned Israel over and over and over like a parent to a child, saying, 'Do that one more time and I will'. Finally, He did. But He also leaves a remnant, a place to start over. God's judgment and grace are there at the same time."

Nine years later, in 2006, I read Ezekiel 4-6 on the same day. I was also reading the New Testament because I was reading the whole Bible that year; so I also read a few verses in Hebrews 10. Concerning Ezekiel 6, I made no notes.

In 2016, I was reading various books of the Bible, so it was a little bit slower pace. I read Ezekiel 6 and 7 on the same day. Concerning chapter 6, I wrote, "Ezekiel is far from Israel, captive in Babylon, but God instructs him to prophesy against the mountains and the land of Israel. Israel is being destroyed and judged by God because of idolatry, their whoring hearts, evils they have committed, and their abominations.

Such behavior of His people breaks God's heart, *'I have been broken'* (v. 9). We are behaving the same today, breaking God's heart. Yet in judgment and punishment, God always leaves a remnant."

Let's take a look at Ezekiel 6. The very first verse says, *"The word of the Lord came to me."* It is always important to know what we are reading comes from the Lord. We see in these opening verses idolatry upsets God, *"I, even I, will bring a sword upon you, and I will destroy your high places. Your altars shall become desolate, and your incense altars shall be broken, and I will cast down your slain before your idols. And I will lay the dead bodies of the people of Israel before their idols"* (vv. 3-5). God Himself will destroy the high places where idol worship was taking place. He does so to demonstrate He alone is the Lord.

Verses 8-9 remind us God always leaves a remnant, a place to start over, *"Yet I will leave some of you alive. When you have among the nations some who escape the sword, and when you are scattered through the countries, then those of you who escape will remember me among the nations where they are carried captive."* Those whom God preserves shall know He and He alone is the Lord.

He goes on to say, *"I have been broken over their whoring heart that has departed from me and over their eyes that go whoring after their idols"* (v. 9). As the chapter closes, He says for the second time:

> *I will spend my fury upon them. And you shall know that I am the Lord, when their slain lie among their idols around their altars, on every high hill, on all the mountaintops, under every green tree, and under every leafy oak, wherever they offered pleasing aroma to all their idols. And I will stretch out my hand against them . . . Then they will know that I am the Lord* (vv. 12-14).

My definition of an idol is anything that gets between you and God.

As part of The Gideons International, I have had the privilege to travel to over thirty-five countries. I have seen idol worship in various places. I have seen Muslim mosques, temples to Buddha, offerings of voodoo. Idol worship still exists in our world today.

It also exists in my own homeland in America. Statistics tell us only about ten percent of people go to church today. My definition of an idol is anything that gets between you and God. That can be selfish ambition, worship of creation rather than the creator, or striving for money and status. It can be worshiping pleasure over worshiping the God of pleasure. Yes, in the United States of America, and many other countries, there are many things that keep us from God.

We see in Ezekiel 6, God is not pleased with idol worship. He reminds us twice in fourteen verses, "I am the Lord." He wants our recognition of that statement. When He is not Lord in our lives, His heart is broken.

DIGGING DEEPER

Our practical application from Ezekiel 6 is this: is He Lord to you or are you breaking His heart? Let's pray.

Prayer

Father, thank You for the reminder You despise idol worship. Eventually, You will have enough and You will destroy it. You did then, You will again. But thank You also for the reminder You always have a remnant, people who have not fallen to idol worship who You can rebuild with. Having a remnant and starting over are examples of Your love, Your mercy, and Your grace toward us.

Thank You for the reminder in Ezekiel 6, that we must choose. Are You the Lord in our lives or are we breaking Your heart? May we be part of the remnant coming back to You. Use us, Lord, to rebuild Your kingdom here on earth. In the name of Jesus, we pray. Amen.

MY THOUGHTS

EZEKIEL 7

Fasting and Prayer

E zekiel 7 describes the wrath of the Lord. Have you ever fasted and prayed? Please read or listen to Ezekiel 7.

COMMENTS

As I looked at my journal in 1997, I noticed something about prayer and fasting while I was reading Ezekiel. I go back a couple of days in my journal to explain. I do not know what you think about fasting and prayer or if you have it as a habit in your Christian life. I do it from time to time, and in 1997, it was November when I was reading Ezekiel. On November 12th, I wrote, "National Fasting and prayer Conference in Dallas. We will participate through a downlink satellite at our church. I am participating for the following reasons:

1. Need to confess our sins as a nation; seek forgiveness and grace from God.

2. To stir up the church of Jesus Christ; to lead and serve in leadership positions with boldness to follow Christ.

3. To seek God's divine intervention in our nation with demonstrative signs and wonders.

4. Personally, to seek how I can be part of revival; how God can use me, The Ezra Project, God's specific confirmation and direction on that ministry.

5. Transformation of my attitude and character into love."

So there was a national fasting and prayer conference being organized across our nation and I participated. Those notes were on Wednesday of that week. The notes now are from Friday of that week. "Fasting and prayer, third day. Have not eaten anything since Tuesday evening dinner. Had some headaches but feel fine. Had a little juice yesterday at noon to try to eliminate the headache, didn't work, so I took some Tylenol last night and I'm fine. Been praying for those five items, mostly our nation. How does revival happen? A leading of the Holy Spirit or a movement by God's people. What is my part? How can I serve God more? What is He doing? How can I be part of it?"

On Saturday morning of that week, I wrote, "Fast over last night. Three days, felt fine." So I fasted Wednesday, Thursday, and Friday as part of a nationally organized fasting and prayer conference. Again, I do not know what you think about fasting. I think it is a scriptural spiritual discipline, so it is something I do from time to time.

Now let's take a look at my notes in 1997, concerning Ezekiel 7 (NKJV), "*'I will repay you according to your ways'* (v. 9). God showed Ezekiel the abominations of Israel, why He judged them."

In 2006, I carried that same theme on when writing, "God shows Ezekiel His judgment on Israel caused by their idolatry and complete disregard for the one, true God."

> **Spiritual war is raging around us, but we won't fight.**

In 2016, I wrote, "God gets broken and angry. *'I will judge you according to your ways'* (v. 3). We get what we deserve. *'The end has come'* (v. 2). God gets to the point where He has had enough. Judgment, punishment, is so we will come back to Him. Our wealth will not be able to save us from God's wrath. Spiritual war is raging around us, but we won't fight. We want peace, but there shall be none. We may even cry out for spiritual help, guidance, but it will be too late. And it's not God's fault, it's ours."

Ezekiel 7 is a tough chapter. It is all about the day of wrath. It reminds me a lot of the Book of Revelation. Ezekiel 7:2-3 say, *"An end! The end has come upon the four corners of the land. Now the end is upon you, and I will send my anger upon you."* Verse 5 says, *"Disaster after disaster! Behold, it comes."* Verse 10, *"Behold, the day! Behold, it comes! Your doom has come."* Yes, there have been days in the past of the wrath of God, and there will days to come when the wrath of God fills the earth.

Why? He tells us many times in this chapter, *"I will judge you according to your ways, and I will punish you for all your abominations"* (v. 3). As I said in my journal, it is not His fault. It is our fault. His judgment is based on our ways.

In those days, our wealth, our money, will not save us. *"They cast their silver into the streets, and their gold is like an unclean thing. Their silver and gold are not able to deliver them in the day of the wrath of the Lord"* (v. 19). In that day, our pride and our strength will not be able to save us. *"I will put an end to the pride of the strong . . . When anguish comes, they will seek peace, but there shall be none"* (vv. 24-25).

Lastly, we may even seek the Lord, but that will not save us. *"They seek a vision from the prophet, while the law perishes from the priest and counsel from the elders"* (v. 26). It came about in the days of Ezekiel as Jerusalem was destroyed. It will also come about at the end of the age.

The chapter closes with these words, *"According to their way I will do to them, and according to their judgments I will judge them, and they shall know that I am the Lord"* (v. 27). Yes, God has demonstrated His wrath in the past. The Book of Revelation describes His wrath to come.

DIGGING DEEPER

How do we avoid the wrath of God? Consider our ways. Consider the things I fasted and prayed about back in 1997. Maybe it is time to fast and pray again. If you choose to, pray and confess our sins as a nation and seek forgiveness and the grace of

God. Ask the Lord to stir up the church of Jesus Christ and have our leaders follow Christ with boldness once again. Seek God's divine intervention in our own nation with signs and wonders. And let's pray for transformation of our own attitude so we may be part of revival.

Prayer

Lord, we lift these things to You. Draw us closer to You through fasting and prayer. In the name of Jesus, amen.

MY THOUGHTS

EZEKIEL 8

Abominations in the Temple and in Our Churches

Ezekiel 8 describes abominations in the temple. Abominations were occurring in the temple and God was not pleased. Are abominations occurring in your church? Please read or listen to Ezekiel 8.

COMMENTS

Concerning Ezekiel 8, I will only use my journal from 2016, when I was sixty-one years old, "God gives Ezekiel a vision of being in the temple in Jerusalem. He shows Ezekiel what they are doing *'to drive me far from my sanctuary'* (v. 6). God doesn't leave us. We drive Him away with our sin, disobedience, idol worship. The seventy elders, the leaders of Israel, were guilty of abominations before God. The twenty-five men, most likely temple priests, are in the inner court worshiping the sun. Man rejects God, causing God's wrath."

Let's take a look at Ezekiel 8. Remember Ezekiel is not in Jerusalem, he is not in Israel, he is in captivity in Babylon. Yet, in Babylon, God takes Ezekiel on a vision trip. Let's begin with verse 3, *"He put out the form of a hand and took me by a lock of my head, and the Spirit lifted me up between earth and heaven and brought me in visions of God to Jerusalem, to the entrance of the gateway of the inner court that faces north."*

> **God doesn't leave us. We drive Him away with our sin, disobedience, idol worship.**

God transports Ezekiel by vision to the temple in Jerusalem. Then God begins to show him the abominations happening in His temple. *"And he said to me, 'Son of man, do you see what they are doing, the great abominations that the house of Israel are committing here, to drive me far from my sanctuary?'"* (v. 6).

Next, He brings Ezekiel to the entrance of the court. He sees a hole in the wall and peers in. God shows him the elders of Israel have been painting pictures of idol worship on the walls in the temple. They have been offering unauthorized smoke, incense, to foreign gods. He says in verse 12, *"Son of man, have you seen what the elders of the house of Israel are doing in the dark, each in his room of pictures? For they say, 'The Lord does not see us, the Lord has forsaken the land.'"*

Next, He takes Ezekiel to the entrance of the north gate. There he sees women weeping for Tammuz, celebrating the shepherd king and god of vegetation.

Next, He brings Ezekiel into the inner court of the temple. There, twenty-five men are worshiping the sun in the temple of the Lord! According to my English Standard Version Study Bible footnote, "The twenty-five men are not further identified, but the location between the porch and the altar would normally be reserved for priests" (p. 1511).

In the vision, God finishes with a question for Ezekiel in verse 17, *"Then he said to me, 'Have you seen this, O son of man? Is it too light a thing for the house of Judah to commit the abominations that they commit here'."*

The vision is concluded in the last verse of the chapter, *"Therefore I will act in wrath. My eye will not spare, nor will I have pity. And though they cry in my ears with a loud voice, I will not hear them."*

We must harken back to the days when Solomon finished the temple, and the glory of the Lord filled the temple. Yet now we see in Ezekiel 8, these terrible abominations. Idol worship inside the temple of God. No wonder God is angry.

DIGGING DEEPER

How does this relate to our day today? I do not know what kind of church you go to or even if you go to church. I have had the privilege to visit churches all over this country and all over the world. There are many great churches that worship the Lord and preach His Word. Yet we also know there are many churches where abominations are occurring today. In our day, many denominations and various pastors and priests have been accused of sexual immorality. There are several denominations ordaining homosexuals as priests or pastors. There are rituals and ceremonies in churches certainly not pleasing to the Lord.

Abominations occurred in the temple of God back then. They occur in our churches today. God was not pleased then; He certainly cannot be pleased today. Yet, we might pray what Jesus said, *"I will build my church, and the gates of hell shall not prevail against it"* (Matt. 16:18). Our application from Ezekiel 8 may be to pray for our churches. We will do so as we close.

Prayer

Father, we lift up Your church. In Ezekiel 8, You were displeased with the abominations happening in the temple of God. You sent Jesus to re-create the church. He said, *"upon this rock I will build my church, and the gates of hell shall not prevail against it"* (Matt. 16:18). Yet we see abominations in several of our churches today. Father, raise up Your church. Cleanse Your church like You did the temple. Restore pastors and priests today. Continue to use houses of worship so people can come and learn about You, people can come and worship You, people can come and grow deeper in their relationship with You. Almighty God, protect Your church. Raise it up anew. As the world gets darker, might Your church shine the light of Jesus all around. We pray for Your church. In the name of Jesus, amen.

MY THOUGHTS

EZEKIEL 9

Pastors and Priests Be Warned

Ezekiel 9 follows chapter 8, the abominations in the temple. Chapter 9 will be the consequences because of those abominations. I am not a pastor or a priest, but if I were, I would heed the warnings of Ezekiel 9. If you are, will you heed these warnings while you still can? Please read or listen to Ezekiel 9.

COMMENTS

In 1997, at forty-two years old, I read Ezekiel 7-9 (NKJV) on the same day, and wrote in my personal Bible reading journal, *"I will repay you according to your ways'* (7:9). God showed Ezekiel the abominations of Israel; why He judged them. Then He marked those who were faithful and the rest were killed. He only judges those who deserve judgment. He always saves the righteous, the faithful."

Nine years later in 2006, I was fifty-one years old when I read Ezekiel 7-9 (NASB) on the same day and wrote, "God shows Ezekiel His judgment on Israel caused by their idolatry and complete disregard for the one true God." Then I quoted 9:10, *"But as for Me, My eye will have no pity nor will I spare, but I will bring their conduct upon their heads."*

Ten years later, in 2016, at sixty-one years old, I read Ezekiel 8 and 9 together. Concerning this chapter, I wrote, "Gods sees, protects, spares the faithful. Remain faithful. Judgment begins at the house of God, the temple, the church."

Judgment begins at the house of God, the temple, the church.

Let's take a look at this chapter. The chapter begins with the word, "Then." That word follows chapter 8. Chapter 8 was filled with abominations occurring in the temple. God showed them to Ezekiel. Chapter 8 ends with these words, *"Then he said to me, 'Have you seen this, O son of man? Is it too light a thing for the house of Judah to commit the abominations that they commit here . . . I will act in wrath. My eye will not spare, nor will I have pity. And though they cry in my ears with a loud voice, I will not hear them'"* (8:17-18).

Ezekiel 9 begins with, *"Then he cried in my ears with a loud voice, saying, 'Bring near the executioners of the city, each with his destroying weapon in his hand.'"* In the next verse, six men come with weapons of slaughter in their hands, but *"with them was a man clothed in linen, with a writing case at his waist"* (v. 2). According to verse 4, that man is instructed to, *"Pass through the city, through Jerusalem, and put a mark on the foreheads of the men who sigh and groan over all the abominations that are committed in it."* To the other six, he said, *"Your eye shall not spare, and you shall show no pity. Kill old men outright, young men and maidens, little children and women, but touch no one on whom is the mark. And begin at my sanctuary"* (vv. 5-6). So they began with the elders who were before the house.

The slaughter is so great Ezekiel intercedes, *"Ah, Lord God! Will you destroy all the remnant of Israel in the outpouring of your wrath on Jerusalem?"* (v. 8). God responds, *"The guilt of the house of Israel and Judah is exceedingly great. The land is full of blood, and the city full of injustice"* (v. 9).

DIGGING DEEPER

In Ezekiel 9, we get a picture of the wrath of God poured out on a people. It is not a pleasant sight. God says, *"As for me, my eye will not spare, nor will I have pity; I will bring their deeds upon their heads"* (v. 10). Judgment for abominations and idol worship began in the sanctuary then spread out across the city.

If I were a priest or pastor today, I would take this warning very seriously. Judgment begins at the house of God. Here is what my English Standard Version Study Bible footnote says about this scene, "A team of seven angels carries out the execution of the unfaithful in Jerusalem at God's command. Only one of them is assigned the job of protecting the faithful" (p. 1511). Yes, God's angels carry out His judgment.

Prayer

Father, we are thankful for the reminder You will execute judgment on idol worship and abomination. In Ezekiel 9, we see You started in the sanctuary. May priests and pastors of our day take warning. If there is anything displeasing in Your sight going on in their churches, may they cleanse their temples today.

We know Your Word says You are the same yesterday, today, and forever. You executed Your judgment then, You will not spare us today. But just like You marked those who were faithful then, may You mark us faithful today. Spare us as a remnant so we can continue to build Your kingdom here on earth. To God be the glory. Amen.

MY THOUGHTS

EZEKIEL 10

God Leaves His Temple

In Ezekiel 10, the glory of the Lord leaves the temple. Is the presence of God still in you? Please read or listen to Ezekiel 10.

COMMENTS

In 1997, I read Ezekiel 10-12, but I did not write any notes on this chapter.

In 2006, I also read Ezekiel 10-12 and wrote, "The glory of the Lord departs the temple and Jerusalem. How sad. I hope God's glory never leaves my life. He leaves if He is not wanted. Israel preferred to follow the nations around them rather than God, so God gives them the desire of their hearts and leaves."

In 2016, I read Ezekiel 10 and 11 on the same day and wrote, "How does one describe the glory of God? I think I would struggle, too. Ezekiel's description of the throne, cherubim, burning coals is like Isaiah's in 6:1-7. It seems Ezekiel is seeing the heavenly throne with a man clothed in linen getting burning coals and at the same time seeing the temple in Jerusalem, the east gate of the house of the Lord. God's presence in the temple is again poised to depart."

As we look at Ezekiel 10, let's set the stage based on the last couple of chapters. Chapter 8 was filled with abominations occurring in the temple. God was not pleased.

In chapter 9, He sends executioners, and they clean out the temple and execute judgment across the city of Jerusalem. That sets the stage for Ezekiel 10.

> **He leaves if He is not wanted.**

Chapter 10 looks and sounds a bit like the first vision in Ezekiel 1. The vision Ezekiel sees is filled with wheels and cherubim and burning coals. Ezekiel sees the glory of the Lord, *"And the glory of the Lord went up from the cherub to the threshold of the house, and the house was filled with the cloud, and the court was filled with the brightness of the glory of the Lord"* (v. 4).

Next, Ezekiel compares the voice of God with the sounds of the wings of the cherubim. *"And the sound of the wings of the cherubim was heard as far as the outer court, like the voice of God Almighty when he speaks"* (v. 5). The only way Ezekiel could make that comparison was because he heard God speak. Imagine that.

Let's now jump down to verses 18-19, *"Then the glory of the Lord went out from the threshold of the house, and stood over the cherubim. And the cherubim lifted up their wings and mounted up from the earth before my eyes as they went out, with the wheels beside them. And they stood at the entrance of the east gate of the house of the Lord, and the glory of the God of Israel was over them."* The glory of the Lord is departing the temple. My English Standard Version Study Bible footnote says, "At the **threshold** of the **east gate**, the **glory of the God of Israel** is poised to depart from the midst of his sinful people slowly and in stages (perhaps symbolizing how he gives the people every opportunity to repent)" (p. 1512).

What a sad scene as the glory of God departs from the temple. Why? We have to go back to Ezekiel 7:4, *"And my eye will not spare you, nor will I have pity, but I will punish you for your ways, while your abominations are in your midst. Then you will know that I am the Lord."*

In the same chapter, verse 9 says, *"I will punish you according to your ways, while your abominations are in your midst."* As mentioned many times, it is our actions that cause God's presence to leave us.

DIGGING DEEPER

How do you feel after hearing a chapter like this? Do you sense God's presence in your life? Or has His presence departed? If you feel God's presence, give Him the glory. If you sense His presence has departed, you know what to do. Repent, fall on your knees before a Holy God. Confess your sins and ask Him to come back.

As He sees the sincerity of your heart, He will respond. As the footnote said about the departure here, it was done slowly and methodically, giving people every chance to come back to God. He desires nothing more than to return and have an intimate relationship with you.

Prayer

Father, we pray that would be the case. We pray Your glory would return to each one of us. We would hear the wings of the cherubim, we would feel the burning of the coals, we would hear the wheels bringing Your glory back into our lives. Father, we open our hearts to You. We welcome You. We ask You to return. And may we experience the joy of the Lord as You do. Hallelujah! Amen.

MY THOUGHTS

EZEKIEL 11

A New Heart

Today, we are in Ezekiel 11. In chapter 10, God's glory left the temple. In chapter 11, wicked counselors will be judged, but there is hope for Israel. Do you have a heart of stone or a heart of flesh? Do you need a heart transplant? Please read or listen to Ezekiel 11.

COMMENTS

In 1997, I read Ezekiel 10-12 (NKJV) on the same day. Concerning chapter 11, I wrote, *"Although I have cast them far off among the Gentiles, and although I have scattered them among the countries, yet I shall be a little sanctuary for them in the countries where they have gone"* (v. 16). Then I referred to verse 19, "God promises to give us a new heart, not a stony one."

In 2006, I also read Ezekiel 10-12 on the same day, and wrote concerning these chapters, "The glory of the Lord departs the temple in Jerusalem. How sad. I hope God's glory never leaves my life. He leaves if He is not wanted. Israel preferred to follow the nations around them rather than God, so God gives them the desire of their hearts and leaves."

In 2016, I read Ezekiel 10 and 11 on the same day, and concerning this chapter, wrote, "God instructs Ezekiel to prophesy against the leaders of Israel, *'You shall fall . . . For you have not walked in my statutes, nor obeyed my rules, but have acted according to the rules of the nations that are around you'"* (vv. 10, 12). I continued, "In the midst of judgment, there is hope. Though God scatters, He gathers. He gives a new heart. He puts His Spirit within."

> **Though God scatters,**
> **He gathers.**

Let's take a look at Ezekiel 11. Verse 1 amazes me. It says, *"The Spirit lifted me up and brought me to the east gate of the house of the Lord."* Imagine what Ezekiel is experiencing. The Spirit is moving him around. The Spirit is giving him these visions.

What Ezekiel sees this time is twenty-five men, probably leaders in the city. According to verse 2, they are giving wicked counsel in the city. They say they are a cauldron. A cauldron is a large cast iron pot for cooking or boiling over an open fire. They say they are the meat. The meat is what is cooked in the cauldron. The phrase in verse 3, *"This city is the cauldron, and we are the meat"* can mean, "we are cooked" or it could mean, "we will not get burned."

Verse 5 is like verse 1. Ezekiel says, *"And the Spirit of the Lord fell upon me."* There is a great warning here as God speaks, *"For I know the things that come into your mind"* (v. 5). It was then and it is now; God knows what we are thinking.

Next, God, through Ezekiel, tells the city they will be judged and be given into the hands of foreigners. They shall fall by the sword. Why? *"For you have not walked in my statutes, nor obeyed my rules, but have acted according to the rules of the nations that are around you"* (v. 12). That verse is another warning to us not to fall to the culture around us.

Today, our culture is mostly anti-Christian. We are probably living in a post-Christian world. But we are not to fall to the culture around us. Because they did, God scattered them among the nations. But He always keeps a remnant, a place to rebuild. Verse 16 says, *"Therefore say, 'Thus says the Lord God: Though I removed them far off among the nations, and though I scattered them among the countries, yet I have been a sanctuary to them for a while in the countries where they have gone.'"*

In the next verse, the Lord says to them, *"I will gather you from the peoples and assemble you out of the countries where you have been scattered, and I will give you the land of Israel.*" Though God scatters, He also gathers. And He gives them an amazing promise, *"And I will give them one heart, and a new spirit I will put within them. I will remove the heart of stone from their flesh and give them a heart of flesh, that they may walk in my statutes and keep my rules and obey them. And they shall be my people, and I will be their God"* (vv. 19-20).

What a beautiful promise in the midst of judgment. Praise the Lord, He keeps a remnant. Praise the Lord, He is a God of restoration.

DIGGING DEEPER

How does Ezekiel 11 touch your heart? Are you being scattered because of your disobedience? Are you being judged because you are following the culture around you? Do you have a heart of stone or a heart of flesh? Have you been away from the Lord and is He bringing you back?

The chapter closes with the glory of God leaving the city of Jerusalem, *"And the glory of the Lord went up from the midst of the city and stood on the mountain that is on the east side of the city"* (v. 23). That mountain is the Mount of Olives. May the glory of God never leave you. It happens when we do not walk in His statutes, we do not obey His rules, and we cave-in to the godless culture around us. Yes, God is a God of judgment, but He is also a God of restoration. Let's pray.

Prayer

Father, regardless of where we are on the journey, You can be with us. Maybe we have fallen, maybe we have chased after the gods of the culture around us. Thank You that You are a God of forgiveness. You are a God of restoration.

Here, You promise to remove our heart of stone and replace it with a heart of flesh. Here, You promise we can be Your people once again and You will be our God. Thank You for such hope. Thank You for such promises.

Lord, give us a heart of flesh. Give us a desire to walk in Your statutes and keep Your rules and obey them. Allow us, once again, to be Your people and You be our God. Thank You for the hope in Ezekiel 11. In the name of Jesus, we pray. Amen.

MY THOUGHTS

EZEKIEL 12

A Rebellious House

In Ezekiel 12, we will see another demonstration by Ezekiel. This time he symbolizes Judah's captivity with baggage. Do you dwell in a rebellious house? Please read or listen to Ezekiel 12.

COMMENTS

On Ezekiel 12, I will only use my journal from 2016, "I too have a rebellious house. Kids who won't see, won't hear, what God has for them. Ezekiel is the actor prophet. God speaks and he acts out the Word. This prophecy is about the second and final exile of Jerusalem, Judah. Ezekiel was in the first one and is Babylon. The people don't listen, they don't believe. They've heard it all before and nothing happens. But God's Word is true. It will come to pass. He always warns through prophets or His Word before He acts."

> He always warns through prophets or His Word before He acts.

Ezekiel 12 begins with these words, *"Son of man, you dwell in the midst of a rebellious house, who have eyes to see, but see not, who have ears to hear, but hear not, for they are a rebellious house"* (v. 2). I mentioned in my journal, I had a rebellious house. We had a Christian home, a Christian family. Our kids are all grown and have their own families today. They saw much of Christianity as they grew up in our home. Yet, today, they *"have eyes to see, but see not, (they) have ears to hear, but hear not"* (v. 2). For the most part, they chose to go their own way, which I guess is what God means by saying, *"a rebellious house"* (v. 2). Why is it so hard for us to follow the Lord? Why is it so hard to see what He has for us to see, and hear what He has for us to hear? Why do we rebel against a God who loves us?

Ezekiel faced the same thing, so God again makes him the actor prophet. He actually acts out an exile so they can understand they will be exiled from Jerusalem, from Judah, to Babylon, the land of the Chaldeans. Yet God's mercy is demonstrated once again, *"And they shall know that I am the Lord, when I disperse them among the nations and scatter them among the countries. But I will let a few of them escape from the sword, from famine and pestilence, that they may declare all their abominations among the nations where they go, and may know that I am the Lord"* (vv. 15-16).

As we are learning through Ezekiel, God always keeps a remnant, a small group of people to rebuild with.

DIGGING DEEPER

I mentioned in my journal, these people heard it all before and they did not believe it would come to pass. They actually have a saying for it, a proverb, *"The days grow long, and every vision comes to nothing"* (v. 22). God said:

> *Tell them therefore, "Thus says the Lord God: I will put an end to this proverb, and they shall no more use it as a proverb in Israel." But say to them, The days are near, and the fulfillment of every vision. For there shall be no more any false vision or flattering divination within the house of Israel. For I am the Lord; I will speak the word that I will speak, and it will be performed. It will no longer be delayed, but in your days, O rebellious house, I will speak the word and perform it, declares the Lord God* (vv. 23-25).

God had given them warning after warning. Why? Because He is so patient. He is loving. He is kind. He is merciful.

But the people take it for granted. They think it is never going to happen. We are so much like them today. We see the Book of Revelation. We see the judgment coming. Just as in those days, these days will also come upon us. But we are complacent. We say, "It has been a long time. It will not come to pass."

Well, heed God's warnings here in Ezekiel 12, *"For I am the Lord; I will speak the word that I will speak, and it will be performed"* (v. 25). God warns them and us in the last verse of this chapter, *"None of my words will be delayed any longer, but the word that I speak will be performed, declares the Lord God."* Yes, the prophecies of God do, and will, come true. They may not be on our timetable; they are on God's timetable. But He has spoken His Word, and He will perform it.

Prayer

Father, may we heed the warning of Ezekiel 12. We have Your Word. It is full of prophecies. As in Ezekiel's day, these prophecies, in our day, will come true. It will not happen on our timing; it will happen on Yours. But may we not become like the people we are reading about. People who had eyes, but saw not, or people who had ears, but heard not. May we hear what You have to say to us here in Ezekiel 12. No more delay. Judgment is on its way.

Father, thank You for Your warnings. You do so to allow us to repent, to confess our sinfulness, our rebellion, and come back to You. We cannot thank You enough for being a God of restoration, a God of forgiveness, a God of love. Again, may we heed Your warning here in Ezekiel 12. Open our eyes and open our ears to Your Word as You perform it. In the name of Jesus, amen.

MY THOUGHTS

EZEKIEL 13

False Prophets, Pastors, and Priests

In Ezekiel 13, we will learn what happens to false prophets. Does your pastor or priest preach the Word of God, or is he a false teacher? Please read or listen to Ezekiel 13.

COMMENTS

In 1997, at forty-two years old, I read Ezekiel 13-15 on the same day and made no notes concerning Ezekiel 13.

Nine years later, in 2006 at fifty-one years old, I also read Ezekiel 13-15 on the same day, and wrote, "God is against false prophets and poor leaders. Those who lead people astray are held accountable by God. But we are also responsible for our spiritual direction. Even Noah, Daniel, and Job could not save us if we continue to reject God, His Word, and follow idolatry and false prophets."

Ten years later, in 2016 at sixty-one years old, I read Ezekiel 13 and wrote in my personal Bible reading journal, "God instructs Ezekiel to prophesy from Babylon against false prophets of Israel. How will they ever get this message? Were there runners between Babylon and Israel?" Then I wrote, "Substitute priests and preachers for prophets in this chapter. We have many false priests and preachers today, who speak to their churches from their own hearts, referring to verse 2. We expect God to fulfill their word, but it's not from Him, according to verse 6. For example, denominations who ordain women and gays."

> The righteous are disheartened and the wicked encouraged thanks to false priests, pastors, and prophets then and today.

I continued, "People are being misled, referring to verse 10. The Lord instructs Ezekiel to come *'against the daughters of your people, who prophesy out of their own minds'* (v. 17). People are dying spiritually, who should not die, because they listened to lies or false prophets. The righteous are disheartened and the wicked encouraged thanks to false priests, pastors, and prophets then and today."

Let's take a look at Ezekiel 13. God, through Ezekiel, condemns false prophets, those who prophesy from their own hearts or from their own minds. Those who claim to hear from God but do not. Verse 6 declares, *"They have seen false visions and lying divinations. They say, 'Declares the Lord,' when the Lord has not sent them, and yet they expect him to fulfill their word"* (v. 6). God clarifies what He means, *"Have you not seen a false vision and uttered a lying divination, whenever you have said, 'Declares the Lord,' although I have not spoken? Therefore thus says the Lord God: 'Because you have uttered falsehood and seen lying visions, therefore behold, I am against you, declares the Lord God'"* (vv. 7-8).

Part of the false prophetic utterances of that day was there would be peace in Jerusalem. The fact was, there would be no peace; God would judge, and He would scatter the people out of Jerusalem. False teaching, false prophesies, lead people to die. As I mentioned in my journal, spiritually die. The end of verse 19 declares it, *"putting to death souls who should not die and keeping alive souls who should not live, by your lying to my people, who listen to lies."*

DIGGING DEEPER

In my journal, I mentioned we could substitute priests and preachers today for the prophets of old. We have much false teaching in our churches today. And people under those teachings may die spiritually. It is both the fault of the preachers and priests, but also the fault of the listener. As verse 19 indicates, we have a tendency to want to listen to lies. This passage in Ezekiel 13, reminds me of 2 Timothy 4:1-4:

> *I charge you in the presence of God and of Christ Jesus, who is to judge the living and the dead, and by his appearing and his kingdom: preach the word; be ready in season and out of season; reprove, rebuke, and exhort, with complete patience and teaching. For the time is coming when people will not endure sound teaching, but having itching ears they will accumulate for themselves teachers to suit their own passions, and will turn away from listening to the truth and wander off into myths.*

Priests and pastors are charged with preaching the Word. The people are forewarned to listen to sound teaching and not have itching ears. We are not to be interested in teaching that will suit our own passions. We are not to follow teachings that take us away from the truth and lead us into myths or false doctrines. God was serious about the proper declaration of His Word then and now. Priest, pastors, prophets, teachers, all will be held accountable by God Himself. We the listeners will also be held accountable if we continually listen to lies.

What is our practical application from Ezekiel 13? Attend a Bible-teaching, Bible-believing church. Do not subject yourself to false teaching. Pay attention to what your church is doing. Pay attention to the Word of God yourself, so you will be able to identify false teaching.

Prayer

Father, thank You for this chapter in Ezekiel, a warning against false teaching. It was relevant then; it is relevant in our day. Holy Spirit, protect us from false doctrine, from false teaching. Lead us into truth. Guide and direct our steps to a Bible believing, Bible teaching church. We ask for Your help. We ask for Your guidance. In Jesus' name, amen.

MY THOUGHTS

EZEKIEL 14

A Flicker of Hope

In Ezekiel 14, elders will be condemned and Jerusalem will not be spared. Let's find out why. Even when we sin against God and deserve His judgment and punishment, there is always a flicker of hope. Do you need hope today? Please read or listen to Ezekiel 14.

COMMENTS

In 1997, I read Ezekiel 13-15 (NKJV) on the same day, and wrote in my personal Bible reading journal concerning chapter 14, *"When a land sins against Me by persistent unfaithfulness, I will stretch out My hand against it'* (v. 13). It is because of our sin that God finally has to judge a people or a person. He is righteous and would rather bless a people or a person. He is patient and willing to forgive. But after pervasive disobedience over a long period of time, He must act. We do the same thing as parents or as a nation. We tolerate sin and try to correct it with love. But, finally, after enough of it, we punish."

In 2006, after reading Ezekiel 13-15, concerning chapter 14, I wrote, "Even Noah, Daniel, and Job cannot save us if we continue to reject God and His Word and follow idolatry and false prophets."

In 2016, I read Ezekiel 14 and 15 on the same day, and, concerning chapter 14, wrote, "The elders or leaders of Israel in exile, have taken their idols into their hearts. Should God be consulted by them? God says yes because He wants their hearts back. What does He answer? *'Repent and turn away from your idols'* (v. 6). If not, *'I will set my face against that man'* (v. 8). When God has had enough, no one can intervene. Not Noah, Daniel, or Job. One can save himself but no one else, according to 14:12-20. Yet, God preserves a remnant."

> **If we have idolatry in our hearts, if we have a rebellious spirit, or disobedience, do you think we can consult God?**

Let's take a look at Ezekiel 14. In the opening verses, the leaders, the elders of Israel, had taken idolatry into their hearts. Because of this, God asks, *"Should I indeed let myself be consulted by them?"* (v. 3). What does that tell us about having a pure heart when we go to God? If we have idolatry in our hearts, if we have a rebellious spirit, or disobedience, do you think we can consult God? Maybe that is why some of our prayers are not answered. What is your heart condition when you go to God?

In the following verses, God shows His grace and mercy once again. He says, if they come to Him with idolatry in their hearts, He will answer them because He wants to lay hold of their hearts. He wants to lay hold of your heart too.

What is the action step He asks of them and of us? *"Repent and turn away from your idols, and turn away your faces from all your abominations"* (v. 6). It is either that or God will turn His face against you, *"I the Lord will answer him myself. And I will set my face against that man"* (vv. 7-8).

Ezekiel 14:9-10 contain another strong warning against pastors and priests who listen to those who have idolatry in their hearts, *"And if the prophet is deceived and speaks a word, I, the Lord, have deceived that prophet, and I will stretch out my hand against him and will destroy him from the midst of my people Israel. And they shall bear their punishment—the punishment of the prophet and the punishment of the inquirer shall be alike—."*

Both are guilty and both will receive the same punishment. We can see God is serious about idolatry, He is serious about false prophets, He is serious about false inquiries, because He wants to be our God.

Verses 13 through the end of the chapter, concern Jerusalem, *"Son of man, when a land sins against me by acting faithlessly, and I stretch out my hand against it and break its supply of bread and send famine upon it, and cut off from it man and beast, even if these three men, Noah, Daniel, and Job, were in it, they would deliver but their own lives by their righteousness, declares the Lord God"* (vv. 13-14).

DIGGING DEEPER

In Ezekiel 14, we see a land that sins against the Lord cannot be delivered by such great men in the hall of faith as Noah, Daniel, or Job. What is the condition of our land today, the United States of America, or the country you are in? Is it a land sinning against the Lord by acting faithlessly? If so, He did not spare Jerusalem. He will not spare our lands either.

In verse 21, God describes His disastrous acts of judgment: the sword, famine, wild beasts, and pestilence. Today, in our world, those things may be war, economic woe, nature, sickness, or plagues. Those four things God allowed to come against nations as judgment. We do not see things that way today. Maybe we should use our spiritual eyes as we see events occurring around us.

Ezekiel 14 closes, as so many chapters do in this book, with hope, with grace, with mercy:

But behold, some survivors will be left in it, sons and daughters who will be brought out; behold, when they come out to you, and you see their ways and their deeds, you will be consoled for the disaster that I have brought upon Jerusalem, for all that I have brought upon it. They will console you, when you see their ways and their deeds, and you shall know that I have not done without cause all that I have done in it, declares the Lord God (vv. 22-23).

There is that remnant once again. God preserves a way to start over. It is true in your own life. If you have idolatry in your own heart, if you have a rebellious spirit, if you have been disobedient, there is still a spark within you, a remnant, so to speak, God can use to start over in your life. Hallelujah, praise the Lord!

Prayer

Father, we have read much about judgment, but each and every time we see You care for people. You love us so much You leave a place to start over. I pray that is the case for all of us; anyone who is struggling, anyone who is on their way back. Thank You for the reminder there is a flame within them You will fan. You want to be their God. All You ask is we repent and turn away from our sinful ways. With that, You will stretch out Your hand toward us. Thank You. May we respond by reaching our hand back to You. To God be the glory. Amen.

MY THOUGHTS

EZEKIEL 15

Why, why, why?

Ezekiel 15 is a short chapter comparing Jerusalem to a worthless vine. Did you raise teenagers and ask them concerning their behavior, why, why, why? Concerning your behavior, do ask yourself, why, why, why? Please read or listen to Ezekiel 15.

COMMENTS

In 1997, I was forty-two years old. Terry and I had three children. Two of them were out of the home by then; we had our daughter still at home. By using my personal Bible reading journals for these devotions, I never know what I am going to discover. This is the case on this day. If you are a parent of teenagers, you will probably relate to this journal entry, especially if you are a Christian.

I wrote, "Devastated, hurt, brokenhearted. Yesterday, I learned, for the first time, my daughter smokes. She has a juvenile drinking ticket, smokes, caught outside on the trampoline with a guy with hickeys on her neck last month. Then to find out Jason gave her her first cigarette and that he smoked through high school. Why do kids have to go look hell in the eye to appreciate good? Why do they need to experiment with evil rather with good? Why is sin so attractive? Why? Why? Why? What happens, God, to our efforts to raise kids right? In prayer, in Bible reading, and by Christian example our whole lives. Where is the heavenly reward for that? Why do kids (my own) not believe or understand moral absolutes? Why is everything relative? Why? Why? Why? Why do Ryan and Desiree think it's okay to stay here when we're not home? Why is it okay for Ryan to spend the night at Desiree's place in Boulder with the excuse that, 'We're not sleeping together, Dad. She has roommates.' Why? Why? Why? Why can't they find their way to Christian friends, church groups, church at all? Why can't they get into the Word of God and understand right from wrong and moral absolutes? Why? Why? Why? Why can't I understand them? Why can't they understand me? Why? Why? Why?"

> **Why do kids have to go look hell in the eye to appreciate good?**

I recorded part of my prayer that day, "To regroup. To get God's help. To respond to Shannon in love. To forgive Jason. To reach out to Ryan. To not give up. To understand life."

You can see from my journal entry, we as Christian parents, became very frustrated with raising our teenage children. Many of you may have had similar experiences. Or maybe you are raising teenagers at the moment. We did all we could to raise our children with Christian principles in a Christian home. Yet, you can see the impact the world had on our kids then and now.

Though I hesitated to share that journal entry, I think it is important to be transparent. I did not grow up with Christian principles all around me. O, I had good parents. They went to church. But the relationship between them and God was more of a private matter. When I became a born-again Christian, hot for the Lord, initially I had problems with my parents and most of my siblings.

Terry and I continued to grow in our faith, and we did all we could to pass it on to our children. I guess we learned Christian parents were not exempt from the challenges teenagers face in the world, though we thought we would be. Maybe, as a Christian parent, you thought the same or you think that way today. It did not happen for us. It may not happen for you.

What is the parallel to Ezekiel 15? We are God's children. He does all He can to raise us right. Yet, we seem to do all we can to avoid His rules, His statutes, His laws, His way of living our lives. We act just like teenagers! I wonder if He asks the same thing I did, "Why? Why? Why? Why won't My children follow Me? Why do My children need to look into the gates of hell? Why can't My children follow My absolutes? Why? Why? Why?"

We see throughout the Book of Ezekiel, God is asking us, "Why?" Why would we rather follow idols than follow the one, true God? Why do His children put great abominations in His own temple? Why do prophets spew false doctrine? Why did the leaders of Israel lead the people astray instead of toward God? Why? Why? Why?

What I recorded in my journal in 1997, was basically an isolated incident, though it challenged me and my Christianity as a parent. My kids are great. They turned out fine. But what about God's kids? How are we turning out? In Ezekiel 15:4-5, He compares us to a useless vine, *"Behold, it is given to the fire for fuel. When the fire has consumed both ends of it, and the middle of it is charred, is it useful for anything? Behold, when it was whole, it was used for nothing. How much less, when the fire has consumed it and it is charred, can it ever be used for anything!"*

Verses 6-7 are the devastating verses in this chapter, *"Therefore thus says the Lord God: Like the wood of the vine among the trees of the forest, which I have given to the fire for fuel, so have I given up the inhabitants of Jerusalem. And I will set my face against them. Though they escape from the fire, the fire shall yet consume them, and you will know that I am the Lord when I set my face against them."*

DIGGING DEEPER

How are we doing as children of God? How does He see us? How does He see you today? Does He look down from His heavenly throne at you and ask, "Why? Why? Why?" How are you treating Your Heavenly Father?

As we go through prophetic books like Ezekiel, the language gets tough. God appears harsh and judgmental, but we see over and over, He leaves a remnant. He leaves a place to start over, because He is a God of mercy, grace, and love. What kind of child of the King are you today?

Are you a worthless branch that cannot be used for anything by God? Or are you one of those survivors, one of those He calls a remnant He wants to preserve so He can build again His kingdom here on earth? Books like Ezekiel challenge us. They challenge our complacency as Christians. They stir us up to faith and good works. Let's pray.

Prayer

Father, thank You for not giving up on us as teenagers. Thanks for looking past our disobedience, our rebellion, our sinfulness, and continually reaching out to us. Thank You for not letting the gates of Hell prevail against us, Your church. After Ezekiel 15, Lord, reach down to us and may we reach back to You. In the name of Jesus, amen.

MY THOUGHTS

EZEKIEL 16

What Kind of Bride Are You?

In Ezekiel 16, we will learn about God's faithless bride. Have you been a faithful or unfaithful bride of Christ? Please read or listen to Ezekiel 16.

COMMENTS

Because of the length of the reading, I will only refer to my journals; however, they are pretty insightful on Ezekiel 16. We begin in 1997, when I wrote, "God raised up Israel from birth. Clothed her, blessed her as she grew. He wanted her for a bride, but as she got older, she spurned God and played the harlot with other nations. She was worse than a harlot. She was an adulterer and God wanted her to come back, but she didn't. She fell deeper and deeper into sin. Worse than Samaria and Sodom. So God judged her, but also made an everlasting covenant with her. One He will honor until the end. Help me relate this story to my kids. I raised them right. They may go out whoring around, walk away from God and me, but I planted good seed, and, though it's winter, springtime is coming, and they will bear fruit for Jesus."

In 2006, I wrote, "God reminds Israel of its selection and blessings by God. Its response, though, was spiritual idolatry and harlotry. Though God faithfully loved Israel, it was not faithful, and, like a prostitute, went whoring around after other nations and their gods. As a parent punishes a child, God punishes Israel for a season, but always promises and renews His everlasting, loving covenant with Israel."

> You misused all the blessings bestowed upon you and forgot where you came from.

In 2016, I wrote, "God, through Ezekiel, rips Jerusalem. You were just like a regular city, wallowing aimlessly until I made you flourish. I *'entered into a covenant with you . . . and you became mine'* (v. 8). I blessed you, raised you up. *'You grew exceedingly beautiful and advanced to royalty'* (v. 13), but you used all I had given you to turn away from Me. You misused all the blessings bestowed upon you and forgot where you came from.

"You *'provoke me to anger'* (v. 26), so I withdrew and turned you over to your enemies. *'How sick is your heart'* (v. 30). *'Because you have not remembered the days of your youth, but have enraged me with all these things, therefore, behold, I have returned your deeds upon your head'* (v. 43). Jerusalem became more corrupt than Samaria and Sodom. I judge them; I will judge you, according to 16:51-52. *'You bear the penalty'* (v. 58). I judge righteously, for you broke the covenant, not Me. But I will restore, not because you deserve it, but because I am true to my word." Then I wrote, "Exactly how most nations have acted. God raises up. He bestows blessings. We take credit for them, misuse them, leave Him to serve self. He did not spare Jerusalem; He will not spare us either."

DIGGING DEEPER

What kind of bride are you? Have you walked faithfully with Jesus since He saved you and entered a marriage relationship with you? Or, have you been unfaithful, whoring around with worldly pleasures and self-interest at the expense of His faithfulness to you? Regardless of your past, you can renew your marriage vow with Him today, "til death do us part," this time!

Prayer

Father, thank You for wanting us to be Your bride. Thank You for making us beautiful. Thank You for bestowing blessing after blessing after blessing upon us. Thank You for being faithful, even though we are not. Forgive us for taking You for granted. Forgive us for not being faithful to You. Forgive us for whoring after other gods, self-pleasures, everything but You.

Thank You for Your righteous judgment. And thank You for providing Your Son Jesus to stand in the gap for our unrighteousness. Thank You for providing a way of escape that we may be able to endure. And thank You for Your everlasting covenant. We bless You, we praise You, and we ask You to take us back as Your heavenly bride. In Jesus' name, we pray. Amen.

MY THOUGHTS

EZEKIEL 17

What Kind of Tree Are You?

I n Ezekiel 17, Ezekiel shares two parables with us. Are you a green tree bearing fruit for Jesus or are you a dry tree, with few branches, and little or no fruit? Please read or listen to Ezekiel 17.

COMMENTS

In 1997, at forty-two years old, I read Ezekiel 17-19 on the same day. My notes are on chapter 18, so we will look at those notes in another devotion.

Nine years later, at fifty-one years old, I again read Ezekiel 17-19 on the same day, and my notes again refer to chapter 18, so we will save those as well.

Ten years later, in 2016, at sixty-one years old, I read Ezekiel 17 and 18 on the same day, and concerning chapter 17, wrote, "Ezekiel 17:1-10 is like a parable the Lord gave Ezekiel; this time, for those of Israel in exile with him in Babylon. God gives the explanation of the parable much like Jesus did in the New Testament, referring to verse 11-18. Israel was brought to Babylon, the remnant left in Israel, but even they disobeyed by seeking an alliance with Egypt. Will the remnant survive? No. They too will be exiled to Babylon, yet God still always provides a remnant of Israel, His people. He Himself will plant and grow the nation of Israel again."

Let's take a look at Ezekiel 17, the parable of two eagles and a vine. In verse 1, the Lord speaking, calls it a riddle as well as a parable. The riddle, or the parable, has to do with two eagles and a vine. The first eagle is the king of Babylon. After his defeat of Jerusalem, he took the people as exiles to Babylon. The second eagle is the king of Egypt. So part of the vine, the nation of Israel, is planted in Babylon while some remained in Jerusalem, the remnant.

The remnant tried to make a covenant with Egypt. The question God asks in verse 9 is, will the remnant in Jerusalem survive? God Himself explains the riddle or parable:

> *Then the word of the Lord came to me: "Say now to the rebellious house, Do you not know what these things mean? Tell them, behold, the king of Babylon came to Jerusalem, and took her king and her princes and brought them to him to Babylon. And he took one of the royal offspring and made a covenant with him, putting him under oath (the chief men of the land he had taken away), that the kingdom might be humble and not lift itself up, and keep his covenant that it might stand. But he rebelled against him by sending his ambassadors to Egypt"* (vv. 11-15).

We see the explanation of this riddle or parable by the Lord Himself. The question of survival is now answered by God, *"As I live, declares the Lord God, surely in the place where the king dwells who made him king, whose oath*

> O, what love God continues to demonstrate toward a rebellious people.

he despised, and whose covenant with him he broke, in Babylon he shall die. Pharaoh with his mighty army and great company will not help him in war" (vv. 16-17).

The answer is no. The remnant in Jerusalem that tried to make a covenant with Egypt will fail. They too will be exiled to Babylon, *"I will spread my net over him, and he shall be taken in my snare, and I will bring him to Babylon"* (v. 20). But it is not over. God, once again, will intervene, *"Thus says the Lord God: 'I myself will take a sprig from the lofty top of the cedar and will set it out. I will break off from the topmost of its young twigs a tender one, and I myself will plant it on a high and lofty mountain. On the mountain height of Israel will I plant it, that it may bear branches and produce fruit and become a noble cedar'"* (vv. 22-23).

Once again, God provides a remnant, a place to start over.

DIGGING DEEPER

The events of chapter 17 happened because of the whoredom in chapter 16. Chapter 17 finishes with this verse, *"And all the trees of the field shall know that I am the Lord; I bring low the high tree, and make high the low tree, dry up the green tree, and make the dry tree flourish. I am the Lord; I have spoken, and I will do it"* (v. 24). O, what love God continues to demonstrate toward a rebellious people. He kept a remnant, then He poured out His love, then He does the same to us, a rebellious people today.

Aren't you thankful He can *"bring low the high tree, and make high the low tree"* (v. 24)? He can *"dry up the green tree, and make the dry tree flourish"* (v. 24)? Hallelujah! Praise the Lord! What kind of a tree are you? Are you a high tree God has brought low? Are you a low tree God has lifted up? Were you a green tree once that has dried up, or are you a dry tree God is going to make green once again? Let's pray.

Prayer

Father, thank You for always keeping a remnant. Thank You for always keeping Your promises. Thank You that You are a God of justice. You bring the low tree high and the high tree low. Father, thank You for planting each one of us. You expect us to bear much fruit. Like Israel of old, if we are not bearing fruit, we will be cut off. But if we are bearing fruit, You will lift us up.

How do You see us, Lord? What kind of trees are we? Regardless of whether we have been green or dry in the past, Lord, thank You for the reminder in Ezekiel 17 You want us to flourish. May we, like the trees, reach our branches up to You. May You make us all green again. Allow us to flourish for You.

You said, *"I am the Lord; I have spoken, and I will do it"* (v. 24). Do it with us again this day. Allow us to bear branches and produce fruit for Your kingdom. We ask it, in Your name. Amen.

MY THOUGHTS

EZEKIEL 18

We Are All on Our Own

In Ezekiel 18, we learn there are no spiritual children or grandchildren. Do you want to see your kids saved, or your parents saved? We all do, so what can we do? Please read or listen to Ezekiel 18.

COMMENTS

In 1997, I read Ezekiel 17-19 (NKJV) on the same day. Concerning chapter 18, I wrote, *"'Behold, all souls are Mine; The soul of the father As well as the soul of the son is Mine'* (v. 4). Each of us get to heaven on our own. As much as I want to be, I cannot be responsible for my children."

In 2006, I also read Ezekiel 17-19 (NASB) on the same day, and concerning chapter 18, wrote, "We are on our own. *'The person who sins will die. The son will not bear the punishment for the father's iniquity, nor will the father bear the punishment for the son's iniquity'* (v. 20). Yet, *'I have no pleasure in the death of anyone who dies,'* declares the Lord God. *'Therefore, repent and live'"* (v. 32).

In 2016, I read Ezekiel 17 and 18 on the same day. Concerning chapter 18, I wrote, *"'All souls are mine'* (v. 4), God declares. A father cannot save a son, nor a son save a father. We are all on our own spiritually. God would that none would perish; all would repent and live. His ways are just, but we keep ourselves out of heaven, according to verse 25. We will all face His judgment, and He offers life, according to verses 30-32."

As I said in my journals, in Ezekiel 18, we understand we are all on our own. God reminds us in verse 4, *"Behold, all souls are mine; the soul of the father as well as the soul of the son is mine: the soul who sins shall die."* The next several verses include examples of righteous living and sinful living. And then there is the discussion about the sins of the father and the sins of the son. God concludes the matter in verse 20, *"The soul who sins shall die. The son shall not suffer for the iniquity of the father, nor the father suffer for the iniquity of the son. The righteousness of the righteous shall be upon himself, and the wickedness of the wicked shall be upon himself."* So, as I said in my journals, we are all on our own. There are no spiritual children or grandchildren.

Then there is another one of those 'buts' in scripture, *"But if a wicked person turns away from all his sins that he has committed and keeps all my statutes and does what is just and right, he shall surely live; he shall not die"* (v. 21). Praise God for forgiveness which is described in verse 22, *"None of the transgressions that he has committed shall be remembered against him; for the righteousness that he has done he shall live."* Wow. Praise God! If we turn away from our wicked ways, we turn away from the sins we have committed, we turn back to obedience, and keep God's laws and His statutes, we can live!

All of our transgressions can be forgotten. Why? Verse 23, God speaking, *"Have I any pleasure in the death of the wicked, declares the Lord God, and not rather that he should turn from his way and live?"* It reminds us of the New Testament passage in 2 Peter 3:9, *"The Lord is not slow to fulfill his promise as some count slowness, but is patient toward you, not wishing that any should perish, but that all should reach repentance."*

> **The message in the Old Testament and the New Testament is consistent. God prefers we all live. He prefers none would die.**

The message in the Old Testament and the New Testament is consistent. God prefers we all live. He prefers none would die. That is the desire of God's heart. We are the ones who choose to rebel. We are the ones to choose a sinful life.

Let's look at verse 25, *"Yet you say, 'The way of the Lord is not just.' Hear now, O house of Israel: Is my way not just? Is it not your ways that are not just?"* Yes, it is our ways that keep us out of heaven. It is our ways that cause us to die and not live.

The chapter concludes with these verses:

Therefore I will judge you, O house of Israel, every one according to his ways, declares the Lord God . . . Cast away from you all the transgressions that you have committed, and make yourselves a new heart and a new spirit! Why will you die, O house of Israel? For I have no pleasure in the death of anyone, declares the Lord God; so turn, and live (vv. 30-32).

DIGGING DEEPER

There are some key applications from Ezekiel 18. First, all the souls are the Lord's. Second, the soul who sins will die. Third, fathers cannot save their sons. Sons cannot save their fathers. No one can save anyone. We are all on our own before the Lord.

Next, God prefers none of us would die, that we all live! And how can that happen? By casting away all of our transgressions we have committed and making ourselves a new heart and a new spirit, referring to verse 31. How does that happen? By coming humbly to the foot of the cross of Jesus.

Prayer

Father, thank You for providing a way so we can turn and live! We turn to Jesus. Jesus, thank You for turning our filthy rags into righteousness. You are the One who casts away all of our transgressions. You are the One who cleanses us from our sin. You are the One who creates in us a new heart and a new spirit. Turn today to Jesus and live. May God add an extra blessing to the reading of His Word today in Ezekiel 18. Amen.

MY THOUGHTS

EZEKIEL 19

God Is Watching

E zekiel 19 is a lament for the princes of Israel. As God watches your behavior, what does He see? Please read or listen to Ezekiel 19.

COMMENTS

You can see as I share from various personal Bible reading journals, I vary my Bible reading from year to year. In 1997, I read just the Old Testament. In 2006, I read the whole Bible. In 2016, I read various books of the Bible. You can also see on different days I read a different number of chapters. For example, in 1997, I read Ezekiel 17-19 on one day. I focused my attention on chapter 18 that year and wrote nothing concerning chapter 19.

In 2006, I read the whole Bible. I read portions of the Old Testament and portions of the New Testament each day. On this day, I read Ezekiel 17-19, and Hebrews 13. The focus of my journal that year was on chapter 18 of Ezekiel and Hebrews 13, so I made no notes concerning Ezekiel 19.

In 2016, I read eighteen books: ten Old Testament books and eight New Testament books. When you read the Bible that way, you can oftentimes slow down the pace. So in 2016, I read Ezekiel 19 all on one day, and wrote, "Lamentation or lament. Melancholy dirge. Description of a problem. Protest of innocence. A plea for help. A statement of faith and a pledge of service when the situation changes. All that according to the Book of Lamentations." Then I wrote, "Kings of Israel rose and fell according to their behavior and the watchful eye of God. It is the same today. Leaders of nations, some good, some corrupt, rise and fall based on their own behavior and the watchful eye of God Almighty. We are electing a new president in the USA. Neither candidate is appealing. God help us, please."

> Leaders of nations, some good, some corrupt, rise and fall based on their own behavior and the watchful eye of God Almighty.

Concerning Ezekiel 19, I did not make very many notes in several of my journals because I did not understand the passage. Some chapters in scripture are just hard to understand. This chapter is one of them. So I turn to my English Standard Version Study Bible footnotes. It appears the writers of the footnotes are as confused as I am about this chapter, so I did not find much help in my footnotes concerning Ezekiel 19.

We do not seem to know who the mother is, nor the lions. Neither of these mother's cubs seem to end up successful. The first was brought with *"hooks to the land of Egypt"* (v. 4). Verse 5 says, *"When she saw that she waited in vain, that her hope was lost."* That cub did not turn out so well, so how about cub number two? Verse 9 says, *"With hooks they put him in a cage and brought him to the king of Babylon; they brought him into custody, that his voice should no more be heard on the mountains of Israel."* So, he too did not turn out so well.

The mother is then compared to a vine in a vineyard. She started out well, but she did not finish well either. *"Your mother was like a vine in a vineyard planted by the water, fruitful and full of branches"* (v. 10). She initially bore much fruit; but then we go to verses 12-14:

> *But the vine was plucked up in fury, cast down to the ground; the east wind dried up its fruit; they were stripped off and withered. As for its strong stem, fire consumed it. Now it is planted in the wilderness, in a dry and thirsty land. And fire has gone out from the stem of its shoots, has consumed its fruit, so that there remains in it no strong stem, no scepter for ruling.*

DIGGING DEEPER

Let's position Ezekiel 19 and the previous few chapters. In chapter 16, it was the faithless bride, worse than Samaria and worse than Sodom. God's judgment was about to fall. Chapter 17 was the parable of the two eagles and the vine. The key there was judgment. The high tree was made low; the low tree was made high. The green tree was dried up and the dry tree flourished.

Moving to chapter 18, God declared the soul who sins shall die. The father could not save the son and the son could not save the father. Next, we come to chapter 19, a lioness and her cubs. God's judgment seems to fall on the cubs and the lioness and the vine, until there is no stem remaining. No scepter for ruling. Judgment is falling on Israel. It is getting bleak. There does not appear to be much future. In the summary of the preceding chapters, we already know why this is happening.

So what do we take away from a chapter like Ezekiel 19? How is your life? Are you being fruitful? Are you being used by God to grow His kingdom here on earth? Or have you been rebellious? Are you whoring around with other gods? Is your success rising or falling? In my journal, I mentioned these kings were judged based on their behavior under the watchful eye of God. I said, it is no different today. We are all being watched by God.

Our behavior is under the watchful eye of God today. What is He seeing in our lives? Is judgment at the door of your own home? Is your success, your future, about to be snuffed out? If so, we were reminded at the end of chapter 18, *"Cast away from you all the transgressions that you have committed, and make yourselves a new heart and a new spirit! . . . turn, and live"* (18:31-32).

After reading Ezekiel 19, that may be what to do. Confess your sins for He is faithful and just to forgive your sins and cleanse you from all unrighteousness, referring to 1 John 1:9. Turn to Him and live today.

Prayer

Father, thank You for reminding us in this chapter, our behavior is under the watchful eye of You. We pray what You see may be pleasing in Your sight. If not, may we turn and live even this day. Draw us closer to You through chapters like chapter 19 of Ezekiel. In Jesus' name, amen.

MY THOUGHTS

EZEKIEL 20

Naturally Rebellious

In Ezekiel 20, we learn about Israel's continual rebellion, but God's plan for restoration. How about you? Are you naturally rebellious to God and His Word? Are you willing to rely on the Holy Spirit to steer you toward obedience? Please read or listen to Ezekiel 20.

COMMENTS

Because of the length of the reading today, I will only share from my journals. We start in 1997, when I read Ezekiel 20 and 21 on the same day. Concerning this chapter, I wrote, "Rebellion of Israel reviewed since deliverance from Egypt. One key area of disobedience was not keeping the Sabbath, God's gift of rest to man. We may be guilty too of not resting and honoring God on the Sabbath. We are too busy. I never work on Sundays, but I don't think I really rest or take enough of the day to honor God either."

> God gives rules and statutes for our good. If we would just obey Him, we would live.

In 2006, I read Ezekiel 20 and 21 on the same day, and concerning this chapter, wrote, "God constantly warns us, but we don't listen, so He acts. Then we cry out to Him, but He decides not to listen. But He always has a remnant to start over with. I don't want God's wrath, so I try to listen and obey."

In 2016, I read Ezekiel 20 and wrote, "The history of a rebellious nation from God's perspective. God has had enough. *'I will not be inquired of by you'* anymore (v. 3). He tells them why. While in Egypt, He searched out a land for them, *'the most glorious of all lands'* (v. 6). What God does with and for Israel is for His honor, His namesake, not because they deserve anything. God gives rules and statutes for our good. If we would just obey Him, we would live. But they and we will not. It's always been pretty simple. God loves us. He created us. He has the right to tell us how to live our lives and He does. We reject and rebel against His laws and Him. And when things don't work out so well, we go running to Him. Because He is faithful and just to who He is, He brings us back. He restores. He blesses. Finally, He warns, *'What is in your mind shall never happen—the thought, "Let us be like* (other) *nations"'''* (v. 32).

DIGGING DEEPER

Are you like the nation of Israel looking the other way from God, His Word, His statutes, and His commandments? Above, I said if we would just obey Him, we would live a very different life. But we will not. Why? Do you believe His Word, His statutes, His commandments are for our good? He loves us, knows what is best for us, and put it in an "owner's manual" for our good pleasure. Why not commit to obey? Why not try it and see if He keeps His Word to bless us exceedingly abundantly, beyond what we can think or imagine?

Prayer

Father, thank You for the reminder in Ezekiel 20, that You watch us. You watch our behavior. And You become disappointed as we rebel, as we refuse to listen to You, as we won't obey Your laws, Your statutes, Your commandments.

You also remind us all the way back in Egypt, You went out and searched out a land for the nation of Israel. You gave them *"the most glorious of all lands"* (v. 6). You will do the same for us today. That is who You are, Lord. You give us beautiful, wonderful gifts.

You remind us, in this chapter, of Your patience. You withhold Your hand for Your namesake. Then You remind us sometimes we push You too far and You will not hear our inquiries anymore. And You remind us even though You get so disappointed in us, You are a promise keeper. You deliver. You restore. You constantly have Your hand reaching out to us. Because we were in Ezekiel 20 today, may we reach our hand back to You, may we trust You as we commit to obey.

Thank You for Your love, Your grace, and Your never ending mercy. We give You praise and thanks, in Jesus' name. Amen.

MY THOUGHTS

EZEKIEL 21

God Wields a Sword of Judgment

Ezekiel 21 describes how the Lord readies His sword. Do you believe in the God of the Old Testament, or only in the loving, merciful, graceful God of the New? Please read or listen to Ezekiel 21.

COMMENTS

In 1997, I read Ezekiel 20 and 21 on the same day, and all my journal notes were related to chapter 20.

In 2006, I also read Ezekiel 20 and 21 on the same day, as well as the New Testament passage of James 1, as I was reading the whole Bible that year. I made most of my notes on Ezekiel 20 and James 1 and nothing on chapter 21 of Ezekiel.

In 2016, I read Ezekiel 21 and 22 together and wrote this about Ezekiel 21, "The Word of the Lord is what Ezekiel speaks as now he sets his face toward Jerusalem though he is captive in Babylon. God is against the Promised Land. A sword of judgment and destruction is drawn this time against both righteous and wicked. God satisfies His fury against His own people. God is giving the sword to Babylon to execute His judgment on Israel. *Things shall not remain as they are* (v. 26). Ruin is on the way, according to verse 27."

Let's take a look at Ezekiel 22. Most Christians think about God as described in the New Testament: a God of love, a God of mercy, a God of forgiveness. If we do not spend time in the Old Testament, we do not see the character of God we see in Ezekiel 21. The description of God here is much different. In verse 2, God instructs Ezekiel to set his *"face toward Jerusalem and preach against the sanctuaries. Prophesy against the land of Israel."* Verse 3 continues *"Thus says the Lord: Behold, I am against you and will draw my sword from its sheath and will cut off from you both righteous and wicked."* Verses 6-7 is God speaking:

"As for you, son of man, groan; with breaking heart and bitter grief, groan before their eyes. And when they say to you, 'Why do you groan?' you shall say, 'Because of the news that it is coming. Every heart will melt, and all hands will be feeble; every spirit will faint, and all knees will be weak as water. Behold, it is coming, and it will be fulfilled,'" declares the Lord God.

Then, God describes His sword of judgment. Polished, sharpened, ready for slaughter. Again, this is not a description of God we are accustomed to. Ezekiel 21:14-15 describe what is going to happen, *"As for you, son of man, prophesy. Clap your hands and let the sword come down twice, yes, three times, the sword for those to be slain. It is the sword for the great slaughter, which surrounds them, that their hearts may melt, and many stumble."*

> God describes His sword of judgment. Polished, sharpened, ready for slaughter.

Through Ezekiel, God is describing a great slaughter. Where? In Israel, His own Promised Land. Verse 19 declares this sword will be in the hand of Babylon. Yes, throughout scripture, God uses nations to bring judgment on other nations. Why is all this happening? Look at verses 24-26:

Therefore thus says the Lord God: Because you have made your guilt to be remembered, in that your transgressions are uncovered, so that in all your deeds your sins appear—because you have come to remembrance, you shall be taken in hand. And you, O profane wicked one, prince of Israel, whose day has come, the time of your final punishment.

Yes, there are times when God has had enough. He says in the next two verses, *"Things shall not remain as they are"* (v. 26). *"A ruin, ruin, ruin I will make it"* (v. 27).

DIGGING DEEPER

Where are you at with your life today? Do you love God with all your heart, soul, mind, and spirit? Do you love your neighbor as yourself? Or are you full of guilt, transgressions, and sin? As the Lord declares, things shall not remain as they are. Praise God we all have a chance to come before Him and confess our sins, to appeal to Him for His grace and His mercy.

Ezekiel 21 unveils a God with a sword of judgment. If He decides to remove that sword from its sheath, how will your life measure up? God says, *"I will judge you. And I will pour out my indignation upon you; I will blow upon you with the fire of my wrath, and I will deliver you into the hands of brutish men, skillful to destroy"* (vv. 30-31). Let's not forget, God is still a God of judgment. And His judgment is true, righteous, and just. He is watching. What is He seeing in your life?

Prayer

Father, we come humbly before You. We do not like chapters like this in Your Word. But it is healthy for us to be reminded You are a God of judgment, a God of wrath, as well as a God of mercy, love, and grace. We are reminded You have a sword and You alone will divide the living and the dead. Thank You, Father, for this stark reminder. But thank You also You are a God of love and forgiveness, and, if we come to You, You always reach out and bring us back to You. But it is up to us to come back to You. May we do so today because we read or listened to Ezekiel 21. Renew a right spirit in each one of us and we will give You the glory. In Jesus' name, we pray. Amen.

MY THOUGHTS

EZEKIEL 22

I Found None

In Ezekiel 22, God through Ezekiel reminds Israel of its shedding of blood. He looks for someone to stand for Him, to stand in the gap. Is He looking again today? If so, will He find one? Please read or listen to Ezekiel 22.

COMMENTS

At forty-two years old, in 1997, I read Ezekiel 22 and 23 (NKJV) on the same day. Concerning this chapter, I wrote in my personal Bible reading journal, "In the midst of the decline of Israel, *I sought for a man among them who would make a wall, and stand in the gap before Me on behalf of the land, that I should not destroy it; but I found no one*" (v. 30).

At fifty-one years old, in 2006, I again read Ezekiel 22 and 23 on the same day, as well as James 2, as I was reading the whole Bible that year. I made no notes on Ezekiel 22.

At sixty-one years old in 2016, I read Ezekiel 21 and 22 on the same day, and concerning chapter 22, wrote, "Jerusalem, the bloody city, because they have shed blood, been defiled by idols, and brought judgment from God. The list of infractions is listed in 22:6-12, mostly sexual sin. God is angry, according to verse 20. He melts Jerusalem with fire and His wrath." I continued to write, "The *priests have done violence to my law and have profaned my holy things. They have made no distinction between the holy and the common'* (v. 26). This is true again today: churches have faded from God's Word, teaching what they want, caving into cultural pressure, women and gay priests, pretending to speak for God when they do not, according to verse 28. God seeks someone to stand for Him. He finds no one this time," again referring to verse 30.

> Churches have faded from God's Word, teaching what they want, caving into cultural pressure.

Let's take a look at Ezekiel 22. As we read these kinds of chapters, it is important to remember, *"Thus saith the Lord."* This is God speaking. He says in verse 4, *"You have become guilty by the blood that you have shed, and defiled by the idols that you have made, and you have brought your days near, the appointed time of your years has come."* Certainly, it is true all of us have appointed times of our years. God knows our birthday; He also knows the day our sojourn will end on earth. It must also be true for nations, as we read here in verse 4.

Verses 6-12 declare the reasons why. They were *"bent on shedding blood"* (v. 6). Fathers and mothers were treated with contempt. The sojourner in the land suffers extortion. *"The fatherless and the widow are wronged in you. You have despised my holy things and profaned my Sabbaths"* (vv. 7-8). *"There are men . . . who slander to shed blood . . . men uncover their fathers' nakedness; . . . they violate women who are unclean in their menstrual impurity. One commits abomination with his neighbor's wife; another lewdly defiles his daughter-in-law; another in you violates his sister, his father's daughter. In you they take bribes to shed blood; you take interest and profit and make gain of your neighbors by extortion; but me you have forgotten, declares the Lord"* (vv. 9-12).

Many of those sins outlined in verses 6-12 are common in our day today. In verse 18, the accusations continue, *"The house of Israel has become dross to me."* God describes His own people, the tribes of Israel, as dross. What is dross? I asked Siri on my smartphone, "Dross is a mass of solid impurities floating on a molten metal or dispersed in the metal." So God is describing the house of Israel as dross, impurities.

He levels another accusation against them in verse 26, *"Her priests have done violence to my law and have profaned my holy things. They have made no distinction between the holy and the common, neither have they taught the difference between the unclean and the clean."* He also accuses the priests of *"saying, 'Thus says the Lord God,' when the Lord has not spoken"* (v. 28).

The people have forgotten the Lord their God and the priests are not teaching the Word of God. They cannot even distinguish between the holy and the common. But, once again, God shows His mercy and His grace, *"And I sought for a man among them who should build up the wall and stand in the breach before me for the land, that I should not destroy it, but I found none"* (v. 30).

DIGGING DEEPER

Do you think one person could have made a difference? Do you think you can make a difference? If God would have found one, do you think He would have spared Israel? What can He do with you in your life, in our day? Let's pray.

Prayer

Father, then and now, You look for a man who will build up a wall, who will stand in the breach. That day, You found none. Today, may that not be the case. Might You find many. Might You find some. Might You find one.

Father, call us out to serve You. Call us out to stand and build up a wall. Call us out to stand in the breach before the land. Call us out to serve You here in our culture this day. And, Holy Spirit, give us the courage to heed the call. Like Ezekiel, send us forth to declare Your Word. And may we go with Your peace and Your blessing. In the name of Jesus, amen.

MY THOUGHTS

Two Sisters

In Ezekiel 23, we are going to learn about two women symbolizing Samaria and Jerusalem. Have you remained faithful in your walk with the Lord, or are you whoring around with other gods? Please read or listen to Ezekiel 23.

COMMENTS

In the previous chapter, Ezekiel 22, God accuses Israel of not only shedding much blood but committing many, many sins. In chapter 23, He accuses both Samaria and Jerusalem of whoring around. Due to the length of the reading, I will only share from my personal Bible reading journals.

In 1997, I wrote, "Jerusalem put on same plane as Samaria. Sisters who were harlots. Yet, Jerusalem, the younger sister, even more than Samaria, the older."

In 2006, I wrote, "Samaria and Jerusalem played the harlot, running after other nations and leaving God. Because of their sins, God judges them. The husband, God, remained faithful."

In 2016, I wrote, "'Oholah', means her tent, represents Samaria or Israel. 'Oholibah', means my tent is in her, is Jerusalem or Judah. Both played the whore, meaning they were not faithful to God, their husband, but loved their enemies, Egypt, Assyria, Babylon. God is disgusted with both Israel and Judah, so He gives them over to their own desires. So often, we get what we deserve, not what God wants for us. They were not only guilty of whoring but of adultery, defilement of the sanctuary, profaning My Sabbaths, sacrificing their children to idols *and you shall bear the penalty for your sinful idolatry*" (v. 49).

> So often, we get what we deserve, not what God wants for us.

DIGGING DEEPER

In both Ezekiel 22 and 23, God is making the case for judging Israel. How about you? Have you remained faithful to God, your husband? Or are you like Samaria and Jerusalem, whoring around with other gods? Let's pray.

Prayer

Father, in Ezekiel 23, we learn You are serious about our relationship with You. You use the illustration of two sisters. You desired faithfulness from them, but they both failed You. You too desire faithfulness from us. May You protect us so we do not fail You. May we stay in loving relationship with You all the days of our lives. May You find us faithful. Amen.

MY THOUGHTS

EZEKIEL 24

Do Not Mourn the Death of Your Wife

Toiloday we reach chapter 24, the halfway point in our forty-eight-day journey through the Book of Ezekiel. We will hear about the siege of Jerusalem and the death of Ezekiel's wife. What kind of God would not even let you mourn the death of your wife? Please read or listen to Ezekiel 24.

COMMENTS

In 1997, I read Ezekiel 24 (NKJV) on its own, and wrote, "God takes Ezekiel's wife, but he is not allowed to mourn. *'So I spoke to the people in the morning, and at evening my wife died; and the next morning I did as I was commanded'* (v. 18). Wow. What obedience."

Nine years later, in 2006, I read Ezekiel 24-26 on the same day with James 3. Concerning this chapter, I wrote, "Ezekiel's wife dies but he cannot mourn. His whole life was an object lesson for the people. His life was not his own. Is he special or does God desire similar commitment from us? Live our lives the way we want or seek God's purpose and live the life He wants out of us?"

Ten years later, in 2016, I read Ezekiel 24 and 25 on my anniversary. That is interesting, isn't it, as Ezekiel's wife dies? I wrote, "The end is beginning in Jerusalem as Babylon lays its siege against the city. Israel falls, not because of God's judgment, but because of its wicked lewdness. In other words, it falls on its own. Finally, God, who is just, has enough and acts, *'I will not go back; I will not spare; I will not relent; according to your ways and your deeds you will be judged'* (v. 14). The USA will not be spared either. We are falling from within, just like Israel." I continued, "On my anniversary, I read about God taking *'the delight of your eyes'* (v. 16). And at evening, Ezekiel's wife dies, but Ezekiel is not allowed to mourn nor weep for his wife. How hard. Sometimes God's assignments are over the top."

Let's take a look at Ezekiel 24. Ezekiel in Babylon, 880 miles away from Jerusalem, sees the siege of Jerusalem begin on the very day it starts. Verse 2 says, *"this very day."* It is amazing how God works. He uses a prophet 880 miles away from the scene to announce the fall of Jerusalem. Why? *"On account of your unclean lewdness, because I would have cleansed you and you were not cleansed from your uncleanness, you shall not be cleansed anymore till I have satisfied my fury upon you"* (v. 13).

> I wonder if we consider God harsh, but we do not consider the harshness of our sinful ways.

We see once again, God is a God of mercy. He would have cleansed Israel if they wanted to be cleansed. But now it is too late. The next verse says, *"I will not go back; I will not spare; I will not relent; according to your ways and your deeds you will be judged, declares the Lord God"* (v. 14). I wonder if we consider God harsh, but we do not consider the harshness of our sinful ways. The reason God judges is because of our behavior.

The next thing to happen is God announces to Ezekiel He is going to take his wife. Is that the reward for being a prophet of God? Verse 16, *"Son of man, behold, I am about to take the delight of your eyes away from you at a stroke; yet you shall not mourn or weep, nor shall your tears run down."* What?!? Remember, in 2016, I read that on my anniversary. Terry has been the delight of my eyes for over four decades. If God took her from me, I would certainly mourn and weep, and tears would run down my cheeks.

Not so for Ezekiel. His whole life was a drama unfolded by God before the people; even here, the death of his wife. Verse 18 describes what happened, *"So I spoke to the people in the morning,"* just like any other day, *"and at evening my wife died. And on the next morning I did as I was commanded."* O, the obedience of Ezekiel.

The people questioned Ezekiel's behavior, and God puts in the mouth of Ezekiel the words He wants to share. Let's pick it up in verses 22-24:

> *And you shall do as I have done; you shall not cover your lips, nor eat the bread of men. Your turbans shall be on your heads and your shoes on your feet; you shall not mourn or weep, but you shall rot away in your iniquities and groan to one another. Thus shall Ezekiel be to you a sign; according to all that he has done you shall do. When this comes, then you will know that I am the Lord God.*

Yes, Ezekiel's whole life was a demonstration for the Lord.

DIGGING DEEPER

How about your life? Is your whole life a demonstration unto God? Whether you think it is or not, people are watching. What are they learning as they watch you live your life? Will they be drawn closer to the Lord we love, or will they be pushed away by our behavior?

Prayer

Father, thank You for this difficult example here in Ezekiel 24. You remind us our life is on display, just like Ezekiel's was. May we, like him, do as we are commanded even when the going gets tough. Father, strengthen us so You can find us faithful. Use us to draw people to You. In the name of Jesus, we pray. Amen.

MY THOUGHTS

EZEKIEL 25

Do We Care About God's People?

Ezekiel 25 contains prophecies about the surrounding nations of Israel. They did not treat God's people well. Do we? Please read or listen to Ezekiel 25.

COMMENTS

Throughout Ezekiel, I have been using three of my personal Bible reading journals from 1997, 2006, and 2016. These are not the only journals I could have used. I could have selected others since I have been journaling my Bible reading since 1983. I actually looked at ten different years before picking these three. I select journals oftentimes because of the ways I read the Bible in various years. In 1997, I was reading the whole Old Testament, a great way to spend time in the scriptures. In 2006, I read the whole Bible, both Old and New Testaments. And in 2016, I selected various books and slowed down the pace and enjoyed the scriptures that way.

In 1997, I read Ezekiel 25-28 on the same day and wrote, "God judges the nations and their leaders." The rest of my journal entry had to do with the other chapters.

In 2006, when reading the whole Bible, I read Ezekiel 24-26 on one day, with James 3, combining Old and New Testament readings each day. On chapter 25, I did not make any notes.

In 2016, I selected eighteen books to read. Actually, I selected sixteen books in 2016, but I finished early, so I added a couple of books at the end. I read ten Old Testament books and eight New Testament books that year. In the Bible reading journals published by the Ezra Project, there are Bible reading trackers in each, so you can look back and see the books you read and the dates you read them. If something like that interests you, visit our website, ezraproject.net, and order an Ezra Project Bible reading journal.

> **God is God. He will make Himself known.**

In 2016, I read Ezekiel 24 and 25 on the same day. Concerning chapter 25, I wrote, "Not only is Israel to face God's wrath, but also the surrounding nations will be judged. *Then they will know that I am the Lord'* (v. 7). God is God. He will make Himself known."

Concerning Amon:

> *For thus says the Lord God: Because you have clapped your hands and stamped your feet and rejoiced with all the malice within your soul against the land of Israel, therefore, behold, I have stretched out my hand against you, and will hand you over as plunder to the nations. And I will cut you off from the peoples and will make you perish out of the countries; I will destroy you. Then you will know that I am the Lord* (vv. 6-7).

Concerning Moab and Seir, the accusation is in verse 8, *"Because Moab and Seir said, 'Behold, the house of Judah is like all the other nations.'"* Obviously, God does not think that. The house of Judah, Israel, was a special nation to God. Verse 11 says, *"and I will execute judgments upon Moab. Then they will know that I am the Lord."*

Concerning Edom, he wrote, *"Thus says the Lord God: Because Edom acted revengefully against the house of Judah and has grievously offended in taking vengeance on them"* (v. 12). Verse 14 says, *"And I will lay my vengeance upon Edom by the hand of my people Israel, and they shall do in Edom according to my anger and according to my wrath, and they shall know my vengeance, declares the Lord God."*

Concerning Philistia, *"Thus says the Lord God: Because the Philistines acted revengefully and took vengeance with malice of soul to destroy in never-ending enmity"* (v. 15). And verse 17, *"I will execute great vengeance on them with wrathful rebukes. Then they will know that I am the Lord, when I lay my vengeance upon them."*

DIGGING DEEPER

How do we apply Ezekiel 25 to our lives today? First, what do we think about the nation of Israel? Do we care about God's land? Do we care about God's people? Do we pray for the peace of Jerusalem?

Secondly, we might consider how we treat other Christians or other church denominations. Do we treat them with honor and respect, even if they think differently or have different theological views than we do? Ezekiel 25 reminds us to question how we treat God's people. Maybe we never think about it, and maybe we can do better.

Prayer

Father, You judged those around the nation of Israel for various reasons. The bottom line was they did not treat Your people well. May we not be accused of the same. May we lift up the nation of Israel. May we lift up our fellow Christians. May we honor Christian denominations that may be slightly different than our own. Use us, Lord, to be an example of Christianity. Use us to be a blessing to others. We ask it, in Jesus' name. Amen.

MY THOUGHTS

EZEKIEL 26

Tyre

Ezekiel 26 is a continuation of the prophecies against the surrounding nations of Israel. Today, it is Tyre. Do you believe all prophecy in the Bible must come true? Please read or listen to Ezekiel 26.

COMMENTS

As I look at my journal from 1997, I read Ezekiel 25-28 on the same day, and made no notes concerning chapter 26.

In 2006, I read Ezekiel 24-26 on the same day, and I made no notes again concerning this chapter.

In 2016, I read Ezekiel 26 and wrote, "Not only is Israel falling, nations around it are too. Tyre will also fall to the Babylonians. Tyre *'shall never be rebuilt'* (v. 14). According to my English Standard Study Bible footnotes, there is a modern city of Tyre today, but it is not on the previous site. 'No city has ever been rebuilt over its ruins' (p. 1538). When God speaks, it happens. He alone judges the nations of the world then and now."

Actually, three chapters have to do with this country or this place called Tyre, Ezekiel 26-28. Why so much attention on Tyre? First, a little geography. Tyre was a coastal city on the edge of the Mediterranean and a part of Israel. It was actually two places. It was an island and a coastal city. I refer to my English Standard Version Study Bible footnote, "Why so much about Tyre? The answer seems to be that, of the states addressed by Ezekiel, only Tyre and Egypt had the power to withstand Babylon: Egypt's power was military, Tyre's was economic" (page 1537).

Why is God against Tyre? Let's begin with verse 3, *"Behold, I am against you, O Tyre, and will bring up many nations against you."* Why? Go back to verse 2, *"Aha, the gate of the peoples is broken; it has swung open to me. I shall be replenished, now that she is laid waste."* Tyre took advantage of Israel when it was down. This did not please God.

DIGGING DEEPER

In Ezekiel 26:7, the Lord says He will bring Nebuchadnezzar and Babylon against Tyre. In verse 14, the Lord declares, *"You shall never be rebuilt, for I am the Lord,"* but today, there's still a place called Tyre. So, is Ezekiel's prophecy against Tyre fulfilled or unfulfilled? My English Standard Version Study Bible footnote has a lot to say about this. In some ways, the prophecies have been fulfilled; in other ways, they have not been fulfilled. I did a little research on my phone and found out the city of Tyre still exists and there are lots of questions about whether these prophecies from Ezekiel were ever really fulfilled.

Is Ezekiel's prophecy against Tyre fulfilled or unfulfilled?

Due to the brevity of these devotions, I cannot get into all those questions. If it interests you, I encourage you to do some research. You may find it very interesting, as I have. The bottom line is, Babylon did come against Tyre, but it did not destroy it. Two-hundred and fifty years after Babylon, Alexander the great attacked Tyre and also destroyed most of it, but not all of it. So, today, Tyre, either the island or the city, still exists and is certainly not a bare rock as predicted in Ezekiel 26. However, I will conclude with a couple of quotes from the ESV footnotes, "In the conquests of Alexander the Great, Tyre was indeed destroyed and made like a **bare rock"** (p. 1538). Concerning, *"You shall never be rebuilt"* (v. 14):

Tyre was rebuilt and reconquered several times after Alexander the Great, so the complete fulfillment of this prophecy did not come immediately. The modern city of Tyre is of modest size and is near the ancient site, though not identical to it. Archaeological photographs of the ancient site show ruins from ancient Tyre scattered over many acres of land. No city has been rebuilt over these ruins, however, in fulfillment of this prophecy (p. 1538).

Some claim the prophecy to be fulfilled, others question it. And that is what I love about scripture. There is so much to see, so much to discover, so much to wonder about. But we are not finished with the city of Tyre. We will continue to see more about it in Ezekiel 27 and 28.

Prayer

Father, we pray You will give us wisdom, knowledge, and understanding as we read the Book of Ezekiel, as we try to glean spiritual insights from these few chapters concerning Tyre. Holy Spirit, teach us, speak to us, as we seek to learn. We bless You and we praise You. In Jesus' name, amen.

MY THOUGHTS

The USA Like Tyre?

In Ezekiel 26, we discussed the city of Tyre. Today, that discussion continues with a lament over Tyre. Tyre was rich, wealthy, and enriched others. Is the USA the Tyre of our day? Please read or listen to Ezekiel 27.

> **Is the USA the Tyre of our day?**

COMMENTS

In my personal Bible reading journals from 1997 and 2006, I have nothing related to this chapter, so we will look at 2016 when I read chapters 27 and 28 on the same day. Concerning Ezekiel 27, I wrote, "The glory, beauty, importance, and success of Tyre are outlined in 27. Reflected in beauty, *'great wealth of every kind'* (v. 12), your abundant jewels, *'you satisfied many peoples . . . you enriched the kings of the earth'* (v. 33). Sounds like a great place, like Paris, Singapore, London, New York today, or the USA. Yet, Tyre falls:

Now you are wrecked by the seas, in the depths of the waters; your merchandise and all your crew in your midst have sunk with you (v. 34).

You have come to a dreadful end and shall be no more forever (v. 36).

"Even the mighty fall."

We learned in chapter 26, Tyre was an island and a coastal city on the coast of Israel. We see here in chapter 27, it was economically blessed. It sounds like it was a beautiful city, a rich city, a city bustling with activity. It was *"perfect in beauty"* (v. 3), and great in wealth of every kind, according to verse 12. Abundant in goods and great wealth, according to verse 18. It seemed like the place to be, according to verse 33, *"you satisfied many peoples; with your abundant wealth and merchandise you enriched the kings of the earth."* Yet, the tide turns in verse 34, *"Now you are wrecked by the seas, in the depths of the waters; your merchandise and all your crew in your midst have sunk with you."* Concluding with verse 36, *"The merchants among the peoples hiss at you; you have come to a dreadful end and shall be no more forever."*

DIGGING DEEPER

The questions raised in chapter 26 still remain in chapter 27. Was Tyre destroyed? Did it become a bare rock? Did it have a dreadful end forevermore? We need to keep going into chapter 28 to find more answers. But, as I referred to in one of my journals, it seemed much like the USA, yet God judged it.

We too seem to think we are perfect in beauty. We have great wealth of every kind. We are filled with abundance of goods, and we trade with countries all over the world. We satisfy many peoples, and we enrich kings all over the earth. God judged Tyre, and we will find out why in chapter 28. If He did not spare Tyre, will He spare the USA? Are we guilty of the same sins as Tyre? We will find out in Ezekiel 28.

Prayer

Father, we thank You for your abundance of blessings. Tyre sounds like a beautiful place. You blessed it with beauty and abundance. You satisfied people, and You made people wealthy. That is probably Your heart's desire, Lord. You want to bless us exceedingly, abundantly, beyond what we think or imagine. Tyre sounded like such a place. Teach us, Lord, what happened to Tyre so it does not happen to us. Continue to reveal Your truth to us in this wonderful Book of Ezekiel. We ask it, in Your name. Amen.

MY THOUGHTS

EZEKIEL 28

I Am a God

E zekiel 28 is the third chapter on the country of Tyre. The king claims he is a god. Have you ever claimed such a thing? Please read or listen to Ezekiel 28.

COMMENTS

In 1997, at forty-two years old, I read Ezekiel 25-28 (NKJV) on the same day. Concerning this chapter, I wrote, "God judges the nations and their leaders. The king of Tyre said, *'I am a god'* (v. 2). Ezekiel said, *'Yet you are a man, and not a god'* (v. 2). He will be thrown into the pit because of his pride and non-recognition of the one true God. We have lots of leaders today who are not honoring or giving glory to God." That was in 1997. Not much has changed today with our political leaders here in the United States and across the world.

In 2006, at fifty-one years old, I read Ezekiel 27 and 28 (NASB) on the same day, and wrote, "Is God judging the king of Tyre or Satan himself? In 28:12-19, it says, *'You were in Eden, the garden of God'* (v. 13). *'You were an anointed cherub'* (v. 14). *'You were on the holy mountain of God; You walked in the midst of the stones of fire'* (v. 14). *'You will cease to be forever'"* (v. 19).

In 2016, at sixty-one years old, I read Ezekiel 27 and 28 and concerning this chapter, wrote, "Even the mighty fall. Why? *'Because your heart is proud, and you have said, "I am a god" . . . yet you are but a man, and no god'* (v. 2) and *'your heart has become proud in your wealth'* (v. 5). God blesses with His goodness to nations, peoples, families, and individuals. Rather than recognize our blessings, wealth, success come from Him, we take the credit. Why? We are a sinful people unwilling to recognize God in our success. No wonder He gets upset, angry, and judges."

Ezekiel 28 is a continuation of Ezekiel 26 and 27 concerning the city of Tyre. In this chapter, we learn why God is upset with Tyre, why He is judging them, *"Because your heart is proud, and you have said, 'I am a god'"* (v. 2).

> So often, as God blesses, we take the blessings for granted. We end up proud.

We learned in Ezekiel 27, Tyre was a beautiful city. It had great wealth of every kind. It was abundant in goods. Many people were satisfied there, and kings became wealthy. So often, as God blesses, we take the blessings for granted. We end up proud. We end up thinking it is because of us. It sounds like that is what happened to Tyre. But God reminds the prince of Tyre that he is not a god, he is *"but a man"* (v. 9). Tyre and its political leadership had become proud based on its success and its wealth.

I mentioned in reference to Ezekiel 27, the USA seems much like Tyre:

Because you make your heart like the heart of a god, therefore, behold, I will bring foreigners upon you, the most ruthless of the nations; and they shall draw their swords against the beauty of your wisdom and defile your splendor (vv. 6-7).

Will you still say, 'I am a god,' in the presence of those who kill you (v. 9).

Later in the chapter, the king of Tyre is described with allusions toward Satan:

You were the signet of perfection, full of wisdom and perfect in beauty. You were in Eden, the garden of God (vv. 12-13).

You were an anointed guardian cherub. I placed you; you were on the holy mountain of God; in the midst of the stones of fire you walked. You were blameless in your ways from the day you were created, till unrighteousness was found in you (vv. 14-15).

Your heart was proud because of your beauty; you corrupted your wisdom for the sake of your splendor. I cast you to the ground (v. 17).

I turn to my English Standard Version Study Bible footnote, "Tyre is likened to a second Adam, clearly a created being (vv. 13, 15) and yet a 'cherub' (v. 14). It is in the 'garden of God' in v. 13, and on the 'mountain of God' in vv. 14 and 16. Some would see v. 17 as a poetic allusion, where in Ezekiel likens the downfall of the proud king of Tyre to the fall and curse on Satan in Gen. 3:1-15" (p. 1542). There may be similarities to Tyre and Satan. Both, in their beauty, fell because of their pride. I also mentioned similarities between Tyre and the United States of America. We too, in our beauty, are guilty of pride.

DIGGING DEEPER

In chapter 28, we now know the "why" of why God judged Tyre. Why? Not only pride, but because they said, *"I am a god"* (v. 9). When we become so successful, so wealthy, so beautiful we think we are a god, God has problems with us. May we in the United States, be reminded of this prophecy against Tyre. May we, as successful, beautiful people, those with wealth and abundance, never forget where the blessings come from.

There is one more passage concerning Tyre in the next chapter. Until then, let's pray.

Prayer

Father, we thank You for the great lessons we are learning from Tyre in the Book of Ezekiel. We understand Your desire may be to bless us abundantly and we thank You. We also thank You for the great warning in these chapters that those blessings cannot translate into pride. They cannot translate into patting ourselves on the back. And, most certainly, they cannot translate into idol worship.

Thanks for the reminder we are but mere men. You and You alone are God. We thank You for our blessings. We thank You for the reminder that You are God. Amen.

MY THOUGHTS

EZEKIEL 29

Pride

In Ezekiel 29, we have a prophecy against Egypt; but there is one small paragraph concerning Tyre, which we reviewed in the last couple of chapters. Both Tyre and Egypt fall because of pride. Do you remember where all your blessings come from, or are you taking credit? Please read or listen to Ezekiel 29.

COMMENTS

Before we get to the prophecy on Egypt, let's finish with Tyre. Did you find those verses concerning Tyre in Ezekiel 29? They begin with verse 17:

> *In the twenty-seventh year, in the first month, on the first day of the month, the word of the Lord came to me: "Son of man, Nebuchadnezzar king of Babylon made his army labor hard against Tyre. Every head was made bald, and every shoulder was rubbed bare, yet neither he nor his army got anything from Tyre to pay for the labor that he had performed against her"* (vv. 17-18).

Back in Ezekiel 26:3-4, the prophecy against Tyre was, *"Behold, I am against you, O Tyre, and will bring up many nations against you . . . They shall destroy the walls of Tyre and break down her towers, and I will scrape her soil from her and make her a bare rock."* The prophecy continues in 26:7-10:

For thus says the Lord God: Behold, I will bring against Tyre from the north Nebuchadnezzar king of Babylon, king of kings, with horses and chariots, and with horsemen and a host of many soldiers. He will kill with the sword your daughters on the mainland. He will set up a siege wall against you and throw up a mound against you, and raise a roof of shields against you. He will direct the shock of his battering rams against your walls, and with his axes he will break down your towers. His horses will be so many that their dust will cover you. Your walls will shake at the noise of the horsemen and wagons and chariots, when he enters your gates as men enter a city that has been breached.

Down to verse 12, *"They will plunder your riches and loot your merchandise."* Now we jump back to 29:18, *"Son of man, Nebuchadnezzar king of Babylon made his army labor hard against Tyre. Every head was made bald, and every shoulder was rubbed bare, yet neither he nor his army got anything from Tyre to pay for the labor that he had performed against her."*

DIGGING DEEPER

Did the prophecy in chapter 26 come true or not? My English Standard Version Study Bible footnote says this about Ezekiel 29:17-21, "Nebuchadnezzar's siege of Tyre had ended with Tyre intact, albeit subject to the Babylonians, who had little to show for 13 years of effort" (p. 1545). Yes, much of what was predicted in Ezekiel 26 happened. Babylon did come and put siege ramps up against the city. They tried hard for thirteen years to break down Tyre. By chapter 29, it appears it did not work. So, what do we conclude about the prophesies of Tyre? I will leave that to biblical scholars.

As I mentioned in chpater 26, my footnotes had much to say about whether the prophecies of Tyre were fulfilled or left unfulfilled. The questions may remain in your mind and mine, so this might be a path of study for you. It can become very important because if the prophecies of Ezekiel did not come true, what do we do with the rest of his prophecies, and what do we do with the entire Bible?

My lack of knowledge about Tyre does not equate with questioning the Word of God. Most likely, through much study, there is an answer. But because *Day by Day Through the Bible* is a daily devotion, not a Bible study, we do not have time to do the research on Tyre. That is something we can do individually, and I encourage you to do so. By the way, if you do, and you want to let me know, you can contact me at ezraproject.net where there is a contact page.

> If the prophecies of Ezekiel did not come true, what do we do with the rest of his prophecies, and what do we do with the entire Bible?

Let's go on to the prophecy on Egypt. Once again, we see pride, this time in the nation of Egypt. God speaks in verse 3, *"Behold, I am against you, Pharaoh king of Egypt, the great dragon that lies in the midst of his streams, that says, 'My Nile is my own; I made it for myself.'"*

Judgment will come against Egypt so all of Egypt will know the Lord is God. But in Egypt's case, they will only suffer for forty years. Their fortunes will be restored after forty years. Yet, Egypt will never become a great power again. Of course, Egypt exists today, but it is not a world-ranked power.

The prophecy of Babylon coming against Egypt occurred in 571 B.C. and Egypt was conquered by Nebuchadnezzar and Babylon in 568 B.C. In this instance, the prophecies of Ezekiel came true. There is more to be said about Egypt in the next few chapters. Let's wrap up our study of Ezekiel 29 in prayer.

Prayer

Father, in Tyre and Egypt, pride was a big issue. Both nations took credit for their success. So, Lord, when our nations do likewise, may we remember our success is because of Your blessings. When we get prideful, very likely You will judge us as well.

But pride also occurs for us as people and families. When You grant us success, Lord, it is from Your hand. May we never put our strength in our self-accomplishment. Thank You for the reminders here on Tyre and Egypt. May we attribute our success to You. Thank You for any measure of success we have experienced. We thank You for it. In Jesus' name, amen.

MY THOUGHTS

EZEKIEL 30

Where Does Your Success Come From?

I n Ezekiel 29, we started discussing Egypt. In chapter 30, it continues with the lament over Egypt. God accuses Egypt of pride. Are you guilty as well? Please read or listen to Ezekiel 30.

COMMENTS

In 1997, I read Ezekiel 29-31 on the same day, and wrote, "God's judgment against Egypt. Israel will run to Egypt for protection and be enslaved. God pronounces judgment for Egypt's pride, arrogance, and lack of godliness taking credit for the Nile, a river of life in the desert. But God limited Egypt's desolation to forty years. Egypt still exists, whereas Assyria and Babylon are gone forever."

Nine years later, in 2006, I was reading both Old and New Testament, and I read Ezekiel 29-31 on the same day with James 5. Concerning this chapter, I wrote, "Egypt will fall and not rise as a power again."

Ten years later in 2016, I read Ezekiel 30 and 31 on the same day, and wrote, "Four chapters on the fall of Egypt from God through Ezekiel and Babylon, 29-32." I quoted various verses:

Her wealth is carried away, and her foundations are torn down (v. 4).

Those who support Egypt shall fall and her proud might shall come down (v. 6).

I will put an end to the wealth of Egypt (v. 10).

I will destroy the idols (v. 13).

I will dry up the Nile (v. 12).

I will execute judgments on Egypt (v. 19).

"God will use Babylon to judge Egypt, verses 10-11, 24."

DIGGING DEEPER

Do you notice in these prophecies against other nations, they are always so people will know God is God?

The prophecy against Egypt began in Ezekiel 29. As I mentioned in one of my journals, it will continue until chapter 32. Do you notice in these prophecies against other nations, Tyre and Egypt for example, they are always so people will know God is God? Verse 19, *"Then they will know that I am the Lord."* The last verse of the chapter, *"Then they will know that I am the Lord."*

Do you think it is important to God that we understand He is the Lord? Do you think He not only judges nations, but individuals, so we will understand and know He is God and there is no other? When nations get out of line, He judges them to bring them back to the knowledge that He is God. Do you think it is the same case for us? When we get out of line, do you think He judges us so we will know He is God?

In both prophetic judgments against Tyre and Egypt, it was because of pride; a failure to recognize where our success comes from. Do you think that might be true in your life? Based on these chapters in Ezekiel, do you think it is time to bend the knee and acknowledge God for your success? That is an easier action step than waiting for the judgment of God to fall on you.

Might we all humble ourselves before an Almighty God, the creator of all things; the One who blesses; the One who gives us our talents and abilities; the One who endowed the earth with wealth; the One who gives us our very breath each and every day; the One who wants us to know He is the Lord.

Prayer

Father, thank You for these great reminders in Ezekiel that You are God, there is no other. All of our success comes from Your hand. These are great reminders, and we thank You for them. We humble ourselves before You. We pray You will receive our praise, honor, and glory so You will not have to administer Your judgment against us to get our attention. Praise God from whom all blessings flow. Praise Him all creatures here below. Amen.

MY THOUGHTS

EZEKIEL 31

Where Does Your Help Come From?

The last couple of chapters have been about Egypt; Ezekiel 31 is the same. We are going to learn Pharaoh is not going to make it. Like Israel, do you look to others for help? Do you depend on others to protect and provide for you? Please read or listen to Ezekiel 31.

COMMENTS

In 1997, I read Ezekiel 29-31 on the same day. Concerning the judgment on Egypt, I wrote, "God's judgment against Egypt. Israel would run to Egypt for protection and be enslaved. God pronounces judgment for Egypt's pride, arrogance, lack of godliness and taking credit for the Nile, a river of life in the desert. But God limited Egypt's desolation to forty years. Egypt still exists, whereas Assyria and Babylon are gone forever." I wrote in my prayer, "You decide the fate of nations. Forgive our land and our leaders. Honor the Christians who pray and act as intercessors."

In 2006, I read Ezekiel 29-31 on the same day, along with a New Testament passage from the Book of James. Concerning these chapters in Ezekiel, I wrote, "Egypt will fall and not rise as a power again. Assyria's fall was an example for Egypt. God knows in advance what nations rise and fall."

In 2016, I was in Nashville, Tennessee on a Gideon assignment when I read Ezekiel 30 and 31, and wrote, "Four chapters on the fall of Egypt, from God through Ezekiel, and Babylon, *her wealth is carried away . . . her foundations are torn down'* (30:4), *'her proud might shall come down'"* (30:6). I continued, "God speaks, *'I will put an end to the wealth of Egypt'* (30:10). *'I will destroy the idols'* (30:13). *'And I will dry up the Nile'* (30:12). *'I will execute judgments on Egypt'* (30:19). God will use Babylon to judge Egypt. 'Egypt, you think you're cool? You think you're strong and mighty? Like who?' According to 31:2, 'Like Assyria? They too were brought down and so will you.'"

Ezekiel 29-32 are a judgment on Egypt. Chapter 31 focuses on Pharaoh himself, *"Son of man, say to Pharaoh king of Egypt and to his multitude: 'Whom are you like in your greatness?'"* (v. 2). Then, God, through Ezekiel, compares Pharaoh and Egypt to Assyria. What happened to Assyria is about to happen to Egypt. What happened to Assyria? *"Because it towered high and set its top among the clouds, and its heart was proud of its height, I will give it into the hand of a mighty one of the nations. He shall surely deal with it as its wickedness deserves. I have cast it out"* (vv. 10-11).

In verse 18, Ezekiel says, *"Whom are you thus like in glory and in greatness among the trees of Eden?"* In other words, if you think you are as cool as Assyria, there is not much hope. If you think you are as good as the trees of the Garden of Eden, there is still not much

> **If you think you are as good as the trees of the Garden of Eden, there is still not much hope.**

hope. The verse continues, speaking of Egypt and Pharaoh, *"You shall be brought down with the trees of Eden to the world below. You shall lie among the uncircumcised, with those who are slain by the sword. 'This is Pharaoh and all his multitude, declares the Lord God.'"*

The might of Egypt will evaporate just like the might of Assyria. Pharaoh and Egypt will not stand. They will not be a place of refuge for Israel.

DIGGING DEEPER

What is the practical application from Ezekiel 31? Do not look to others for protection. Do not look to others for salvation. Look to the Lord. Stay faithful and true to God Almighty, not other nations, not your friends. Trust wholly in the Lord. He is enough.

Prayer

Father, we thank You for Ezekiel 31. Father, thank You for reminding us not to depend on the nations around us for our strength or for our protection. Thank You for reminding us, as Your children, not to depend on those people around us who look stronger, happier, healthier. Thank You for the reminder we are to depend on You and You alone. Reach down to us, Lord, as we reach up to You. Amen.

MY THOUGHTS

EZEKIEL 32

The Pit

I n Ezekiel 32, the judgment on Egypt continues. Pharaoh will end up in a pit along with many other enemies of God. Do you believe in the pit? Do you believe in hell? Please read or listen to Ezekiel 32.

COMMENTS

In 1997, I was forty-two years old. I read Ezekiel 32-34 on the same day and wrote nothing concerning Ezekiel 32.

In 2006, I was fifty-one years old. I read Ezekiel 32 and 33 on the same day with 1 Peter 1, as I was reading the whole Bible that year. I wrote nothing on Ezekiel 32.

In 2016, I was sixty-one years old. I read Ezekiel 32 and 33 on the same day and did write concerning Ezekiel 32. "Ezekiel knows exactly when he hears from the Lord. Time after time, in his book, he names the exact year, month, and day, referring to verses 1 and 17. Do I know when I hear from the Lord? Yes, sometimes. This year, April 1st, and August 2nd, concerning the Ezra Project." I continued to write, "God is going to destroy Egypt by the sword of Babylon. Egypt will end up in the pit with Assyria, Elam, Meshech-Tubal, Edom, princes of the north and Sidon. Hell is crowded with the enemies of Israel, the enemies of God. There is a hell."

Let's take a look at Ezekiel 32. As noted in one of my journals, Ezekiel is very specific about when he hears from the Lord. *"In the twelfth year, in the twelfth month, on the first day of the month, the word of the Lord came to me"* (v. 1). *"In the twelfth year, in the twelfth month, on the fifteenth day of the month, the word of the Lord came to me"* (v. 17). Have you ever heard from the Lord specifically? Can you mark the year, the month, the day? Do we think God only spoke to prophets of old or does He still speak to us as specifically today? I believe He does, as a couple of days were noted in my journal, concerning the Ezra Project in 2016.

> **Do we think God only spoke to prophets of old or does He still speak to us as specifically today?**

In this chapter, the first time Ezekiel heard from the Lord, he was to do a lament over Egypt. He reminds Egypt, *"You consider yourself a lion of the nations"* (v. 2), but *"I will cast you on the ground"* (v. 4). *"I will strew your flesh upon the mountains and fill the valleys with your carcass"* (v. 5). *"I will trouble the hearts of many peoples, when I bring your destruction among the nations"* (v. 9). *"I will make many peoples appalled at you, and the hair of their kings shall bristle with horror because of you"* (v. 10).

Then Ezekiel reveals very specifically how they will be destroyed. *"For thus says the Lord God: The sword of the king of Babylon shall come upon you"* (v. 11). That is a very specific prophecy. God names the very nation that will come against Egypt.

He concludes the lamentation in verse 15, *"When I make the land of Egypt desolate, and when the land is desolate of all that fills it, when I strike down all who dwell in it, then they will know that I am the Lord."*

In verses 17-18, Ezekiel again hears from the Lord and tells Egypt it will be destroyed and put down into the pit. Verse 19, *"Whom do you surpass in beauty? Go down and be laid to rest with the uncircumcised."* Verse 21, *"The mighty chiefs shall speak of them, with their helpers, out of the midst of Sheol: 'They have come down, they lie still, the uncircumcised, slain by the sword.'"* Egypt will join other nations in Sheol, the place of death. *"Assyria is there"* (v. 22). *"Elam is there"* (v. 24). *"Meshech-Tubal is there"* (v. 26). *"Edom is there"* (v. 29). *"The princes of the north are there, all of them, and all the Sidonians"* (v. 30).

The chapter ends with Pharaoh joining them there, *"When Pharaoh sees them, he will be comforted for all his multitude, Pharaoh and all his army, slain by the sword, declares the Lord God. For I spread terror in the land of the living; and he shall be laid to rest among the uncircumcised, with those who are slain by the sword, Pharaoh and all his multitude, declares the Lord God"* (vv. 31-32). Yes, Egypt will join the others in Sheol.

Starting in chapter 29 and rolling right through chapter 32, Ezekiel has proclaimed the judgment on Egypt. I mentioned in one of my journals, hell is a crowded place. All these people, enemies of Israel, are there in the pit.

DIGGING DEEPER

What is our practical application from Ezekiel 32? First, we go back to verses 1 and 17. Do you know when you hear from God? Have there been years, months, and days when you know you heard the voice of God? I believe He still speaks to us today. Listen. Hear what He might have to say to you.

Second, there is a hell, there is a pit. In Ezekiel 32, many people are described as inhabiting the pit. May we do all we can to avoid the pit. Heaven is real and so is hell. We learned that here in Ezekiel 32.

Prayer

Father, we thank You for this chapter. Thank You for the illustration You spoke specifically to Ezekiel, and You still speak to people today. May our ears be attuned to Your voice. Speak into our hearts, O Lord. Thank You for the reminder of the pit, of hell. Holy Spirit, dwell within us. Help each of us do all we can to avoid the pit.

May we live our lives according to Your Word, according to Your rules, according to Your statutes. Might we find grace at the foot of the cross. Might we walk according to Your ways. May we be pleasing in Your sight. In Jesus' name, we ask it. Amen.

MY THOUGHTS

EZEKIEL 33

Watchmen

Ezekiel 33 describes Ezekiel as the watchman for Israel. Do we have watchmen today? Is anybody warning us about our culture and pronouncing God's judgment on our society? Please read or listen to Ezekiel 33.

COMMENTS

In 1997, I read Ezekiel 32-34 (NKJV) on the same day, and wrote in my personal Bible reading journal, "We are instructed that in judgment, God appoints those to warn us. If they do not warn us, they are held accountable. If they warn us and we do not listen, we are accountable. God is fair. He warns us. We think the way of the Lord is not fair, but God is just. *'I will judge every one of you according to his own ways'* (v. 20). Personally and individually, He judges us."

Then I wrote, "When Jerusalem fell. God opened the mouth of Ezekiel. He was no longer a mute, according to verse 22. People often want to hear from God, but *'they hear your words, but they do not do them; for with their mouth they show much love, but their hearts pursue their own gain'"* (v. 31).

Nine years later, in 2006, I read Ezekiel 32 and 33 on the same day with 1 Peter 1. Concerning this chapter, I wrote, "Jerusalem has been defeated. Ezekiel hears of it and God opens his mouth. He becomes a watchman for his nation proclaiming hope to the captives."

Ten years later, in 2016, I read Ezekiel 32 and 33 on the same day, and wrote concerning chapter 33, "Ezekiel was made a watchman in 3:16-21. The watchman is responsible to deliver God's message of warning. He is not responsible for the response of the hearers. Who and where are God's watchmen today? Are they sounding the trumpet or remaining silent? God has no pleasure in the death of the wicked. He desires them, all of us, to turn back and live. Is, 'I am a good person' good enough?" I was referring to Ezekiel 33:12-20. I continued, "A powerful repudiation of being good gets one into heaven. Jerusalem falls, fulfilling all of Ezekiel's prophecies, and exiles in Babylon probably get the same news, and they gather around Ezekiel to see what he has to say next, but they are not really interested. They will not act on what they hear."

> The watchman is responsible to deliver God's message of warning. He is not responsible for the response of the hearers.

Let's go back to one of the references I made in one of those journals, that Ezekiel was made a watchman in 3:16-21. As we turn there, verses 16-17 say, *"And at the end of seven days, the word of the Lord came to me: 'Son of man, I have made you a watchman for the house of Israel'."* The verse goes on to explain the role of the watchman, *"Whenever you hear a word from my mouth, you shall give them warning from me"* (v. 17).

To paraphrase the rest of these verses, the watchman's role is to give the warning. For example, if a warning is given to the wicked, but Ezekiel does not deliver the warning, the blood is on Ezekiel's head. But if he warns the wicked and the wicked ignore his warning, the blood is on their own head. The same is for a righteous man. If Ezekiel does not warn him, then the blood of the righteous man is on Ezekiel's head. But if he does warn the righteous man and the righteous man ignores Ezekiel, his blood is on his own head.

Here in chapter 33, the role of the watchman is described again, *"and if he sees the sword coming upon the land and blows the trumpet and warns the people, then if anyone who hears the sound of the trumpet does not take warning, and the sword comes and takes him away, his blood shall be upon his own head"* (vv. 3-4). Down to verse 6, *"But if the watchman sees the sword coming and does not blow the trumpet, so that the people are not warned, and the sword comes and takes any one of them, that person is taken away in his iniquity, but his blood I will require at the watchman's hand.*"

I questioned in one of my journals, are there watchmen today? Are they blowing the trumpet, or are they remaining silent? I do not know the answer to that question. I do not really see or hear Christians being watchmen, warning our nation or any other nation what is going on. I wonder if there will be pastors or priests held accountable by God because they were appointed watchmen, but they did not warn the people. Or, is it more like the end of this chapter:

> *"As for you, son of man, your people who talk together about you by the walls and at the doors of the houses, say to one another, each to his brother, 'Come, and hear what the word is that comes from the Lord.' And they come to you as people come, and they sit before you as my people, and they hear what you say but they will not do it; for with lustful talk in their mouths they act; their heart is set on their gain. And behold, you are to them like one who sings lustful songs with a beautiful voice and plays well on an instrument, for they hear what you say, but they will not do it. When this comes—and come it will!—then they will know that a prophet has been among them"* (vv. 30-33).

In his day, Ezekiel was a watchman. He cried out warning after warning, and the people did not listen. Today, Lord, have You appointed watchmen? Are they warning us? Are we not listening?

DIGGING DEEPER

Our practical applications are pretty easy. First, the Word of God is a watchman. It provides the warnings. Stay close to the Word. Understand the warnings of God. Second, attend a church where the Bible is preached and taught to be warned about what is happening in our culture, in our society. Third, heed the warnings we know. May we be on the alert for warnings from God.

Prayer

Father, give us ears to hear, give us eyes to see what You are doing all around us. We ask it, in the name of Jesus. Amen.

MY THOUGHTS

God Provides a Good Shepherd

I n Ezekiel 34, we will see a prophecy against the shepherds of Israel. He is not pleased with them, so He provides a good shepherd. Do you know who it is? Please read or listen to Ezekiel 34.

COMMENTS

In 1997, I read Ezekiel 32-34 on the same day and concerning this chapter, wrote, "Chapter 34 is beautiful. God judges the shepherds, pastors who aren't feeding His sheep. Then He declares He will be our Shepherd. He will feed His flock."

In 2006, I read Ezekiel 34 and 35 on the same day with 1 Peter 2. Concerning chapter 34 (NASB), I wrote, "'*Woe, shepherds of Israel who have been feeding themselves! Should not the shepherds feed the flock? You eat the fat and clothe yourselves with the wool, you slaughter the fat sheep without feeding the flock*' (vv. 2-3). God takes away the sheep from the shepherds and provides a good shepherd for them. Jesus is the Good Shepherd."

> Shepherds, leaders, rulers, feed themselves not the sheep or their people.

In 2016, I read Ezekiel 34 and 35 again on the same day, and wrote concerning chapter 34, "Shepherds, leaders, rulers, feed themselves not the sheep or their people.

This is true throughout history and today. Government leaders in many countries are well off while the people are not. Sometimes also true in the church. Again, God has had enough. He comes against the shepherds. He intervenes and becomes the Shepherd. And He is the Good Shepherd. God refers to David as His servant and a good shepherd. And of the line of David, Jesus the Lamb, and the Shepherd. Again, God promises restoration of the people in exile with the consistent purpose that we know Him."

DIGGING DEEPER

Let's take a look at Ezekiel 34. First, God comes down pretty hard on the shepherds:

Thus says the Lord God: Ah, shepherds of Israel who have been feeding yourselves! Should not shepherds feed the sheep? You eat the fat, you clothe yourselves with the wool, you slaughter the fat ones, but you do not feed the sheep. The weak you have not strengthened, the sick you have not healed, the injured you have not bound up, the strayed you have not brought back, the lost you have not sought, and with force and harshness you have ruled them (vv. 2-4).

The shepherds referred to here are the leaders of Israel. I mentioned in my journal, we have many government leaders like this today that are feeding themselves and not feeding their sheep. I have been to many countries where I saw government palaces and peasant neighborhoods.

God has enough, *"For thus says the Lord God: Behold, I, I myself will search for my sheep and will seek them out"* (v. 11). Thank You, Jesus. Thank You. Thank You that You love Your sheep, us, and You seek us out.

He later says, *"I will feed them with good pasture . . . There they shall lie down in good grazing land . . . I myself will be the shepherd of my sheep"* (vv. 14-15). Once again, thank You, Jesus. Verse 16 goes on to say, *"I will seek the lost, and I will bring back the strayed, and I will bind up the injured, and I will strengthen the weak."* O, Hallelujah! Yes, Jesus does all those things.

In verse 25, the Word continues, *"I will make with them a covenant of peace."* These sheep will once again be protected. They will be secure in the Promised Land once again. Verses 27-28 say, *"And they shall know that I am the Lord, when I break the bars of their yoke, and deliver them from the hand of those who enslaved them. . . . They shall dwell securely, and none shall make them afraid."* The chapter closes with, *"And they shall know that I am the Lord their God with them, and that they, the house of Israel, are my people, declares the Lord God. And you are my sheep, human sheep of my pasture, and I am your God, declares the Lord God"* (vv. 30-31).

As I said in my journal, Ezekiel 34 is a beautiful chapter. Praise God, He is our Shepherd. Praise God, He will feed us, His sheep. Praise God, He will seek the lost. He will bring back the strays. He will bind up the injured. He will strengthen the weak.

Prayer

Thank You for being our Shepherd. Jesus, thank You for being the Good Shepherd. Thank You for declaring here in this chapter, *"I am your God"* (v. 31). We bless You. We worship You. We praise You. Amen.

MY THOUGHTS

EZEKIEL 35

You Are Always Here, and You Always Hear

E zekiel 35 is a prophecy against Mount Seir. God reminds us in this chapter, He is always here, and He always hears. Do you realize "always" means always? Please read or listen to Ezekiel 35.

COMMENTS

In 1997, when I was forty-two years old, I read Ezekiel 35-37 on the same day. I made no notes concerning this chapter.

Nine years later, in 2006, at fifty-one years old, I read Ezekiel 34 and 35 on the same day and made no notes concerning chapter 35.

Ten years later, in 2016, at sixty-one years old, I read Ezekiel 34 and 35 on the same day. I do have notes concerning chapter 35, "Mount Seir, Edom, God is against because they did not support Israel. As Edom tried to take possession of Israel and Judah, the Lord was there. And as they magnified themselves against the Lord, He heard it. God is here, and He sees and hears His enemies. He acts, so once again, You *'will know that I am the Lord'* (v. 15). God wants to be known. He wants to be recognized. He wants to be worshiped."

Let's take a look at Ezekiel 35. As one of my journals indicates, Mount Seir is identified with Edom. An oracle against Edom already appeared in Ezekiel 25. Ten chapters later, God declares He is against Edom, or Mount Seir, once again. What was the charge against them? *"Because you cherished perpetual enmity and gave over the people of Israel to the power of the sword at the time of their calamity, at the time of their final punishment"* (v. 5). Here is another indication of a nation that was against Israel.

> God wants to be known. He wants to be recognized. He wants to be worshiped.

Verse 7 describes the punishment for Mount Seir, *"I will make Mount Seir a waste and a desolation, and I will cut off from it all who come and go."* I do not know any Edomites today, do you?

For the fun of it, I asked my smartphone, Siri, about Edom. Here is what she came up with, "Edom was an ancient kingdom in Transjordan located between Moab to the northeast, the Arabah to the west, and the Arabian Desert to the south and east. Most of its former territory is now divided between Israel and Jordan." Notice the words, "ancient kingdom" and "its former territory." Ezekiel 35:9 says, *"I will make you a perpetual desolation, and your cities shall not be inhabited. Then you will know that I am the Lord."* It is pretty clear this prophecy has come true.

In verse 10, we see Edom tried to capture both Israel and Judah. The verse says, *"Because you said, 'These two nations and these two countries shall be mine, and we will take possession of them'—although the Lord was there—."* So God declares Himself that He was present in Israel and Judah at that time. Not only did they try to take the Promised Land, they reviled with language against God's people, *"I have heard all the revilings that you uttered against the mountains of Israel, saying, 'They are laid desolate; they are given us to devour.' And you magnified yourselves against me with your mouth, and multiplied your words against me; I heard it"* (vv. 12-13).

DIGGING DEEPER

Let's get to some practical applications as we conclude Ezekiel 35. First, the Lord was there. Second of all, *"I heard it"* (v. 13). Do you realize God is here? Do you realize God is there? Wherever you are, God is. You cannot hide from the presence of God.

Second, do you realize, *"I heard it"* (v. 13), God hears? There is nothing you can say, or nothing you can think that God does not hear. So how is your behavior when you think God is not there? How is your language when you think God is not listening?

Ezekiel 35, about some obscure mountain called Mount Seir, has some pretty interesting applications for us today. God is here and He hears. Maybe those realizations will help us act and speak a bit more Christ-like.

Prayer

Father, thank You for the challenges, even from books like Ezekiel and chapter 35. Thank You for reminding us You are always here, and You always hear. When we realize You are always here, and You always hear, might we also be reminded in this book, seventy-three times you said, *"That they will know that I am the Lord."* Thank You for reminding us of that as well in this chapter, You are the Lord. That is why You are always here, and You always hear. We thank You that You are the Lord. Amen.

MY THOUGHTS

EZEKIEL 36

Clean Water and New Hearts!

Today, we are in Ezekiel 36. In the last several chapters, there were prophecies against the nations around Israel. Now Ezekiel focuses on the nation of Israel itself. God removes hearts of stone and transplants them with hearts of flesh. Do you need a heart transplant? Please read or listen to Ezekiel 36.

COMMENTS

Due to the length of this great chapter, I will only share my journal entries. We begin in 1997 when I read Ezekiel 35-37 (NKJV) on the same day. Concerning this chapter, I wrote, "God will restore Israel. Those He scattered would come back to the land. *'I do not do this for your sake, O house of Israel, but for My holy name's sake'* (v. 22). God promises cleansing, a new heart, a new Spirit within us. He promised Israel would never suffer famine again."

In 2006, I read chapters 36 and 37 (NASB) on the same day, and wrote, "Two great chapters. God promises Israel will return to its land, be restored, grow and multiply again. They will be treated *'better than at first'* (v. 11). God will do it, *'not for your sake, O house of Israel, that I am about to act, but for My holy name'* (v. 22). He will give them a new heart and put a new Spirit within them."

In 2016, I read Ezekiel 36 on one day, and wrote, "In the bleak prophecy of Ezekiel, comes hope, restoration. God makes clear He is speaking. *'Thus says the Lord,'* *'hear the word of the Lord,' 'I have spoken,'* appear ten times in the first seven verses. The land, mountains of Israel, will be inhabited by Jews again and it shall bear fruit. Verse 9 says, *'I am for you'*. Israel defiled the land. God acts justly by removing them. So, it is not because of them the land is restored, it is *'for the sake of my holy name'* (v. 22). God gathers them from the nations and brings them back to Israel. God cleanses them. God gives them a new heart and a new Spirit to obey Him once again.

"It's God!" I wrote. *"'It is not for your sake that I will act, declares the Lord God; let that be known to you'* (v. 32). It is for His namesake, His glory, so that the nations that are left all around you shall know that I am the Lord. *'I have rebuilt the ruined places and replanted that which was desolate. I am the Lord; I have spoken, and I will do it'"* (v. 36). Part of my prayer that day was, "Thanks for hope, for restoration. The nation of Israel exists today as a testimony to Your glory. We get no credit for anything. It's all You, for Your namesake, Your glory."

DIGGING DEEPER

Praise God for chapters like Ezekiel 36, for phrases from the Lord Himself like:

- *I am for you* (v. 9).
- *I . . . will do more good to you than ever before. Then you will know that I am the Lord* (v. 11).
- *And I will vindicate the holiness of my great name* (v. 23).
- *I will sprinkle clean water on you, and you shall be clean from all your uncleannesses* (v. 25).
- *I will give you a new heart, and a new spirit I will put within you* (v. 26).

> God is a God of judgment, but He is also a God of restoration. He is the God of the second chance.

Praise the Lord for the hope of Ezekiel 36. God is a God of judgment, but He is also a God of restoration. He is the God of the second chance.

Do you need encouragement? Do you need a second chance? Let Him sprinkle clean water on you today!

Prayer

Father, we glorify Your name. We thank You these words have all come true. Israel exists today on the land You gave it. We thank You that You have given us a new heart. You can remove our heart of stone and replace it with a heart of flesh. You put Your Spirit within us. Wow. Thank You. Cause us to walk in Your statutes and obey Your rules. May the people around us know You are the Lord because Your Spirit is within us. We give You the praise and all the glory. In Your name, amen.

MY THOUGHTS

EZEKIEL 37

The Valley of Dry Bones

Today brings us to one of the most famous chapters in the Book of Ezekiel, the chapter on the valley of dry bones, Ezekiel 37. Are you spiritually dry? Do your spiritual bones need rattling? Please read or listen to Ezekiel 37.

COMMENTS

In 1997, at forty-two years old, I read Ezekiel 35-37 on the same day. Concerning chapter 37, I wrote, "Vision of dry bones coming to life express hope of chapter 36. God can breathe new life into people, nations, situations that appear very dead without hope. God can rattle dry bones. Judah and Israel would also be united in one kingdom again. These prophesies have come to pass. Israel was regathered back to its land and it is no longer a divided kingdom, but one. Praise God He protects His people and His land."

> **God can rattle dry bones.**

In 2006, at fifty-one years old, I read Ezekiel 36 and 37 on the same day. Concerning this chapter, I wrote, "And the valley of dry bones comes alive!"

And in 2016, at sixty-one years old, I read Ezekiel 37 and 38 on the same day. Concerning this chapter, I wrote, "The vision of the valley of dry bones. May the hand of the Lord be upon me and the Spirit of the Lord in me, referring to verse 1. Will Israel live again? Yes! God will raise them up again. To a people in exile to Babylon, this provided great hope. More hope: Judah and Israel, divided since after Solomon, will be reunited by God." I continued to write, "No more defilement, idol worship, backsliding. *'I . . . will cleanse them; and they shall be my people, and I will be their God'* (v. 23). They will live in peace. Finally! The sanctuary, or the temple, will be restored. Hope for Israel after the fall of Jerusalem."

DIGGING DEEPER

Let's take a look at Ezekiel 37. God offers Ezekiel the vision of dry bones. Can these bones come alive? Of course, and they do. Chapter 37 is the continuation of the hope we saw in Ezekiel 36. It is also our hope. Our dry bones can live. How? Verse 14, *"And I will put my Spirit within you, and you shall live."* Thank You, Jesus, for putting Your Spirit in us.

The next part of the chapter is the illustration of the two sticks that are combined once again. Verse 19, *"Behold, I am about to take the stick of Joseph (that is in the hand of Ephraim) and the tribes of Israel associated with him. And I will join with it the stick of Judah, and make them one stick."* What hope for the nation of Israel again. Remember, Ezekiel is in Babylon and he is seeing these things. He must have become really excited about these visions he shares in chapter 37.

Verse 22 continues the excitement, *"And I will make them one nation in the land . . . they shall be no longer two nations, and no longer divided into two kingdoms."* Hallelujah for the hope of Israel. The promise continues in verse 25, *"They and their children and their children's children shall dwell there forever."* This prophecy has come true. Today, Israel still exists on its land.

Ezekiel probably got really excited about verse 26, *"I will make a covenant of peace with them. It shall be an everlasting covenant with them."* Remember, when Ezekiel's seeing this, Babylon is destroying his country. How has the covenant of peace worked out? Israel has had many, many, many conflicts in its history. But God preserves it.

Verse 26 concludes with this phrase, *"And I will set them in their land and multiply them, and will set my sanctuary in their midst forever."* Yes, the temple has been destroyed, but God's sanctuary, His presence, is still in the land of Israel today. Terry and I have been there. We sensed the presence of God. There is no place like Israel on the face of the earth.

These words in Ezekiel, written centuries ago, have come to pass. We see the prophecies fulfilled in our lifetime. To God be the glory.

Prayer

Father, we thank You for the rattling of our own dry bones as You put life in us. Thank You for the promise You put Your Spirit within us. Thank You for the prophecy fulfilled, that Israel still inhabits the land as one nation today. Thank You that Your presence still exists in Israel.

Lord, we are amazed as we read Your Word that we see these words alive in our world today. I pray, Lord, as people read Ezekiel 37, their own valley of dry bones will rattle with life, the life You alone can give. Breathe in us, Lord, Your Spirit. May we live, stand on our feet, as an exceedingly great army for You. Hallelujah, amen.

MY THOUGHTS

Gog and Magog

E zekiel 38 is the prophecy against Gog. Who, or what, are Gog and Magog? Please read or listen to Ezekiel 38.

COMMENTS

In 1997, the day I read Ezekiel 38 and 39 was Thanksgiving. I am going to share a little bit about my journal entry from Thanksgiving, 1997. I wrote, "We are in Colorado Springs for Thanksgiving. One of my favorite holidays. It is a feast to remember all we can be thankful for. It is not commercialized yet. A day of families gathering together to celebrate blessings. I have much to be thankful for."

On Thanksgiving Day 1997, I read Ezekiel 38 and 39 (NKJV) and wrote in my journal, "God will intervene for Israel when nations come to destroy it. He will show Himself by using natural disasters to protect Israel so *they shall know that I am the Lord*" (v. 23). I continued, "I don't want to see, *'My fury will show in My face'* (v. 18). But His victory will be complete, and all nations will see His judgment and glory."

In 2016, I read Ezekiel 37 and 38 on the same day, and wrote concerning chapter 38, "God is against Gog and Magog, whoever/whatever country it is. It will not prevail against Israel. In the later years, they will come against Israel with evil schemes, but it will not prevail. Though God brings them against My land, *'I vindicate my holiness before their eyes'* (v. 16). Gog will be defeated by a great earthquake, and rain and hailstones, fire and sulfur, pestilence and bloodshed, all to make God known."

Let's take a look at this chapter. The first question is, who is Gog and Magog? Here, I turn to my English Standard Version Study Bible footnotes, "These two names have been the focus of extensive investigation and speculation in both Jewish and Christian literature, but there is no consensus on their meaning" (p. 1561). The footnote contains lots of speculations about what these things mean, but again, without consensus. The footnote ends with, "'Gog' and 'Magog' remain enigmatic, perhaps because the intention of the prophecy is simply to point to a yet-unknown future leader of a great attack against God's people, one whose identity will not be known until the prophecy is fulfilled" (p. 1561). Interestingly, Gog and Magog are the names of the nations led by Satan to attack Jerusalem at the end of the thousand years, according to Revelation 20:8.

DIGGING DEEPER

In much of my Christian life, Gog and Magog have been referred to as Russia. However, according to the footnotes, that is problematic. Whoever it is, whenever it happens, God is against it. The king, the leader, the nation, will not prevail against Israel.

Verse 8 declares, *"In the latter years you will go against the land that is restored from war, the land whose people were gathered from many peoples upon the mountains of Israel."* Chapter 38 follows chapter 37, the restoration of Israel, remember, the dry bones coming back to life. This nation, this Gog and Magog, will attack restored Israel. But again, it will not prevail.

Let's focus on verse 10 for a moment, *"Thus says the Lord God: On that day, thoughts will come into your mind, and you will devise an evil scheme."* Does that ever happen to you? Do thoughts come into your mind? Do you devise evil schemes? All too often, it happens to me. Thoughts come into my mind, and I have no idea where they come from. Those thoughts, oftentimes, drag me down into "what-ifs" and "maybes" that will probably never happen! But God recognizes thoughts like these do come into our minds.

This event will happen, *"You will come up against my people Israel, like a cloud covering the land. In the latter days I will bring you against my land, that the nations may know me, when through you, O Gog, I vindicate my holiness before their eyes"* (v. 16). It is all under the sovereignty of God.

> Lest we forget, God has natural weapons we do not have at our disposal.

The only purpose for Gog and Magog is to glorify God among other nations. How will this enemy of Israel be defeated? Verse 19, *"On that day there shall be a great earthquake in the land of Israel."* Verses 21 and 22, *"I will summon a sword against Gog on all my mountains, declares the Lord God. With pestilence and bloodshed I will enter into judgment with him, and I will rain upon him and his hordes and the many peoples who are with him torrential rains and hailstones, fire and sulfur."* Lest we forget, God has natural weapons we do not have at our disposal.

The chapter concludes with, *"So I will show my greatness and my holiness and make myself known in the eyes of many nations. Then they will know that I am the Lord."* Earlier in one of the devotions, I mentioned the phrase, *"That they may know that I am the Lord,"* appears seventy times in the Book of Ezekiel.

Here, in Ezekiel 38, God is going to use Gog and Magog to make Himself known. The Prophecy against Gog and Magog continues in the next chapter. Until then, let's remember God is sovereign. He orchestrates the activities of the world, oftentimes, around His Promised Land, the land of Israel.

He has at His disposal natural weapons: hail, rain, fire, and pestilence. When we see these things going on around our world today, do we look up to heaven? Do we wonder if God is trying to show His greatness and His holiness and make Himself known in the eyes of our nations? May it be so that we will know He is the Lord.

Prayer

Father, whether it is nation against nation or natural disasters, might we look up and know You are a sovereign God, You are in control. May we surrender to Your greatness and Your holiness. Thank You for the reminder in Ezekiel 38, You are the Lord. Blessed be Your name, amen.

MY THOUGHTS

EZEKIEL 39

The Lord Will Restore

E zekiel 39 is the continuation of Ezekiel 38 on the prophecy against Gog and Magog. He brings them against His own nation! They will eventually be defeated and Israel restored. Is God bringing someone, or something, against you to restore you? Please read or listen to Ezekiel 39.

COMMENTS

In 1997, I read Ezekiel 38 and 39 on the same day. Most of my notes were concerning chapter 38, but I have one line on chapter 39, "His victory will be complete and all nations will see His judgment and glory."

Nine years later, in 2006, I was reading the whole Bible, so I was reading Old Testament and New Testament passages each day. On this day, I read Ezekiel 38 and 39, and 1 Peter 4 (NASB). Concerning chapter 39, I wrote, "God will prevail *'and all the nations will see My judgment . . . And the house of Israel will know that I am the Lord their God from that day onward'"* (vv. 21-22).

Ten years later, in 2016, I was reading various books of the Bible, so I had a slower pace. On this day, I read Ezekiel 39 and wrote, "God orchestrates the attack on Israel, but the attacker, Gog, will fall to Israel. God appears to fight and win the battle, not Israel. That's why God gets the glory. Has this battle happened yet? If it is yet to come, it sounds like a nuclear war. So many bodies everywhere. It takes seven months to bury them to cleanse the land. Why will all this happen? Israel *'dealt so treacherously with me that I hid my face from them and gave them into the hand of their adversaries'* (v. 23). *'I will restore the fortunes of Jacob and have mercy on the whole house of Israel'* (v. 25). By doing all this, God gets the glory. Nations and *'Israel will know that I am the Lord their God'* (v. 22). He wants to be known."

Chapter 39 is a continuation of chapter 38, the prophecies against Gog and Magog. It is amazing God is making all this happen. Let's look at verse 2, *"And I will turn you about and drive you forward, and bring you up from the uttermost parts of the north, and lead you against the mountains of Israel."* So God is leading Gog and Magog against His own nation.

> **So God is leading Gog and Magog against His own nation.**

Verse 4, *"You shall fall on the mountains of Israel, you and all your hordes and the peoples who are with you."* However, they are not going to prevail, *"And my holy name I will make known in the midst of my people Israel, and I will not let my holy name be profaned anymore. And the nations shall know that I am the Lord, the Holy One in Israel. Behold, it is coming and it will be brought about, declares the Lord God. That is the day of which I have spoken"* (vv. 7-8).

God will bring Gog and Magog against Israel to show His glory, *"And I will set my glory among the nations, and all the nations shall see my judgment that I have executed, and my hand that I have laid on them. The house of Israel shall know that I am the Lord their God, from that day forward"* (vv. 21-22).

DIGGING DEEPER

In my journals, I asked the question, 'Why is all this happening?' God explains, *"And the nations shall know that the house of Israel went into captivity for their iniquity, because they dealt so treacherously with me that I hid my face from them and gave them into the hand of their adversaries, and they all fell by the sword. I dealt with them according to their uncleanness and their transgressions, and hid my face from them"* (vv. 23-24).

The problem in Israel was iniquity, treacherous behavior, uncleanliness, and transgressions against God. But God's mercy prevails once again, *"Now I will restore the fortunes of Jacob and have mercy on the whole house of Israel . . . They shall forget their shame and all the treachery they have practiced against me"* (vv. 25-26). *"Then they shall know that I am the Lord their God, because I sent them into exile among the nations and then assembled them into their own land . . . I pour out my Spirit upon the house of Israel, declares the Lord God"* (vv. 28-29).

It is amazing. God brings a nation against Israel. This is going to be a brutal battle. It will take seven months to bury the dead. But God will prevail, and He will restore the fortunes of Israel.

Throughout the Book of Ezekiel, we are learning God is in control. He is in control of the nation of Israel. He is also in control of each of our lives. We are reminded He loved Israel enough to punish them. He loves us the same way, too. He may punish, but He also restores.

Prayer

Father, thank You for Your mercy, Your love, Your grace on display in the Book of Ezekiel. May we gain confidence from this book. It is the same for us; You love us, You have mercy on us, and You extend grace to us. You will punish, but You will also restore. Thank You. In the name of Jesus, amen.

MY THOUGHTS

EZEKIEL 40

A New Temple

The next four chapters, Ezekiel 40-43, are all about the restoration of the temple. What great hope for the nation of Israel. Is your life in ruins? Do you need to be restored? Please read or listen to Ezekiel 40.

COMMENTS

> God is specific, not general. He is a God of detail.

In 1997, after reading Ezekiel 40 (NKJV), I wrote, "*'He took me there'* (v. 1). Ezekiel gets a preview of a new future temple. God is specific, not general. He is a God of detail; therefore, He knows every measurement, every detail of my life."

In 2006, after reading Ezekiel 40, I wrote, "Ezekiel saw visions from God and wrote them down. The temple was never built according to Bible notes but would give people in captivity hope that a temple would be built in Jerusalem again."

In 2016, after reading Ezekiel 40, I wrote, "Fourteen years after the destruction of Jerusalem, Ezekiel, still in exile in Babylon, was shown God's restoration. He sees the new temple in detail escorted around by a heavenly being, *'look with your eyes, and hear with your ears, and set your heart upon all that I shall show you'*" (v. 4).

Then I wrote a question, "Why is there provision for animal sacrifices in the new temple?"

Chapter 40 is a vision of a new temple, fourteen years after the destruction of Jerusalem. This is Ezekiel's second vision of a temple. The first occurred earlier in the book in chapters 8-11. In reference to these two tours of the temple, I refer to my English Standard Version Study Bible footnote, "The vision of chapters 40-48 is a direct counterpart to the pre-destruction vision in chapters 8-11, in which the abominations practiced in Jerusalem drove the holy God from his temple. In chs. 40-42, Ezekiel is again taken on a tour, this time of the new temple, which culminates with the return of the glory of God" (p. 1564).

In my English Standard Version Study Bible, I have a two-page spread of this temple diagrammed. The next few chapters will describe aspects of this new temple, culminating in the glory of the Lord returning to the temple.

DIGGING DEEPER

As we close this chapter, I am reminded Ezekiel is not in Israel. He is not anywhere near Jerusalem. He is in Babylon. In verses 1-2, he says, *"the hand of the Lord was upon me, and he brought me to the city. In visions of God he brought me to the land of Israel, and set me down on a very high mountain, on which was a structure like a city to the south."* How would you like to be transported by God to see visions like Ezekiel saw? How cool would that be?

Prayer

Father, thank You for letting Ezekiel peer into the future. Thank You for the prophets of old. Thank You that You instructed them to record what You showed them and now centuries later, we get to see what they saw. Lord, we know there will be a new temple. We know there will be a New Jerusalem. And we know You are a promise keeper, so we look forward to the day when we see the temple in the New Jerusalem. We know it will be filled with Your glory. Hallelujah! Amen.

MY THOUGHTS

EZEKIEL 41

A Tour of the New Temple

Ezekiel 41 is the second chapter of Ezekiel's vision of the new temple in Jerusalem. The Lord gives Ezekiel a tour. He reminds us how precise, how exact, how intentional He is with not only His temple, but creation, and each of us. Do you see intent and order around you? Please read or listen to Ezekiel 41.

COMMENTS

In 1997, I read Ezekiel 41 and 42 on the same day, and wrote, "More measurements of the temple."

In 2006, while reading the whole Bible that year, I read Ezekiel 41 and 42 along with 2 Peter 1. Concerning Ezekiel, I wrote, "More measurements of the temple. God has a holy place. We need to go to Him with honor, worship, and respect."

In 2016, I read Ezekiel 41 and 42 on the same day. Concerning chapter 41, I wrote, "God shows Ezekiel His temple. It's like when we moved into our house about five years ago. Everyone got a tour. We showed them all the rooms. God is showing Ezekiel all the rooms of His house. However, Ezekiel doesn't enter the most holy place, according to verses 3-4. It appears he only looks in. There are places that are most holy. We need to honor and respect God as most holy. Not a buddy; not 'Yo,

God'; not 'When I get to heaven I got a few questions for God.' No, honor and respect."

> **We need to honor and respect God as most holy. Not a buddy; not "Yo, God"; not "When I get to heaven I got a few questions for God." No, honor and respect.**

As we look into Ezekiel 41, let's go back to the 'he' described in the opening verses. The 'he' is described in chapter 40. We start with verse 1, *"the hand of the Lord was upon me, and he brought me to the city."* Jump down to verse 3, *"When he brought me there, behold, there was a man whose appearance was like bronze, with a linen cord and a measuring reed in his hand."*

The Lord is the "he" in chapter 41. This "he" is giving Ezekiel a tour of the temple. According to my English Standard Version Study Bible footnote:

> The temple structure is now described in detail, including both floor plan and elevations. The **nave** (v. 1) is the main hall of the temple. Ezekiel is guided into its interior but does not follow his celestial guide into the **Most Holy Place** (v. 4). This might have been the climax of the tour, but it continues. Verses 5-11 describe the three-story structure built into the temple's walls. A building is located to the extreme west of the temple complex (v.12), but no purpose is identified for it. . . . The **cherubim**, carved on the walls in relief (w. 18-20), are reminiscent of the cherubim woven into the fabric walls of the tabernacle (Ex. 26:1, 3). The cherubim and palm trees are combined in the decoration of Solomon's temple (1 Kings 6:29-32) (page 1568).

Here in chapter 41, we are getting a tour of the inside of the temple. It is amazing to me the detail God provides in scripture. Exact measurements, exact materials. As I read through the scriptures over and over, I realize God is a God of detail. He is also a God of purpose and a God of specific direction.

As we look at creation around us, we see these characteristics of God. Things are not random. God designed earth. He designed the universe with the same kind of detail we read about here in Ezekiel 41. I am not a scientist, but you can see God's specific design and how scientists try to figure it out. Just like in this temple, there are precise measurements in creation between the sun and the earth or the speed the earth rotates or the path it takes around the sun. All these are so precise if they get out of kilter, the earth would be consumed and all of us on it. Do we really believe this all happened by chance?

DIGGING DEEPER

That is the reminder from Ezekiel 41. It is the application. Our God is a designer. He not only designed a beautiful temple, He designed a beautiful place for us to inhabit here on earth. As you stroll through your day, observe, take in God's precise, exact, orderly creation, and give Him praise.

Prayer

Thank You. Praise God from whom all blessings flow. Praise Him all creatures here below. Praise Him above ye heavenly host. Praise Father, Son, and Holy Ghost. Amen.

MY THOUGHTS

EZEKIEL 42

The Difference Between Holy and Common

E zekiel 42 is a continuation of a tour of the temple as Ezekiel saw it. Do you consider your church a holy place? Are there only common things in your life, or are certain things or places holy? Please read or listen to Ezekiel 42.

COMMENTS

In 1997, I read Ezekiel 41 and 42 on the same day, and just wrote one line, "More measurements of the temple." I also made an interesting note, "Nehemiah 8:1-12, my theme passage for the Ezra Project." Friends, I wrote that in 1997. The Ezra Project did not start until 2002. That is five years after I wrote about a theme passage in 1997. It is amazing God was laying on my heart the ministry of the Ezra Project in the mid-'90s though He did not lead me to start it until 2002!

I think we see in Ezekiel, in these chapters on the temple, God is a planner, He is a designer. Here, in my mind, He was beginning His plans for this thing called the Ezra Project. I do not know these notes are in these journals. I do not go back and look at them until I do devotions like today. So, I too get amazed at what God has done and is doing in my own life as I look at my own journals.

Nine years later, in 2006, I also read Ezekiel 41 and 42 on the same day. I shared this journal entry yesterday but will share it again because it is all I wrote concerning these two chapters, "More measurements of the temple. God has a holy place. We need to go to Him with honor, worship, and respect."

As we ponder what I wrote there, the question is, do we? Do you go to your house of worship with the thought in mind of honor, worship, and respect? In so many churches, we take a casual approach to God. I remember going to speak in one church and asking the pastor what he wore in the pulpit. He said, "We give God our best." That did not mean everybody wore a suit and tie, but they wore their best. Some had a nice pair of pants and a shirt. That was their best. But there is a difference between giving God our best and going to church in shorts, flip flops, torn jeans, or baseball hats.

> Houses of worship ought to be treated as holy places.

I am certainly not telling you how to dress when you go to church, but I am trying to remind us what God is reminding us of in Ezekiel 42. There is a holy place. Houses of worship ought to be treated as holy places. We should go there with honor and respect. That is a practical application from a chapter like this.

Ten years later in 2016, I also read Ezekiel 41 and 42 on the same day. Concerning 42, I wrote, "Even the priests that entered into the holy place left their garments and put on common clothes to go back to the people. Maybe it's still okay to dress up to go to church."

DIGGING DEEPER

You can see, out of all three journals in different decades of my life, the aspect of honor and respect is what I got out of Ezekiel 42. In the chapter, Ezekiel is getting a tour of the outer court of the temple. There was a difference between what went on in the outer court and what went on inside the temple, especially the holy place. Let's look at verse 14, *"When the priests enter the Holy Place, they shall not go out of it into the outer court without laying there the garments in which they minister, for these are holy. They shall put on other garments before they go near to that which is for the people."*

There is a difference between the outer court and the holy place in the temple. There ought to be a difference like that in our lives between the commonplaces of our lives, our homes, our work, our shopping centers, and our houses of worship.

The last verse in this chapter reminds us of the difference between the holy and the common, *"to make a separation between the holy and the common"* (v. 20). He was talking about a wall between the inside of the temple and the outer court. A separation, again, *"between the holy and the common"* (v. 20).

What do you consider common in your life? What do you consider holy, if anything? I want to go to my house of worship with an attitude of honor and respect. Not for the building, but for the God I am going to worship. May we all be challenged by Ezekiel 42 and the difference *"between the holy and the common"* (v. 20).

Prayer

Father, thank You for insights from chapters like Ezekiel 42. Thank You for reminding us that to You there may be a difference *"between the holy and the common"* (v. 20). Holy Spirit, reveal in our own hearts what is holy to us and what is common. Are there sanctuaries in our own lives we can honor and respect a little more than everything else in our everyday lives?

When we come to You, whether it is in our house or whether it is in a house of worship, may we come with honor and respect. May we treat You holy. Thank You for reminding us in this chapter You are holy, and You want us to be holy. In Jesus' name, amen.

MY THOUGHTS

EZEKIEL 43

God's Glory Fills the Temple Again

Ezekiel 43 is the fourth and final chapter of Ezekiel's tour of the new temple. Today, we see the glory of the Lord return to fill the temple. Have you been away? Do you need the glory of God in your life again? There is hope. Please read or listen to Ezekiel 43.

COMMENTS

What a beautiful picture as Ezekiel sees the glory of the Lord enter the temple. Aren't you glad he recorded it in Ezekiel 43? Let's see how this chapter impacted me in various stages of my life.

In 1997, I read Ezekiel 43 and 44 (NKJV) on the same day and wrote, "The glory of the Lord comes back to Israel and enters the temple again. Ezekiel, *'fell on my face'* (v. 3). Everyone who ever sees God's glory falls on their face. It must be so awesome. There is no other response. God is willing to dwell with us if we don't defile His name, worship idols, and are ashamed of our iniquities. We need to understand and desire holiness."

In another decade of my life, in the 2000s, I read Ezekiel 43 and 44 on the same day and wrote, "Ezekiel fell on his face when he saw the glory of the Lord. We shall do likewise. The glory of God returns to the temple in Ezekiel's vision."

And in a third decade of my life, the 2000-teens, I also read Ezekiel 43 and 44 on the same day, and wrote, "For a third time Ezekiel sees the glory of God. In chapter 1, he sees the glory leave. In chapters 8-11, he sees a vision of the glory of God. Now he sees the glory return to the temple in chapter 43. Can I imagine seeing the glory of God? No. However, my response would be the same, to fall on my face." I continued, "God, not Ezekiel's guide, declares, *'this is the place of my throne and the place of the soles of my feet, where I will dwell in the midst of the people of Israel forever'* (v. 7). God Himself says, Jerusalem and the temple are His dwelling place here on earth. He, God Himself, then describes it. He is a God of detail." I finished with, "Animal sacrifices will be restored. Why?" I was referring to verses 18-27.

> **Everyone who ever sees God's glory falls on their face.**

Let's jump into Ezekiel 43:

> *Then he led me to the gate, the gate facing east. And behold, the glory of the God of Israel was coming from the east. And the sound of his coming was like the sound of many waters, and the earth shone with his glory. And the vision I saw was just like the vision that I had seen when he came to destroy the city, and just like the vision that I had seen by the Chebar canal. And I fell on my face. As the glory of the Lord entered the temple by the gate facing east, the Spirit lifted me up and brought me into the inner court; and behold, the glory of the Lord filled the temple* (vv. 1-5).

What a sight! What a privilege for Ezekiel to see such a thing. This prophet of God has seen the glory of God three times! In every one of those journals in various decades of my life, I wondered what it would be like to see the glory of God. I said I had no idea what it would be like, but my response would be like Ezekiel and everyone else that ever saw the glory of God. Surely, I would fall on my face.

Next, Ezekiel hears God's voice. How many people have ever heard God's voice? Ezekiel hears the voice of God say, *"Son of man, this is the place of my throne and the place of the soles of my feet, where I will dwell in the midst of the people of Israel forever"* (v. 7). Let's remember, Ezekiel is in Babylon. He is seeing this vision after he saw Jerusalem destroyed. Praise the Lord for a God of hope.

In verse 10, God tells Ezekiel, *"describe to the house of Israel the temple."* I said before, aren't you glad he wrote it down? The chapter closes with a description of the altar of the temple. Animal sacrifices purify the altar and make atonement for it. Burnt offerings and peace offerings will once again be offered to the Lord, at this new temple. And the final verse says, *"and I will accept you, declares the Lord God"* (v. 27).

DIGGING DEEPER

What a scene in Ezekiel 43. A people in captivity in Babylon, a people in despair have been given great hope by Ezekiel's vision of the glory of the Lord filling the new temple in Jerusalem once again. We serve a God of hope! Aren't you glad God Himself says, *"I will accept you"* (v. 27)?

We are reminded in these last several chapters about the new temple, that God is holy. There is a difference between the holy and the common. Now we see the Spirit of the Living God fill the temple once again. It is an illustration of how the glory of the Lord fills us when we become Christians and the Holy Spirit dwells within us. I am reminded of the New Testament passage in 1 Corinthians 6:19-20, *"Or do you not know that your body is a temple of the Holy Spirit within you, whom you have from God? You are not your own, for you were bought with a price. So glorify God in your body."*

Yes, God's presence filled the temple. His Holy Spirit fills our temple when we become a child of the King. Blessed be the name of the Lord.

Prayer

Father, thank You for reminding us of Your glory. Thank You for reminding us of Your presence then and now. Thank You for reminding us You are a God of restoration and a God of hope. We fall on our face before You. We worship You. We thank You for saying, *"I will accept you"* (v. 27). You deserve all the glory. You deserve all the praise. You deserve our worship. We bless Your name. Amen.

MY THOUGHTS

EZEKIEL 44

Stand Firm

Ezekiel 44 is about gates and priests. Some Levitical priests stood firm; others fell. Are you standing firm? Please read or listen to Ezekiel 44.

COMMENTS

In 1997, at forty-two years old, I read Ezekiel 43 and 44 (NKJV) on the same day. Concerning chapter 44, I wrote, "The way back to God: sin offerings and repentance." I continued to write, "The east gate where God's glory entered would shut and no man was to enter through it because that is the gate God came through. Priestly duties removed from Levites. They would only be gatekeepers and maintenance crew but could no longer *come near any of My holy things, nor into the Most Holy Place*' (v. 13). I finished with "God is a God of restoration. Hallelujah!"

In 2006, at fifty-one years old, I also read Ezekiel 43 and 44 (NASB) on the same day. Concerning chapter 44, I wrote, "The glory of God returns to the temple in Ezekiel's vision and the priests *shall teach My people the difference between the holy and the profane, and cause them to discern between the unclean and the clean*'" (v. 23).

In 2016, at sixty-one years old, I read Ezekiel 43 and 44 on the same day. Concerning chapter 44, I wrote, "No one enters the east gate to the city ever again until Jesus comes back to reign, referring to verse 23. I have seen the east gate and it is shut. Levites again become gatekeepers and temple attendants but are restricted from altar service because of past failures. Only the Levitical priests in the lineage of Zadok who remained faithful to God can do altar ministry. Holiness matters to God.

> **We still need to be taught the difference between holy living and common living.**

We still need to be taught the difference between holy living and common living. God expects holiness, biblical, not worldly behavior."

Let's look at chapter 44. We just had four chapters of Ezekiel's tour of the new temple. Chapter 44 begins with the end of Ezekiel's tour, *"Then he, (the Lord), brought me back to the outer gate of the sanctuary, which faces east. And it was shut. And the Lord said to me, 'This gate shall remain shut; it shall not be opened, and no one shall enter by it, for the Lord, the God of Israel, has entered by it'"* (vv. 1-2).

As noted in my journals, holiness matters to God. Even a gate He entered through could not be reused by mere humans.

The Lord continues to speak to Ezekiel, *"Son of man, mark well, see with your eyes, and hear with your ears all that I shall tell you concerning all the statutes of the temple of the Lord and all its laws"* (v. 5). Ezekiel obeyed that commandment; thus, we are reading his book today.

As mentioned already, holiness matters to God. Look at verse 10, *"But the Levites who went far from me, going astray from me after their idols when Israel went astray, shall bear their punishment."* God's judgment even came upon the priesthood. That judgment continues, *"They shall not come near to me, to serve me as priest"* (v. 13). They were relegated to gatekeepers and the maintenance crew of the temple. Only the Levitical priests of the sons of Zadok could continue to keep charge of the sanctuary and offer priestly duties at the altar. Why? Because when other priests went astray, they stood firm, *"But the Levitical priests, the sons of Zadok, who kept the charge of my sanctuary when the people of Israel went astray from me, shall come near to me to minister to me . . . They shall enter my sanctuary, and they shall approach my table, to minister to me, and they shall keep my charge"* (vv. 15-16).

DIGGING DEEPER

God watches us. He sees those who go astray and those who stand firm. How are you doing? Are you standing firm in your Christian walk or have you gone astray from time to time? God is faithful and He wants faithfulness from us. He wants consistency, He wants us to endure.

Not only will a priest minister in the temple, they will teach the people, *"They shall teach my people the difference between the holy and the common, and show them how to distinguish between the unclean and the clean"* (v. 23). Those were the duties of priests then. They are the duties of our pastors and priests today. They are to teach us the difference between the holy and the common and distinguish between the unclean and the clean.

The Jews needed that then and we still need such teaching today. We need pastors and preachers who can teach us the difference between the holy and the common, between the clean and the unclean, in the culture we live in today.

The application from chapter 44 of the Book of Ezekiel is to stand firm. Stay consistent even as others go astray.

Prayer

Father, we know from the Book of Ezekiel that many failed You in days gone by. Many fail You today. Many go astray, but You look for those who will stand firm, who will stay consistent, who will endure. Lord, find us faithful. Continue to teach us through Your Word the difference between the holy and the common and the difference between clean and unclean. Help us strive for holiness. May our lifestyle be clean before You. O Father, guide and direct our steps. We ask it in Your name, amen.

MY THOUGHTS

EZEKIEL 45

Daily, Weekly, Annually

I n Ezekiel 45, we are going to see a portion for the Lord and a portion for the prince. We are also reminded God wants time with us daily, weekly, and throughout the year. Do you want time with Him daily, weekly, and throughout the year? Please read or listen to Ezekiel 45.

COMMENTS

In 1997, I read Ezekiel 45 and 46 on the same day and concerning chapter 45, wrote, "Why so many feasts and offerings? To keep God in front of us. Sabbath means weekly honoring God. Feasts mean regularly throughout the year honoring God. Church helps us keep God before us."

In 2006, I read Ezekiel 45 and 46 on the same day. Concerning chapter 45, I wrote, "I do not claim to understand all the Old Testament sacrifices." I continued, "Here God allocates Himself land for His temple and there is no separation of church and state. The princes live on or near the land designated for the temple. They also give offerings daily. Spirituality was to be a part of daily life, not just on the Sabbath or new moon festivals. What is our spiritual sacrifice daily?"

In 2016, I also read Ezekiel 45 and 46 on the same day. Concerning this chapter, I wrote, "These chapters are like Moses all over again. There's a correlation between religion and politics, not separation of church and state. For example, the prince is to furnish the offerings for festivals from the tax or offerings given to him by the people."

Let's look over Ezekiel 45. Remember, Ezekiel saw the destruction of Jerusalem. He saw the destruction of the temple. In the previous chapters, God shows him the restoration of the temple. Now he is carving out some land in the restored Jerusalem for the temple and the princes. Verse 1, *"you shall set apart for the Lord a portion of the land as a holy district . . . It shall be holy throughout its whole extent."*

As mentioned in previous chapters, holiness matters to God. Verse 7, *"And to the prince shall belong the land on both sides of the holy district and the property of the city, alongside the holy district and the property of the city."* After land is designated for the holy temple, the next portion of land near the temple is for the prince of Israel.

But before he goes any farther, he admonishes the princes, *"Thus says the Lord God: Enough, O princes of Israel! Put away violence and oppression, and execute justice and righteousness"* (v. 9). It would be awesome if that could be said today in our halls of government. If only we could depend on our princes to execute justice and righteousness. Verse 10 tells them they are to have just balances. In other words, they are to be truthful.

> Though most of our holidays have been robbed by the secular culture around us, it is up to us Christians to keep them as holy feasts unto the Lord.

The rest of the chapter has to do with provision of sacrifices from the people to the prince so sacrifices could be made regularly at the temple. Verses 16-17 say, *"All the people of the land shall be obliged to give this offering to the prince in Israel. It shall be the prince's duty to furnish the burnt offerings, grain offerings, and drink offerings, at the feasts, the new moons, and the Sabbaths, all the appointed feasts of the house of Israel."* In this system, the people gave their offering to their prince, and the prince provided the offerings for the festivals. As noted in my journals, no separation of church and state here.

I questioned in one of those journals, "Why all these sacrifices?" I said in my journals it was a way to keep God close to the people's hearts. The Sabbath is weekly, so there is weekly recognition of God's influence in our lives. There are festivals throughout the year to draw us close to God so we do not forget the Lord throughout the year. We have the same thing today. We should be offering a daily sacrifice to the Lord, our Bible reading and prayer. Next, we should be going weekly to a house of worship, our honoring of the Sabbath. And we have our feasts throughout the year: Easter, Christmas, Pentecost. Those are times when we are to focus on the Lord. Though most of our holidays have been robbed by the secular culture around us, it is up to us Christians to keep them as holy feasts unto the Lord.

DIGGING DEEPER

The practical application from Ezekiel 45 is: what are we giving to the Lord daily, weekly, and throughout the year? Are we engaged daily with the Lord? Are we engaged weekly with the Lord? And are we celebrating our designated feasts as unto the Lord? Though our culture may be against us, it is up to us to keep stable spirituality daily, weekly, and throughout the year.

Prayer

Father, thank You for the reminder in Ezekiel 45, to keep spirituality in our forefront. Thanks for the reminder to be with You daily through prayer and Bible study, weekly by attending a church, and throughout the year as we celebrate our feasts unto You. Strengthen our daily time with You. Strengthen our houses of worship. And might You preserve our special feasts throughout the year.

Thanks for the reminder You want relationship with us daily, weekly, and throughout the year. May we be as excited to be with You as You are with us. In Jesus' name, we pray. Amen.

MY THOUGHTS

EZEKIEL 46

Morning by Morning

Ezekiel 46 is about the prince, feasts, and offerings. Worshippers came in one gate and left through another. They were to bring daily sacrifices. What do you offer to God daily? Please read or listen to Ezekiel 46.

COMMENTS

In 1997, I read Ezekiel 45 and 46, and concerning chapter 46, wrote, "Worshipers came in one gate but had to leave through another. We should also be changed; leaving not as we came, after worship."

In 2006, I also read Ezekiel 45 and 46 on the same day with a New Testament passage from 2 Peter 3. Concerning chapter 46, I wrote, "The princes live on or near the land designated for the temple. They also give offerings daily. Spirituality was to be part of daily life, not just on the Sabbath or new moon festivals. What is our spiritual sacrifice daily?"

In 2016, I again read Ezekiel 45 and 46 on the same day and concerning this chapter, wrote, "Festivals, offerings, worship, was communal according to verse 3. Offerings were regular, new moons, Sabbath feasts, but also daily. We should offer ourselves to God each day. Burnt offerings and grain offerings daily. Recognize my sinful nature, a need for forgiveness, and God's provision, which I need daily."

As part of my prayer after reading that passage, I wrote, "My celebrations of You would be pleasing in Your sight. My morning by morning offerings are acceptable to You. Be with me, Holy Spirit, I recognize I can do nothing without You."

Let's look at the key points in this chapter starting with verse 9, *"When the people of the land come before the Lord at the appointed feasts, he who enters by the north gate to worship shall go out by the south gate, and he who enters by the south gate shall go out by the north gate: no one shall return by way of the gate by which he entered."* I mentioned in one of my journals, when we go to church, we should be changed. We should not go out the same way we came in. Is that what happens when you go to church? Or has church become so routine we just go but nothing really changes?

DIGGING DEEPER

How many sermons can you remember? When was the last time the pastor said something that touched your heart? When was the last time the worship penetrated your very being? When was the last time you walked out of church different? There is a practical application; may we not enter church and leave the same way anymore. If that is not happening to you, maybe it is time to change churches. But, praise God, when it does happen; you are in the right church.

> When was the last time you walked out of church different?

Another application comes from verses 13-14, *"You shall provide a lamb a year old without blemish for a burnt offering to the Lord daily; morning by morning you shall provide it. And you shall provide a grain offering with it morning by morning."* I also referred to this concept in my journals. Spirituality is supposed to be daily. Today, we do not bring a burnt offering or a grain offering to the Lord, but we can give Him an offering of our time in Bible reading and prayer. To some of you, that is a sacrifice. But imagine how much time it took to take a burnt offering and a grain offering to the temple. This passage encourages us to give something to the Lord each and every day, to give Him a sacrifice of praise in Bible reading and prayer.

From Ezekiel 46, may we pay more attention to what church is doing for us, and may we give the Lord something morning by morning.

Prayer

Father, we thank You for these wonderful reminders in Ezekiel 46. When we attend our houses of worship, may we not go in and come out the same way. And might You call us, Holy Spirit, to spend time with You daily, morning by morning. Touch our hearts with Your presence as we do. In Your name, we ask it. Amen.

MY THOUGHTS

Flowing Water

W e are in the second to the last chapter of the Book of Ezekiel, chapter 47, about water flowing from the new temple. Do you like water? Do you like flowing, spiritual water? Please read or listen to Ezekiel 47.

COMMENTS

I was forty-two years old in 1997 when I read Ezekiel 47 and 48. Concerning these last two chapters in this book, I wrote, "Ezekiel ends with God giving instructions on how to reposition all the tribes of Israel in the new city named Yahweh Shammah, The Lord Is There. Wow, what a roller coaster book: the good, the bad, the ugly, the good. Praise God for restoration."

I was fifty-one years old in 2006 when I read Ezekiel 47 and 48 and finished this book, but I will save that journal entry for the devotion on chapter 48.

I was sixty-one years old in 2016 when I read Ezekiel 47, and concerning this chapter, wrote, "Ezekiel's tour continues. Back into the temple, the inner court. Here, he is shown flowing water, living water. From the inner court out to the temple, out the south gate, they are now wading through the trickle of water that becomes so deep Ezekiel would have to swim to pass through. Wherever this river goes, it causes life, *'so everything will live where the river goes'* (v. 9). There will be fish, fresh fruit every month, and healing in the leaves of the trees along the banks of the river. Next, God gives the boundaries of Israel like He gave to Moses in Numbers 34:1-12. My Bible map shows them almost the same, except this time, it includes a bit more land on the northeast, maybe modern-day Lebanon. Not bad, after Jerusalem had been destroyed by Babylon and Ezekiel is still sitting as a captive in Babylon, God gives hope of restoration then and now."

In chapter 47, Ezekiel's tour continues. He is back to the temple. This time he sees water *"issuing from below the threshold of the temple"* (v. 1). Water issuing from the temple begins as a trickle and becomes a river of life. The heavenly being giving Ezekiel this tour describes it this way, *"And wherever the river goes, every living creature that swarms will live, and there will be very many fish. For this water goes there, that the waters of the sea may become fresh; so everything will live where the river goes"* (v. 9). *"And on the banks, on both sides of the river, there will grow all kinds of trees for food. Their leaves will not wither, nor their fruit fail, but they will bear fresh fruit every month, because the water for them flows from the sanctuary. Their fruit will be for food, and their leaves for healing"* (v. 12).

I love water. I love to sit by water, I love to watch water. I like to see water. But I live in Colorado where there is not a lot of water, so this vision excites me. It also excites me because this river appears again in the last chapter of the Bible, Revelation 22, *"Then the angel showed me the river of the water of life, bright as crystal, flowing from the throne of God and of the Lamb through the middle of the street of the city; also, on either side of the river, the tree of life with its twelve kinds of fruit, yielding its fruit each month. The leaves of the tree were for the healing of the nations"* (vv. 1-2). Praise God for the river of life flowing from the temple of God!

> **Christianity is not a lake; it is not a reservoir. It needs to be like a river continually moving, continually staying alive.**

The chapter closes with a renewed vision of the boundaries of the Promised Land. Remember, Ezekiel is still in captivity in Babylon, but God is showing Ezekiel the restoration of his homeland. The apportionment of that land will continue in the final chapter of Ezekiel.

DIGGING DEEPER

Let's close with a few applications. God is the originator of the river of life. He is the one who provides water flowing from the temple. Water is vital everywhere in our world today. Along the riverbanks of our world, there are trees for fruit. There are leaves for healing. Yes, we are physically dependent on water.

But we are also spiritually dependent on the river of life. Christianity is not a lake; it is not a reservoir. It needs to be like a river continually moving, continually staying alive. Praise God for the river of life.

Secondly, praise the Lord for being a God of restoration. In Ezekiel 47, the land is going to be restored. I noted in my 1997 journal, "What a roller coaster book: the good, the bad, the ugly, the good." Praise God it ends with the good. We will learn about that as the book ends in chapter 48.

Prayer

Father, we praise You. We thank You for the river of life. We thank You for the physical nourishment of water in our daily lives. We thank You for water that provides food and healing. And we thank You that You are a God of restoration.

Our lives are like the Book of Ezekiel. They are roller coaster rides. We experience the good, the bad, the ugly, and, hopefully, we will finish with the good, eternal life with You. Thank You for being a God of restoration. We give You the glory and the praise. Amen.

MY THOUGHTS

EZEKIEL 48

Make Him Known

Today, we conclude the Book of Ezekiel. Chapter 47 ended with the division of the land, which continues here in chapter 48. We will also see the name of the new city. Over seventy times in Ezekiel, God said, *"that they shall know that I am the Lord."* After the Book of Ezekiel, do you know Him better? Will you go forth and make Him known? Please read or listen to Ezekiel 48.

COMMENTS

In 1997, I read Ezekiel 47 and 48 on the same day and wrote about these two chapters, "Ezekiel ends with God giving him instructions on how to reposition all the tribes of Israel in the new city named Yahweh Shammah, The Lord Is There."

Nine years later, in 2006, I read 47 and 48 on the same day again, and wrote, "What an end to Ezekiel. After God's judgment, He offers the promise of restoration, a new temple filled with His glory, a new city designed by God, and a return of the tribes of Israel, a river of life, and the name of His city, The Lord Is There. No place on earth has been specifically designed by God and named as such. No wonder He returns to Jerusalem."

Ten years later, in 2016, I finished Ezekiel with the 48th chapter, and wrote, "The twelve tribes of Israel are once again allocated to the Promised Land, but differently than when Joshua assigned the land the first time. Why? Who knows? Maybe the behavior of each tribe while in the land. The tribes of Judah and Benjamin saddle up to the holy portion. God has a long memory, *'This shall be for the consecrated priests, the sons of Zadok, who kept my charge, who did not go astray when the people of Israel went astray'* (v. 11). Glad He's also the One who forgives." I finished with, "Jerusalem, the holy city. *'The name of the city from that time on shall be, The Lord Is There'* (v. 35). Is He still there today or will He come back and be there in the future?"

Let's close the Book of Ezekiel. In a way, I find this to be a strange ending. It ends abruptly. But it also ends with a great line, *"and the name of the city from that time on shall be, The Lord Is There."*

DIGGING DEEPER

Let's go all the way back to the beginning of Ezekiel, the day we introduced this book. Then, I said, "Ezekiel was a street preacher in Babylon for twenty-two years. Ezekiel is both the name of the prophet and the title of the book that records his messages. His name means 'God strengthens.' He lived out his prophetic career among the community of the exiled Jews in Babylon."

I said throughout this book, Ezekiel was still in Babylon. He saw this entire book, all these visions, while in captivity in Babylon. His first oracle dates in 593 B.C., five years after the first group of exiles showed up in Babylon.

He spoke to Jews forced from their homeland because they had broken faith with their God. His message was to restore God's glory to a people who had spurned Him. His message is unrelenting with language that seems hard and offensive.

Ezekiel was in Babylon for five years before he started preaching. He was deeply concerned about the holiness of God. The sin of the people and their behavior offended their Holy God.

What did we see in the 48 chapters of Ezekiel? We saw the call of God oftentimes comes in the midst of the greatest trials of life. We saw what it takes to do what God asks even when it does not make sense at the time. We saw the valley of dry bones come back to life. And we heard over seventy times God say, *"that they shall know that I am the Lord."*

> I hope because you spent time in Ezekiel, He is more known to you now than before.

In a nutshell, what we saw is God's judgment, His punishment, and His restoration. That cycle of judgment, punishment, and restoration has gone on since the days of Ezekiel and is still going on today. Why? Because as He said over seventy times in this book, *"that they shall know that I am the Lord."* Our God wants to be known. I hope because you spent time in Ezekiel, He is more known to you now than before.

Often, we think of prophetic books as judgmental and discouraging. But as we read the prophets, we see each time they end with hope because God is a God of hope. If you are in despair, if you are downtrodden, if you are discouraged, look up to the God of hope. Look up to the God we learned about in Ezekiel, a God of restoration, a God who wants to be known in your life.

Prayer

Father, we thank You for including the Book of Ezekiel in Your holy scriptures. Thank You for this prophet who wrote down the visions You gave him. Thank You they have been preserved over thousands of years and we get to read these visions today.

We saw Your glory leave the temple and return to the temple. If Your glory has left our lives, Lord, we open our gates to You. Return, Lord Jesus. Come back and restore our lives. We want to help You be known in our families, in our communities, in our world. To God be the glory. Great things You have done. We fall on our faces before You and give You praise and worship. Amen.

MY THOUGHTS

ABOUT THE AUTHOR

Allen J. Huth is the Founder and President of the Ezra Project. The Ezra Project's mission is to connect God's people to God's Word.

At age fifteen, Allen was in a tragic car accident. God saved his life physically and spiritually that day. That night, he started reading the Bible. Allen has been a daily Bible reader for over fifty years. The Bible changed and shaped his life. He started keeping journals of what God was showing him through His Word in 1983 and continues doing so today.

He is a former member of the staff of the Colorado state legislature, a former vice president of the Colorado Association of Commerce and Industry, and was a partner in a business consulting firm when God called him to start the Ezra Project in 2002.

Allen has been an active volunteer in The Gideons International for over forty years. He served as the international president, international vice president, and international treasurer.

He has spoken in churches, banquets, and conferences in nearly forty countries including Australia, Belgium, Brazil, Cambodia, Chile, Egypt, India, Indonesia, Kenya, Korea, Germany, Norway, Papua New Guinea, Romania, Singapore, South Africa, Thailand, and the People's Republic of China.

Allen and his wife, Terry, have been married nearly fifty years. They have three adult children and five grandchildren.

Other *Day by Day Through the Bible* books in the series include:

- *The Writings of Moses – Genesis & Exodus*
- *The Writings of Moses – Leviticus, Numbers & Deuteronomy*
- *The Writings of Solomon*

- *The Writings of the Minor Prophets*
- *The Writings of John*
- *The Writings of Paul*
- *The Writings of Mark, Peter, James, Jude & Hebrews*

He also wrote the *Chronological Bible Reading Journal,* the *Trio Bible Reading Journal,* and *12 Practical Principles of Leadership According to Ezra.* Find his works at **ezraproject.net**.

CPSIA information can be obtained
at www.ICGtesting.com
Printed in the USA
JSHW061659070523
41373JS00001B/2